The Psychology
of Decision Making

FOUNDATIONS FOR ORGANIZATIONAL SCIENCE

A Sage Publications Series

Series Editor

David Whetten, *Brigham Young University*

Editors

Peter J. Frost, *University of British Columbia*
Anne S. Huff, *University of Colorado*
Benjamin Schneider, *University of Maryland*
M. Susan Taylor, *University of Maryland*
Andrew Van de Ven, *University of Minnesota*

The FOUNDATIONS FOR ORGANIZATIONAL SCIENCE series supports the development of students, faculty, and prospective organizational science professionals through the publication of texts authored by leading organizational scientists. Each volume provides a highly personal, hands-on introduction to a core topic or theory and challenges the reader to explore promising avenues for future theory development and empirical application.

Books in This Series

PUBLISHING IN THE ORGANIZATIONAL SCIENCES, 2nd Edition
Edited by L. L. Cummings and Peter J. Frost

SENSEMAKING IN ORGANIZATIONS
Karl E. Weick

INSTITUTIONS AND ORGANIZATIONS
W. Richard Scott

RHYTHMS OF ACADEMIC LIFE
Peter J. Frost and M. Susan Taylor

RESEARCHERS HOOKED ON TEACHING:
Noted Scholars Discuss the Synergies of Teaching and Research
Rae André and Peter J. Frost

THE PSYCHOLOGY OF DECISION MAKING:
People in Organizations
Lee Roy Beach

Lee Roy Beach

The Psychology of Decision Making
People in Organizations

Foundations for
Organizational
Science
A Sage Publications Series

SAGE Publications
International Educational and Professional Publisher
Thousand Oaks   London   New Delhi

For information:

SAGE Publications, Inc.
2455 Teller Road
Thousand Oaks, California 91320
E-mail: order@sagepub.com

SAGE Publications Ltd.
6 Bonhill Street
London EC2A 4PU
United Kingdom

SAGE Publications India Pvt. Ltd.
M-32 Market
Greater Kailash I
New Delhi 110 048 India

Printed in the United States of America

Library of Congress Cataloging-in-Publication Data

Beach, Lee Roy.
 The psychology of decision making : people in organizations / Lee Roy Beach.
  p. cm. — (Foundations for organizational science)
 Includes bibliographical references and index.
 ISBN 0-7619-0079-9. — ISBN 0-7619-0080-2 (pbk.)
 1. Decision-making. 2. Organization. I. Title. II. Series.
HD30.23.B413 1997
153.8'3—dc21   96-51267

This book is printed on acid-free paper.

97 98 99 00 01 02 03 10 9 8 7 6 5 4 3 2 1

Acquiring Editor: Marquita Flemming
Editorial Assistant: Frances Borghi
Production Editor: Sherrise M. Purdum
Production Assistant: Denise Santoyo
Typesetter/Designer: Danielle Dillahunt
Indexer: Teri Greenberg
Print Buyer: Anna Chin

This book is dedicated to the four teachers who made it possible:

David Laberge, Michael Wertheimer,
Kenneth Hammond, and Ward Edwards

Contents

Introduction to the Series

The title of this series, **Foundations for Organizational Science** (FOS), denotes a distinctive focus. FOS books are educational aids for mastering the core theories, essential tools, and emerging perspectives that constitute the field of organizational science (broadly defined to include organizational behavior, organizational theory, human resource management, and business strategy). The primary objective of this series is to support ongoing professional development among established scholars.

The series was born out of many long conversations among several colleagues, including Peter Frost, Anne Huff, Rick Mowday, Ben Schneider, Susan Taylor, and Andy Van de Ven, over a number of years. From those discussions, we concluded that there has been a major gap in our professional literature, as characterized by the following comment: "If I, or one of my students, want to learn about population ecology, diversification strategies, group dynamics, or personnel selection, we are pretty much limited to academic journal articles or books that are written either for content experts or practitioners. Wouldn't it be wonderful to have access to the teaching notes from a course taught by a master teacher of this topic?"

The plans for compiling a set of learning materials focusing on professional development emerged from our extended discussions of common experiences and observations, including the following:

1. While serving as editors of journals, program organizers for professional association meetings, and mentors for new faculty members, we have observed wide variance in theoretical knowledge and tool proficiency in our field. To the extent that this outcome reflects available learning opportunities, we hope that this series will help "level the playing field."

2. We have all "taught" in doctoral and junior faculty consortia prior to our professional meetings and have been struck by how often the participants comment, "I wish that the rest of the meetings [paper sessions and symposia] were as informative." Such observations got us thinking—Are our doctoral courses more like paper sessions or doctoral consortia? What type of course would constitute a learning experience analogous to attending a doctoral consortium? What materials would we need to teach such a course? We hope that the books in this series have the "touch and feel" of a doctoral consortium workshop.

3. We all have had some exposure to the emerging "virtual university" in which faculty and students in major doctoral programs share their distinctive competencies, either through periodic jointly sponsored seminars or through distance learning technology, and we would like to see these opportunities diffused more broadly. We hope that reading our authors' accounts will be the next best thing to observing them in action.

4. We see some of the master scholars in our field reaching the later stages of their careers, and we would like to "bottle" their experience and insight for future generations. Therefore, this series is an attempt to disseminate "best practices" across space and time.

To address these objectives, we ask authors in this series to pass along their "craft knowledge" to students and faculty beyond the boundaries of their local institutions by writing from the perspective of seasoned teachers and mentors. Specifically, we encourage them to invite readers into their classrooms (to gain an understanding of the past, present, and future of scholarship in particular areas from the perspective of their firsthand experience), as well as into their offices and hallway conversations (to gain insights into the subtleties and nuances of exemplary professional practice).

By explicitly focusing on an introductory doctoral seminar setting, we encourage our authors to address the interests and needs of nonexpert students and colleagues who are looking for answers to questions such as the following: Why is this topic important? How did it originate and how has it evolved? How is it different from related topics? What do we actually know about this topic? How does one effectively communicate this information to students and practitioners? What are the methodological pitfalls and conceptual dead ends that should be avoided? What are the most/least promising opportunities for theory development and empirical study in this area? What questions/situations/phenomena are not well suited for this theory or tool? What is the most interesting work in progress? What are the most critical gaps in our current understanding that need to be addressed during the next 5 years?

We are pleased to share our dream with you, and we encourage your suggestions for how these books can better satisfy your learning needs—as a newcomer to the field preparing for prelims or developing a research proposal, or as an established scholar seeking to broaden your knowledge and proficiency.

DAVID A. WHETTEN
SERIES EDITOR

Preface

This book presents an overview of the psychology of decision making. The intent is to be brief so the reader will not get lost in technical details but to be broad so the reader can understand how the field has developed since its inception as a scholarly discipline in the early 1950s.

To achieve both brevity and breadth requires selectivity. No doubt my selection of topics is biased, as is my interpretation of what they mean and how important they are. The fact is, however, that I have made no effort to be unbiased because, no matter how hard I might try, I would please few of my colleagues, each of whom would happily add or subtract from my selection and gladly quarrel with my interpretations. So rather than pretend to be unbiased, I unapologetically warn the reader that what follows is very much my own viewpoint, derived from 35 years of work in the field.

On the understanding that they are blameless for what is deficient in the following pages, I would like to thank my colleagues, Terry Connolly and Amnon Rapoport, for their help and advice.

1 The Preliminaries

Ralph stared at the figures in disbelief; he felt a headache coming on. What happened? After all the planning and work, all the careful analysis and getting his people to buy in, all the sleepless nights and worry, what went wrong? When he took this job he was sure he knew how to deal with the situation—he was the guy who had previously saved three other businesses that had the same problem. Had he been too optimistic? Had his past experience hindered rather than helped? Betty Miller, the company president, clearly believed he was on the wrong track. He hated to prove her right. After all, he was supposed to be the Knight in Shining Armor who would save the firm. Clearly, this knight was going to have to think things through again.

He flipped back over the figures from previous months, comparing them carefully with the latest report. What were they trying to tell him? Had something changed that he had failed to notice? Was he focusing on the wrong things? Slowly he began to see a pattern. Although not broken out in a way that would make it obvious, the figures suggested that the problem was not with the products themselves but in sales. Some salespeople appeared to be doing a great job, but many more were not. That might be it! He had always read the reports from the viewpoint of fixing the product. Maybe that mind-set blinded him to the possibility that the sales people simply do not do a good job. He felt like a fool. Most managers made just the opposite mistake, blaming the people first and the product last. Okay, he was more into product innovation than human resources, everyone knew that. But now that he began to look at the figures this new way, everything began to make sense.

Ralph felt a surge of relief and excitement—all was not lost, not yet anyway. He was going to have to get a lot more information to make the details clear, but he thought he understood the problem. True, it was not something he had ever dealt with before, but he and Betty ought to be able to fix things. Then it was a matter of coming up with plausible options, deciding on the right one, working hard, and watching closely so he didn't get misled again. It could be done. He almost called Betty to tell her. She probably would be so relieved that she wouldn't gloat. But on second thought, maybe he would tell her tomorrow so he could enjoy this feeling of relief a little while longer.

* * *

To better understand the problems Ralph faces, we need some way of structuring our thinking. The customary structure, Figure 1.1, begins with diagnosis of a decision problem, moves on to selection of an action that will solve the problem, and ends with implementation of the selected action until the problem is solved.

Diagnosis

The need for a decision arises when anomalous events occur. Often, these events stem from internal changes (wants) or external changes (demands), but they also can stem from the realization that an earlier decision was wrong and its implementation is not producing the right results. In Ralph's case, the anomalous events were the unexpected figures in the monthly report, resulting in the realization that what he was doing was not making things better.

To make sense of the anomalous events, the decision maker must mentally put the events in the proper context to give them meaning,

Theoretical Viewpoint

Tasks	Prescriptive	Behavioral	Naturalistic
Diagnosis	-----	✓ Lens Model	✓ Recognition
Action Selection	✓ Choice (Probability, Utility)	✓ Choice (Subjective Prob., Utility)	✓ Policy ✓ Screening ✓ Choice
Implementation	-----	-----	✓ Progress-Monitoring

Figure 1.1. A Framework for Examining Decision Theories and Research

which allows him or her to draw on previous experience to decide what to do. If this is a situation that is very similar to a situation that was encountered before, he or she can use that experience to deal with the events. If the situation is substantially different from previously encountered situations, he or she can set about formulating an action plan that deals with its uniqueness. In Ralph's case, the company's problem had been interpreted as a product problem. But the figures in the reports did not make sense in this interpretation, suggesting that the frame was incorrect. When he began to view the situation as a sales problem, the figures suddenly began to make sense.

No matter whether the decision maker's framing of the events results in use of previously acquired knowledge about what to do or in formulation of a new action plan, he or she must use the events to guide the fine-tuning of the response. Even past experience usually provides only a general strategy for dealing with the situation. (When one can do exactly what one did before it is called a conditioned response, which seldom is an effective way of dealing with complex situations and almost never is effective for unique situations.) Therefore, the decision maker must diagnose the situation by evaluating the states of its most salient features. In Ralph's case, his past experience with product problems provided little for dealing with the present sales problem, which probably is really a human resource (HR) problem. Therefore, he anticipated having to obtain more information to make judgments about precisely what was wrong and how serious it was before he could decide what to do about it.

Action Selection

We often speak as though the decision maker has some set of potential plans of action (options) and that decision consists of choosing the best from among them. However, consider your own decision making—you frequently have no idea about what might be reasonable plans of action. Often, you start off in one direction only to change your mind when things go awry. In fact, decisions seldom are made at a single point. Rather, the process seems to feel its way along, changing in the light of feedback and often leading in directions that never were conceived of when it all began. In Ralph's case, he thinks that with Betty's help he can come up with options from which to choose, but the fact is that once he understands the nature of his sales/HR problem he will start to do the most obvious things and then adjust his actions in light of how well they work.

The "feeling along" nature of decision making is very difficult to capture in a readable narration and even more difficult to describe in a tractable theory. It is far easier, for both the theorist and the reader, to talk as though decision options actually exist in full-blown clarity and that the choice among them occurs at a single point in time. But this is merely a useful fiction. In Ralph's case, the fiction is useful because we can think of him making choices among different options— even if he makes a sequence of choices in light of feedback about how things are progressing in his search for a solution to his sales/HR problem. The fiction also is useful to Ralph because it allows him to think in terms of rather specific plans of action—even though he knows that anything he decides to do will surely be modified as he goes along.

Implementation

After a plan of action has been decided on, it must be implemented. That is, the plan must be used to guide behavior and the decision maker must monitor its progress toward resolving the anomaly that started everything in the first place. Again, even though Ralph will feel his way along just like anyone else, he may talk as though he has a well-formulated plan, if only because it is easier to communicate with his colleagues and to help his HR people understand their contribution. He may even believe it himself. But after the dust settles and he has time to review what finally happened, the odds are good that Ralph will see that the route he took to get where he got does not look much like the original plan. Indeed, if he laid a history of what happened side by side with the original plan, the only things they might share is a common starting point and, if he had successfully solved his sales/HR problem, a common ending point.

Some Background

We will return to the structure in Figure 1.1 because it is the blueprint for the remainder of this book. For the moment, let us leave Ralph, who is busy enjoying his new insight about how to frame his problem, and turn to consideration of some of the larger issues in studying decision making.

Prescriptive Theory

First of all, decision making is studied by many different disciplines, each of which seems to regard it as uniquely its own. Economists address decision making by constructing axiomatic models that describe the market forces at work in particular circumstances and that prescribe appropriate actions in light of the assumptions underlying the models. Operations researchers follow a similar logic, except that their models tend to be limited to specific problems encountered in specific enterprises. Applied statisticians also model decisions, either prescriptively (e.g., hypothesis testing) or descriptively (e.g., structural modeling).

With the possible exception of structural modeling, the emphasis in most work on decision making has been on prescribing what should be done rather than on describing what decision makers actually do and certainly not on diagnosis or implementation. This is because the models are designed solely to address the tasks involved in choice, which, as we shall see, is but one kind of decision making. Moreover, their logic need not mimic or even parallel the cognitive processes of the decision maker, even though their authors often use language that implies that it does. As a result, until quite recently, if decision behavior was examined at all, it was evaluated in light of how well it conformed to the prescriptive models rather than the other way around. That is, because the models followed logically from what usually were regarded as very attractive axioms, it did not seem reasonable to evaluate them by comparing them to what decision makers actually do. If such a comparison ever was made, it was the behavior that was evaluated; behavior that conformed to the models was judged to be rational, and behavior that did not conform to the models was judged to be irrational. Prescriptive theory almost always focuses on choices among options and seldom focuses on either diagnosis or implementation.

Because students of organizational behavior are more interested in describing what people do than in prescribing what they should do, we approach decision making in quite a different way. We are interested in the interplay of group and institutional dynamics and their effects on the decisions made within and on the behalf of organizations. As a result, organizational behaviorists are interested in the ways in which decision makers use information to arrive at decisions, and this is where our story begins.

Behavioral Theory

Behavioral decision theory began as the study of the degree to which unaided human decision making conforms to the processes and output of prescriptive decision theory. Almost from the beginning, however, it has gone beyond this rather narrow mandate by "psychologizing" prescriptive theory to make it more descriptive of what decision makers actually do.

Diagnosis

Behavioral research on diagnosis is based on the work of Egon Brunswik. Brunswik (1947) studied perception and in doing so developed a model that describes how observers use sensory cues to infer (diagnose) the nature of the world around them. This model, called the lens model, was generalized by Hammond (1955) to more macrolevel inferences. The result is that diagnosis has come to be thought about in terms of *policies* that decision makers use to evaluate the characteristics of decision situations prior to making decisions about what to do in those situations. The lens model has provided a powerful way of thinking about policies and has contributed greatly to an understanding of how decision makers use policies in situations as diverse as evaluating the quality of pigs (Phelps & Shanteau, 1978) to evaluating the quality of applicants for jobs as insurance salesmen (Roose & Doherty, 1976). These studies form the foundation of an empirical tradition in the study of policy use that has proved to be of enormous theoretical and applied value.

The rather offbeat Phelps and Shanteau (1978) pig study illustrates how this kind of research is done. In the first of two experiments, seven members of the Kansas State University senior livestock-judging team were each given a set of 64 index cards on each of which was written a description of a hypothetical female breeding pig. The descriptions consisted of 11 characteristics of pigs, and each pig was said to be high or low on the characteristic (e.g., high body weight, low quality of nipples). The high and low values of the 11 cues across the 64 hypothetical pigs formed a partially replicated factorial design. Each livestock judge was asked to read each description and rate the pig for breeding quality. Thus, the 11 cues were the independent variables, and each judge's 64 ratings were the dependent variables. The analysis was done using analysis of variance. The results showed that all of the judges used nine or more of the cues to arrive at their ratings, but it was not clear whether some cues counted for more than others. In the second study, the judges were shown pictures of pigs and rated the breeding quality of each pig. This time results showed that most of the cues were used but they were used in clusters. That is, various cues contributed to an inference about size, others contributed to meat quality, and others to breeding quality. This was interpreted to mean that the judges' policies involved a multistage strategy in which cues were integrated into intermediate inferences that then were combined to arrive at a final decision.

Choice

Behavioral research on choice began by comparing decision behavior with the dictates of prescriptive decision theory. The major prescriptive influence has been the work of von Neumann and Morgenstern (1947) who originated game theory. The general idea is that economic inter-actions can be regarded as games, as *gambles*. The participant is viewed as a gambler who must place a bet (select one or another course of action) and then observe the outcome (win or lose).

The key to choosing the best bet is conceptually very simple. The player should select the option that offers the most attractive payoff package. A simple way to summarize the attractiveness of an option's package is to add up the values of the payoffs it offers. However, this fails to take into account the possibility that those payoffs may not materialize if the option is chosen. To fully reflect the structure of the situation, the attractiveness of the payoffs must be tempered by the probability of acquiring them. To include the probabilities, the attrac-tiveness of a bet can be summarized by first discounting each payoff by the probability that it will be acquired and then summing the discounted values of the payoffs. Because a probability is a decimal number, discounting is accomplished by multiplying the payoff's value by the probability. The sum of all possible discounted payoffs is called the option's expected value. It is assumed that the player will select the option that has the greatest expected value.

Research on the behavioral correlates of prescriptive theory usually involves having subjects make choices between two offered bets. We will examine a prototypical study in a later chapter. However, a study by Gray (1975) provides a uniquely interesting illustration of behav-ioral research that uses prescriptive theory. Gray presented third-grade students with an array of six stacks of 10 cards, face down. Each stack contained arithmetic problems of roughly equal difficulty for the children and the stacks ranged from very difficult at one end of the array to very easy at the other end. The subject looked at a problem from each stack and stated how many of the 10 problems he or she would solve correctly if asked to work the problems in that stack. Dividing the estimate by 10 provides the student's assessment of his or her probability of success for each stack. The students' task was to choose a stack from which a problem would be randomly selected for them to solve. They were told that if they chose the most difficult stack and got the correct answer, the payoff would be six red poker chips, the next most difficult paid five chips, and so on down to one chip for the easiest problems. If they got the wrong answer, they had to pay the experimenter the corresponding number of poker chips; they were loaned 10 chips to start out, which were deducted from their winnings at the end of the experiment.

The students' choices of problems to solve can be viewed as gambles—they could try a high-payoff, difficult problem, but the odds were against getting the right answer. They could try a low-payoff, easy problem, but the payoff was so low it hardly was worth the trouble. The students understood the dilemma and selected the problems that prescriptive theory would dictate—the appropriate balance between the risk of failure and the magnitude of the payoff. In fact, these third graders turned out to be very efficient gamblers—with one exception. Like real gamblers, many of the students would play conservatively for a while and then, after having built up a supply of poker chips, would take a flyer on the really difficult stack. They almost invariably lost, whereon they would select easy problems until they had regained their fortune. Then they would gamble conservatively for a while before taking another flyer.

Naturalistic Theory

Naturalistic decision theory departs from both prescriptive and behavioral decision theory in its almost exclusive focus on how decisions actually are made, rather than on how they "should" be made. It borrows heavily from behavioral decision theory (and is viewed by many as a further development of behavioral decision theory rather than as a separate theory), but it goes beyond it both in how decisions are described and in its attention to decision implementation. Naturalistic theory is very much influenced by the need for practical knowledge about real-world decision making.

To a large degree, naturalistic theory is based on the work of Herbert Simon. In his classic *Administrative Behavior* (1945), Simon emphasizes that the behavior of a person in an organization is constrained by the position he or she holds in that organization—something so obviously true that it is easy to overlook both its insightfulness and broad implications. This means that decision making in organizations is strongly influenced by the structure and norms of the organization and that decision makers do not entertain the full array of options that an outsider might consider available. Another feature of Simon's analysis is the emphasis on the individual as a decision-making agent for the organization—emphasizing that organizations do not themselves make decisions. As pointed out by Davis (1992), after all these years this small but important point is still overlooked by many people who study organizational and group decision making.

Simon is a Nobel laureate in economics who has produced a stream of useful insights that have inspired astonishing amounts of research by many people. Two of his most famous insights, based on his observations of behavior in organizations, are *bounded rationality* and *satisficing*. Because decision makers' cognitive capacity is rather limited, they must reduce information processing demands by simplifying the problems they encounter. To do so, Simon contends, they construct "small worlds" that are limited representations of the problem at hand. The representation contains only the most salient information, and the decision maker proceeds to make his or her decision based solely on that "bounded" representation. The decision may in fact be "rational" in that it conforms to the prescriptions of the appropriate prescriptive theory, but the decision maker uses only the information contained in the bounded representation.

Satisficing is another way of reducing the information processing load. This is not a "rational" decision strategy in the sense of following the prescriptions of prescriptive theory, but it allows the decision maker to arrive at a decision without all the computational effort required by prescriptive theory. Here, it is assumed that the decision maker has some set of standards that an option must meet for it to be at least minimally satisfactory. The idea is that the first option that comes along that meets all of the standards is the one that is selected. Satisficing is not rational in the prescriptive sense because the decision maker has no assurance that an as-yet-unseen option might not be superior to the option that has been selected, and he or she therefore would fail to select the best possible option. However, the simplicity of this decision strategy, and its ease of use, presumably makes it worthwhile to risk missing the best option in favor of choosing one that is at least sufficient.

Naturalistic thinking is strongly influenced by decision making in organizations, particularly work-related decisions. Organizational theorists have tended to examine decisions at a higher, more macro, level than do most behavioral decision theorists. The former often treat the organization as the unit and talk as though it makes decisions, presuming something like an organizational mind. The latter focus on individuals, often without specifying the particular context, presuming that an organization's decisions are a function of the collaborative decisions made by its individual members. Things are often confused, however, by a tendency for both organizational and behavioral theorists to switch back and forth between levels of analysis, which muddles things considerably.

Still, observations of individual decision makers in the context of their work provides invaluable information about how decision making takes place. The result has been a number of theories designed to cover some limited kind of decisions but that contribute to an emerging new view about how decision making takes place, particularly in organizational contexts. These small theories are beginning to coalesce into more general theories. It is the coalescence that is called naturalistic decision theory and research.

Paradigms, Theories, and Models

Thirty-five years ago, Thomas Kuhn (1962) pointed out that scientific disciplines adopt central conceptual frameworks, called paradigms, that give meaning to their accumulated observations and that drive how they think about and study the phenomena that constitute their areas of study. Kuhn argued that advances in science come from revolutionary paradigmatic shifts rather than from gradual changes induced by research findings, which was the previous view of how science progressed. In this sense, Kuhn's work was itself an example of precisely what he was talking about. For philosophers of science, the "revolutionary shift paradigm" for how science progresses quickly replaced the "gradualism paradigm"—although a middle ground is widely accepted today.

Evolution is a prime example of a dominant scientific paradigm. It is a central tenet for the biological sciences, providing an underlying logic that unites areas of study that otherwise might have little in common. The evolution paradigm is so pervasive that it goes unquestioned by most biologists; it is a bedrock assumption. Indeed, although some preachers and politicians may regard evolution as heresy, virtually all biologists regard doubts about it as apostasy.

The social sciences also have a dominant paradigm. It is utilitarianism, the view that behavior is motivated by its instrumentality for attaining valued outcomes. The near-universal acceptance of this paradigm is surprisingly recent. Fifty years ago the dominant para-digm was characterological and moral; behavior was explained by strength of character and of moral rectitude. The role of rewards and punishment was acknowledged, but they were seen as ways of control-ling the natural impulses of character (or lack of character). Today, one almost never hears characterological explanations from well-educated people. Instead, behavior is explained in terms of the ends it is assumed to seek. I suspect that your great-grandparents regarded the characterological paradigm as obviously true (as many people still do) just as you regard the utilitarian paradigm as obviously true. The question is whether the shift from character to utility is scientific progress or whether it is just a shift. We will return to this question from time to time in the following chapters.

A Hierarchy

It is useful to differentiate among paradigms, theories, and models. Although the terms are often used interchangeably, they are not the same thing. In fact, they are hierarchically related: Paradigms are the most general—rather like a philosophical or ideological framework. Theories are more specific, based on the paradigm and designed to describe what happens in one of the many realms of events encom-passed by the paradigm. Models are even more specific, providing the mechanisms by which events occur in a particular part of the theory's realm. Of the three, models are the ones most affected by empirical data—models come and go, theories give way when only evidence is overwhelmingly against them (and sometimes not even then), and paradigms stay put until a radically better idea comes along.

Prescriptive (Normative) Models

Prescriptive decision theory and behavioral decision theory more strongly reflect the utilitarian model than is common in the social sciences, largely because both are informed by economic thought. For example, policy research, using the Lens Model, views the decision maker as an intuitive statistician who must make inferences on the basis of fallible cues. The analogy is with the statistician who uses fallible data to make inferences about some underlying process. In-deed, the Lens Model relies on multiple regression as both a method of data analysis and as a structural model of information utilization. The assumption is that performance will be best when the decision maker's cognitive processing mirrors what a statistician would do when applying multiple regression to the information available to the decision maker.

Prescriptive decision theory views the decision maker as a maximizer of expected value. Behavioral decision theory has translated this into the assumption that decision performance will be best if the decision maker's cognitive processes correspond to the dictates of utility theory and probability theory. That is, performance will be best if the attractiveness of an option is summarized as the sum of the probability-discounted utilities corresponding to its potential payoffs and if the decision maker chooses the option that offers the greatest sum. If performance falls short of what an economist could achieve by following these prescriptions, the fault must lie in the failure of the decision maker to behave according to these assumptions. Therefore, by examining the noncorrespondence between what the decision maker *should* do and what he or she actually does, behavioral theory ought to help us to (1) better understand human decision processes and (2) find ways of helping the decision maker perform better. In choice research, utility theory, probability theory, and expected value maximization are all referred to as *normative models* because they are seen as defining the norms for correct processing of relevant information—not because it is a social norm to actually behave this way. Systematic differences between the prescriptions of the normative models and what decision makers actually do are interpreted by behavioral theory as reflections of people's cognitive shortcomings and their systematic processing errors. Techniques for helping decision makers overcome these shortcomings and avoid these errors are called *decision aids.*

Naturalistic theory view also tends to be utilitarian but not as stridently so as prescriptive and behavioral theory. It is influenced by observations of professional decision makers (managers) and recognizes that the process tends to be messy and less analytic than even the decision makers themselves might wish. Most analyses find that decision makers have difficulty comprehending the problems they face and that decision makers tend to simplify things to deal with them. The focus seldom is on doing the best job possible, settling instead on doing a good enough job to keep things rolling along. In fact, decision making is often seen as a way of keeping events headed in a desirable direction rather than as maximization.

Seeds of Doubt

Now, let me plant some seeds of doubt. Everything in this book is driven by the utilitarian paradigm. This is due in part to the fact that the theory and research to be described is done by social scientists, and the utilitarian paradigm has become a "natural" part of our thinking. It is also because decision theory and research have close ties to economics, and economics is the quintessential theoretical elaboration of the utilitarian paradigm. However, as we progress through our story, stresses and strains will begin to emerge; models will be abandoned, theories will collapse, and whispers about a paradigm shift will be vaguely heard. In some ways, it will be like a detective story, with evidence stumping us at every turn, frustrating our desire for a simple clean picture of what is going on, and finally leaving us with only a hazy notion of what the future might look like. But it is not as satisfying as a detective story because the hazy notion is as good as it gets, the story is not yet completed and we can only guess at what will happen next.

Summary

We have characterized decision making as a sequence of events: diagnosis, action selection, and implementation. We have identified three viewpoints for examining decision making: prescriptive, behavioral, and naturalistic. It is important to note that the naturalistic viewpoint grew out of the behavioral viewpoint, which in turn grew out of the prescriptive viewpoint, so it is not entirely correct to think of them as competing with one another. On the other hand, for progress to be made, each viewpoint has defined itself by how it differs from its predecessor, which often makes it look like they all are in competition. Because behavioral theory and its research agenda were dictated by the nature of prescriptive theory, we will begin our exploration of the psychology of decision making by examining how crucial aspects of prescriptive theory were incorporated into behavioral research and what the results were. Then we will examine the pressures put on behavioral theory by studies conducted in organizations and groups and how these pointed out severe problems with the evolving views about how decision making takes place. Finally, we will examine the response to these pressures, naturalistic theory, which both departs from its prescriptive and behavioral ancestry and permits a way of reconciling them with the pressures of organizational research.

We close this chapter with a discussion of the differences between paradigms, theories and models, and this differentiation will be an important part of our subsequent discussion. Historically, behavioral decision work has been driven by the utilitarian paradigm and normative models. Naturalistic theory also is utilitarian but less insistently so. The point to remember is that there are major changes under way in how decision making is viewed and how it is studied, and a paradigm shift may well be under way.

2 Framing the Problem

Ralph and Betty were walking back to their offices from the cafeteria. It had been a working lunch, and Betty had no recollection of what she had eaten—she thought it might have been sort of yellow. She agreed with Ralph that their problem wasn't with production, as he had insisted earlier, and that their top priority was to focus on sales. Then they had discussed the possibility that their hiring procedures were the root of the difficulty. It looked as if they were hiring people who were ill-suited for selling the company's unique line of products. Earlier, she had talked with their human resources (HR) people about hiring procedures, but at the time she hadn't known exactly what to ask. Anyway, it was clear that the HR folks thought they were doing the best that could be done and that hiring was pretty much of a crapshoot at best. She wasn't happy with their attitude, but she didn't know enough to confront them.

At lunch, she and Ralph had agreed that a good salesperson had a mixture of talents, but what that mixture might be was a mystery. In an offhand remark, Betty had joked that it would be nice to clone the salespeople who already do a good job. There had been a moment of silence when they both recognized that the joke was right on target.

Betty turned the cloning notion over in her mind as they walked along. It made sense—not literally, of course, but certainly what they wanted was an entire force of salespeople like the best they now had. This immediately raised two questions: (1) How can you figure out what makes the best people the best? (2) How can you train old people to be like them or select new people who are already like them? And what on earth guided HR's present selection process? Whatever it was, it surely didn't work. Both she and Ralph wanted to swing into action, to solve their problem before things got any worse. But what exactly were they going to do? As they parted to go to their separate afternoon meetings, Ralph suggested they talk with his sister-in-law, who worked at the local college. Maybe she had come across something that might help.

*   *   *

Actually, Betty and Ralph have come farther than they might realize. Common sense tells us that identifying the problem is a large part of solving it, and common sense has much to commend it. In our terms, identifying the problem means framing it properly. Improper framing causes one to invest, as Ralph had earlier, in trying to solving the wrong problem. Betty and Ralph now have reframed the problem from one involving products to one involving their sales force. Then, within this new frame they have begun to explore their options. The key concept is to clone the good performers by getting rid of (or retraining) the poor ones and hiring people who have characteristics of the good performers. After their discussion, they both were ready to get to work.

Getting to work is dangerous when you don't know what to do. It is one thing to know what your goal is, it is another thing to know how to reach it. But, Betty and Ralph are asking good questions, and when you have no answers, it always is a good idea to go to someone who might have them—in this case, Ralph's sister-in-law at the college. But before we see what happened when they talked with her, let us examine framing more closely.

Framing and Reframing

Framing involves embedding observed events in a context that gives them meaning. Events seldom occur in isolation; the decision maker usually has some idea about what led to them—what is going on and why. This knowledge supplies the context, the ongoing story that gives coherence to one's experience, without which everything would appear to be random and unrelated. Incoherent experience sometimes occurs under extreme stress (and can be induced by drugs or may accompany some kinds of brain damage), but under normal circumstances, most of us are aware of a meaningful flow from the past to the present and into the future.

Sometimes, however, events do not fit into this ongoing flow. Often, these anomalous events can quickly be reconciled with experience. For example, you realize that a letter you are awaiting did not arrive, prompting you to recall that yesterday was a holiday and there was no mail delivery. But, when anomalous events cannot be easily reconciled, they may signal the need to reframe the situation. For example, if you are sitting in your office peacefully answering your e-mail and the fire alarm sounds, your first reaction is to be startled by the loud intrusive noise. This may be followed by a moment of confusion about what is going on; then you quickly make sense of things by assuming that the building is on fire. Once you recognize the fire alarm for what it is, the flow of your experience is changed—you no longer are in a peaceful e-mail-answering situation; you are in a fire situation, and your behavior must change accordingly. Now seemingly trivial events that previously had escaped your notice or that might not have made much sense had you focused on them, become meaningful—the smoky smell of which you had been only faintly conscious, the clamor of voices down the hall, the sound of sirens in the distance.

Of course, as was the case with Ralph and the monthly reports, the anomalous events may not be as dramatic as a fire alarm. In fact, events are often so subtle that we miss their importance, or it is so easy to erroneously reconcile them with our current frame that we fail to notice that they in fact signal the frame's inadequacy. Ralph looked at the figures every month and failed to see their message—he thought they were telling him that he still had not solved the product problem. Only when it became clear that his efforts were getting him nowhere and things were getting progressively worse did he realize he had misinterpreted (misframed) the situation. Because the figures did not send an unequivocal message, he had to think hard about what they meant. When the reframing insight came, his entire approach to the problem changed.

Wagenaar and Keren (1986) provide an example of what follows from framing situations in either one way or another. They instructed half of a group of individuals to frame a decision from the viewpoint of a public official and the other half to frame it from the viewpoint of a parent. The decision was about whether to impose a law requiring children to wear seat belts when traveling in an automobile. Information was presented about accidents in which children were hurt. Half of each framing group (parent or public official) received statistical information (each year 100 of 150 juvenile victims of traffic accidents could be saved if they wear seat belts), and half received anecdotal information (a story about a little girl who died because she was not wearing a seat belt). The participants were asked to make a decision about the law and to explain how the information influenced their decision. It was found that participants operating under the parental frame were more likely to favor the law when presented with the anecdotal information about the little girl than when presented with the statistical information, and participants under the public official frame were more likely to favor the law when presented with the statistical information. In short, framing provides the context within which information is used, and different frames put the focus on different kinds of information.

The most prominent line of decision research on framing has focused on how people differentially frame problems that are stated in terms of possible gains or possible losses. Tversky and Kahneman (1981) presented 150 participants with the following problems and asked them to choose which bet in each pair they would prefer to play:

A1: A sure gain of $240
A2: A 25% chance to gain $1,000 and a 75% chance to gain nothing

or

B1: A sure loss of $750
B2: A 75% chance to lose $1,000 and a 25% chance to lose nothing.

It was found that when choosing between A1 and A2, 84% of the participants chose A1, even though $240 is less than the expected value of $250 for A2. When choosing between B1 and B2, 87% chose B2, even though the expected loss for B2 is equal to the loss of $750 for B1. The results illustrate the often repeated finding that people tend to avoid taking risks (choose the sure thing) when outcomes are framed as gains and that they tend to take risks (choose the gamble) when outcomes are framed as losses, even when the only difference is in how the outcomes are stated. That is, the wording of the problem can influence how people frame it and, as a result, how they decide to deal with it.

This research finding ought not come as a surprise. Advertisers, politicians, and anyone else who tries to influence people's behavior know that the way in which things are described influences how people frame situations. Most of us have learned to discount the hyperbole of such descriptions, but clearly, we are not immune to its effects—we still buy heavily advertised products and we still vote for the politicians who use the right words.

Framing goes beyond mere wording. Indeed, the fact that wording has an influence at all merely indicates how pervasive framing is and how sensitive it is to relevant information. As suggested in the previous chapter, Nobel laureate Herbert Simon (1955) suggested that decision makers reduce information-processing demands by constructing limited representations of situations because they cannot cognitively deal with a great deal of information. The representation is called a "small world." The problem with relying on a small world representation is that it might not include the right things, be too simplistic, or just be wrong. Hence, it behooves us to be rather flexible, to be sensitive to signs that the representation needs correction (reframing). Of course, some people appear amazingly inflexible, retaining their frame in the teeth of disconfirming information that other people would regard as overwhelming. Consistent to a fault, their overconfidence in their frame's correctness makes them vulnerable to serious error. At the other extreme, there are those who seem unable to stick with one frame for any length of time. Flighty and inconstant, they see every side of every issue, seeing it first this way and then that; they never resolve much of anything. It is best to be somewhere between the two extremes, flexible but not flighty.

Expertise and Framing

Experts often exhibit the desirable flexibility without flightiness. As a result of research in both cognitive science (Anderson, 1981) and in behavioral decision making (Wright & Bolger, 1992), a great deal has been learned about what makes people experts at one or another task and how they approach problem solving and decision making.

At first the research results appear to be conflicting; sometimes experts are awful and sometimes they do a very good job. Shanteau (1992) has analyzed the results of many studies and found that experts perform better in domains involving physical processes and less well in domains involving human behavior. In short, they do better in inherently predictable domains and worse in inherently unpredictable domains. Even at that, experts generally do better than novices, and they clearly approach tasks differently from novices. Part of this difference is because experts can use their experience to frame situations rapidly and accurately. Then they use the underlying meaning of the situation provided by the frame to guide their task performance— and use of the underlying meaning provides flexibility because it allows the expert to vary his or her approach to the particular problem at hand without losing track of the larger picture. That is, having framed the situation, experts use the frame to draw on their knowledge about what to expect in the situation, what variations are reasonable (and what they mean), what has worked in the past, and how that might be adapted to the present situation. Lacking the depth of experience, novices must rely on the surface characteristics of the situation to guide their performance of the task, with the result that they are more likely to "do things by the book," thereby failing to use the nuances of the situation profitably. In short, framing allows an expert's performance to be informed by a significantly richer store of information than a novice's and at the same time injects a degree of flexibility and adaptability that is unavailable to the novice.

The superiority of expertise is not due merely to having access to memories of past experience, although that plays an important role. Studies of chess experts, for example, show that when they are shown chess pieces randomly arranged on a board, they are no better at remembering the pieces' locations than are novices. Nevertheless, when the pieces are placed in locations that might reasonably occur in an ongoing game of chess, experts are far superior to novices in recalling the locations (Chase & Simon, 1973; de Grott, 1965). What is more, the experts can start with the given arrangement and anticipate what moves might occur two or three steps ahead. The conclusion is that chess experts, and presumably other kinds of experts, can recognize meaningful patterns of events and, having recognized (framed) them, can use them to perform the tasks that the situation demands.

The Nature of Frames

It is reasonable to ask how frames are cognitively represented and how they come to be shared by different people. That is, what is the essence of a frame—how does it give meaning and how does it relate to ongoing experience? And how do different people come to have what they at least think are the same frames for a situation?

I think of the frame of a situation as the decision maker's image of the situation (Beach, 1990) because to me the word *image* implies both visual and narrative representation. To get the idea, recall what you were doing yesterday at noon. Do you have a picture in your mind's eye of where you were and who you were with? Do you remember the conversation? Could you tell me in a phrase or two what was going on?

Now consider the following about your recollection:

- Do you see your companions and the locale in your mental picture? (Can you see yourself? If you can, you know this is not an exact memory because you never see yourself unless you look in a mirror.)
- Can you recall the conversation verbatim—maybe even hear your companions' voices in your head? In fact, you are unlikely to recall the conversation word for word, just the gist of it.
- Is your brief description of what was going on simply a list or does it focus on your understanding of the why and wherefore of what took place? It is probably much more laden with meaning than would be the description of an outside observer who merely recounted the events.

In short, your version of what happened yesterday at noon is a rather complex representation composed of both visual and auditory components that are held together by the storylike meaning of what was going on.

When I ask you about yesterday, I am in effect asking you to recall the frame you placed on events and then to color in the details; by and large, memory is a store of frames and referents from which we reconstruct the past rather than a store of exact recordings of what occurred (Neisser, 1982). The frame you currently are using for yesterday noon might change dramatically if I were to tell you something you did not know about one of the people with whom you were talking (presuming that you were talking with others). Suppose I told you that this morning one of those companions had checked into a hospital for treatment of an acute psychiatric problem? As in the fire alarm example, your first response might be to startle. Your second response might be to review yesterday's conversation to see if something suggested that this could happen. Finally, you might completely reinterpret what was going on yesterday in light of this new information and reframe the situation or parts of the situation.

Researchers have studied the nature of framing, and the results are instructive, if a bit overwhelming. Instead of using the term *frame,* much of the research uses the term *schema* (singular) or *schemata* (plural). Subspecies of schemata are given labels to denote the particular roles they play. Thus, *scenarios* (Jungermann, 1985; Jungermann & Thüring, 1987; Thüring & Jungermann, 1986) and *mental models* (Johnson-Laird, 1983) are researchers' labels for schemata that play a role in forecasting and problem solving. *Knowledge partitions* (Dinsmore, 1987) is the label for schemata that play a role in inference. *Episode schemata* (Rummelhart, 1977) and *causal models* (Einhorn & Hogarth, 1986) are labels for schemata that play a role in reasoning about complex chains of occurrences that lead up to some specified event. *Script* (Schank & Abelson, 1977) is the label for schemata that play a role in dealing with social situations. *Prototype* (Rosch, 1976) and *stereotype* (McCauley, Stitt, & Segal, 1980) are labels for schemata that play a role in classifying people, objects, and events. *Self-concept* (Marcus & Nurius, 1986; Marcus & Wurf, 1987) is the label for schemata that play a role in organizing our knowledge about ourselves. In short, many areas of research, under various labels, have studied schemata and their use in different situations, but the underlying concept is pretty much the same. And this concept is what we mean when we speak about frames in decision making.

As you can see, a considerable amount is known about framing— each of the areas cited above has an enormous literature associated with it. Although it is beyond the scope of this book to present a comprehensive review, we can derive from the literature a formal definition of a frame: A frame is a mental construct consisting of elements, and the relationships between them, that are associated with a situation of interest to a decision maker. The elements are the salient current events and associated past events. Relationships define the expected interactions among the elements—violations of these expectations indicate that the frame is not a valid representation of the situation of interest. If these violations are regarded by the decision maker as sufficiently important, they prompt revision of the frame, either through its complete replacement or through reinterpretation of its various elements or relationships.

It is perhaps impractical to try to think of frames in this formal, rather esoteric way. A more down-to-earth definition is that the frame is the decision maker's interpretation of what is going on. It derives from the decision maker's knowledge about events that led up to the situation in question and his or her private theories about how people behave and what makes things happen. Therefore, it tells the decision maker what to expect. The frame may be in error, but until feedback or some other form of information makes the error evident, the frame is the foundation for understanding the situation and for deciding what to do about it. In fact, knowing the frame the decision maker is using, goes a long way in predicting and understanding the decisions he or she makes—which is useful for other people who must interact with the decision maker.

Shared Frames

Unless one is a hermit, few decisions are made in isolation and few fail to have an impact on someone else. Indeed, decision making is essentially a social behavior, even when there is nobody else present, because one anticipates how others will react and factors this into the decision. And of course, a large proportion of our decisions are made in concert with other people—we ask for advice, we use others as sounding boards as we deliberate, we ask them what they would do. Organizations per se do not make decisions, but individuals in organizations do. And when they do they must take others into account.

To take others into account when making decisions, the decision maker has to assume that he or she knows how they frame the situation of interest. Clearly, if I think your frame is different from mine, to avoid conflict or censure I must try to make decisions that will not be anomalous from the viewpoint of your frame, or I must try to bring our frames into alignment so my decision will not look outlandish or stupid to you. If you are my boss or a colleague with whom I must coordinate my work, this becomes especially important.

People align their frames in two ways. First, they talk about them— discussion permits them to iron out the differences and come to some mutually shared idea about the nature of the situation and its demands and about what their options might be. (Or if they cannot align them, they can at least understand where they differ.)

The second way frames become aligned is more subtle. People who share a similar view of the world, a similar set of beliefs and values, tend to frame situations similarly. This shared set of beliefs and values is called a *culture* (Trice & Beyer, 1993). Thus, we can speak of a country's culture—the inhabitants' shared worldview. And we can speak of an organization's culture—the members' shared worldview. We even can speak of a marriage's culture or a family's culture or a friendship's culture—whenever two or more people have in common a set of beliefs and values that induce similar interpretations of events. In short, people who share cultures often arrive at similar frames for situations, frames that might be very different from those arrived at by outsiders.

If you have traveled in foreign lands, you no doubt have encountered situations that you framed in one way due to your cultural background and that the local people framed in quite another way. I lived in The Netherlands for a while and frequently heard comments about how shallow Americans tend to be (present company always excepted of course). The nub of the argument was that Americans become too familiar too quickly, because we frequently use first names from the moment we meet someone and we are rather open about personal information such as marital status, our families, and our attitudes about things in general. Dutchmen, and many other Europeans for that matter, tend to be much more guarded; friendships are built over years, and one often knows very little about the personal lives of people with whom one has worked for a long time. My usual defense was that this is merely a difference in style, but I do not think I really believed it. In fact, American values favor openness and straightforwardness, and we distrust people who behave otherwise. Dutch values favor discretion and privacy, and they distrust people who behave otherwise. In both cases, our respective values influence how we differentially frame social situations and our subsequent expectations about how we and others should behave. We each interpret observed behavior in light of our respective frames and draw the logical conclusions; they see us as shallow and we see them as unduly reserved.

Organizational cultures induce perhaps even more commonality in framing than do national cultures. The population of any nation will have a variety of subcultures. Whereas they all may share a few core beliefs and values that define them as part of that nation's larger culture, they also will have substantial differences, and the resulting differences in how they frame things are the stuff of which politics is made. Variety also exists in organizations, but there tends to be less of it. If people substantially dislike the dominant culture, it usually is easier to leave than to bring about change. Therefore, most of the people who are attracted to and remain in an organization are fairly comfortable with the beliefs and values that make up its culture and with the way in which the organization's members tend to frame situations. Indeed, it has been shown that there is a substantially greater tendency for people to leave an organization, law firms in this case, when there is a conflict between their values and the organization's than when the two sets of values are similar (Sheridan, 1992).

If this sounds too abstract, consider the members of a religious congregation. Presumably, it is the common core of beliefs and values that makes membership attractive. People who do not hold those beliefs and values are not attracted to the congregation. As a result, there is a greater similarity of worldview among the members than there would be within some randomly selected group of people. This does not mean that there are no disagreements within the congregation, but it means that the things they disagree on are peripheral to their central core of beliefs and values (often, how those beliefs and values ought to be translated into action).

Any organization is like this congregation—there is culture consisting of a central core of shared beliefs and values, sometimes larger, sometimes smaller, but shared nonetheless. The larger the shared core the more similar will be the frames that the organization's members derive for situations. This means that individuals usually can make decisions for the organization that will neither surprise nor outrage other members (Beach, 1993b; Weatherly & Beach, 1996). On the other hand, if the core is small, conflict will tend to arise because everyone with be playing from a different sheet of music, so to speak. That is, if the core is small, different people will tend to have different frames for the same situation, and a decision made by any one member may look wrong, foolish, or malevolent to other members.

Of course, even if two people frame a problem in the same way it does not mean that they will automatically choose the same way of dealing with it. In fact, they may not even arrive at similar options from which to choose. Nevertheless, if the frames are similar, they can at least understand where the other person is coming from and can at least think about the choice using the same assumptions the other person is using. So conflict may arise, but it is conflict about how to deal with the problem, not about what the problem is. Presence of a shared culture does not ensure that things always go smoothly, but absence of one almost certainly ensures that they will not.

There is a downside to a widely shared culture in an organization. Because it predisposes the members to frame things in particular ways, it often makes them overlook alternative frames. This "groupthink" (Janis, 1982) phenomenon is often observed, and its dangers are broadly recognized—in utter unanimity everyone marches off in the wrong direction. Equally bad, however, is the fact that frames that do not fit well with the culture get very short shrift. This means that novel viewpoints and fresh ideas are quickly squelched.

Perhaps more important, a shared culture makes necessary organizational reforms very difficult to bring about. Consider an organization that has been around for a long time and has functioned in a rather stable, predictable environment. People who disliked its culture have left, and people who found the culture attractive have come and stayed. In short, everyone is pretty happy and they all see the world pretty similarly.

Suppose that stable environment begins to change—not radically perhaps, but change nonetheless. The members, who often do not have a very clear view of what is going on outside the organization, fail to see the danger, but the leader does. If the only way to deal with the danger is for the organization to radically change, to try new innovative approaches to problems it does not yet comprehend, the leader may be in for trouble. Often, revolutionary changes clash with the core beliefs and values of the organization's culture, and it is the attractiveness of this core that makes the organization attractive to its members. Anything that threatens this core, which violates these beliefs and values, is framed as a threat and is regarded as patently wrongheaded and dangerous. This frame leads to decisions that protect the core and results in resistance to the proposed changes, often rationalized by a disbelief that the threat is great enough to justify revolutionary change. Every executive can tell stories of sincere efforts to convince employees that change was necessary, efforts that were actively or passively subverted, not because of the effort they would require but because the proposed changes flew in the face of the organization's culture.

Organizational change is an interesting topic, but we must not let it lead us astray. The point is that people who share beliefs and values, and who have a common experience as a result of long association with one another, tend to frame problems in much the same way. This is valuable in that it is efficient—decisions end up being coordinated because they are predicated on the same set of assumptions. Nevertheless, the range of admissible frames is limited by the culture. Frames that fall outside the range tend to be regarded with suspicion or are rejected as out-of-hand. When problems arise that cannot be addressed by the frames within that range, the culture becomes a liability—it does not permit the organization to address the problems because it does not allow its members to understand (frame) problems adequately, and therefore they cannot make the appropriate decisions.

Information and Framing

In much of what has been discussed thus far it may appear that framing is some magical process that through a flash of insight leads to a clear understanding of the situation and the problems it presents. In fact, framing is often the result of hard work and thoughtful examination of events. True, the mind abhors a vacuum and usually frames events almost automatically—but when the stakes are high and we are making a conscious, contentious effort to be careful, this first frame usually is regarded as provisional. In business, for example, going with the first hunch is dangerous and even when it appears to be the overwhelmingly correct frame, people usually make sure by checking it against the facts.

Betty and Ralph arrived at their understanding of their sales problem both by Ralph's analysis of the monthly reports and by Betty's insightful remark about cloning. His use of information showed him that his first framing of the company's problem was wrong and suggested that the real frame had something to do with sales. Her remark further defined the sales frame by focusing their attention more closely on building a good sales force. But, the frame is not yet fully developed—they both want to work on solving the problem, but action is premature until they more clearly delineate the frame—it is still too loose to provide any clear guidance for action. The only way to tighten it is to gather information. Perhaps they ought to speak with their customers about what they value in salespeople and who they think does the best job. In light of what they find out, they should perhaps devise ways of predicting success for job applicants (or design appropriate training programs for older employees). They might also want to find out what HR currently is doing when it evaluates job applicants to learn why current practices are producing such bad results.

In short, initial framing may be fairly swift, but when the stakes are high we seldom settle for that first impression. Instead, we seek information against which to test the validity of the initial frame and to guide us in tailoring a frame that best fits the facts. After that initial, almost instantaneous, framing a lot of time and work is invested in fleshing out our understanding of the situation and making judgments (inferences) about those parts of it that are not wholly clear.

Summary

Framing serves to tie events to the decision maker's ongoing experience, thereby endowing those events with meaning. Nevertheless, a frame is a fragile thing; when challenged by events that conflict with it, the decision maker is quick to amend it or to replace it altogether—although people differ in the degree to which they are flexible in this regard. Experts may well be experts because their training and past experience allow them to recognize situations and apply familiar frames to them. Once the situation is framed, the expert's knowledge about what to expect and what has worked or not worked in the past can be brought to bear on the current problem.

Because almost every decision ultimately is a social decision, people make efforts to understand others' frames. When they perceive differences between those frames and their own, they make efforts to align the frames, through discussion and persuasion. Fortunately, when people have a history of shared experience, they tend to frame situations similarly in the first place, thus reducing the amount of work needed to align their frames. Organizations' cultures, the beliefs and values shared by members of the organization, promote similar frames and therefore can contribute to coordinated decision making.

Having examined the role of framing, its nature and how frames come to be shared, we can move on to the next step, policy-based decision making.

3 Policy

PART 1

————

Dr. Karma Howell not only had a unique first name, she had a smile warm enough to melt steel. Her students loved her and so did Ralph, in a proper brother-in-law-like sort of way.

Ralph and Betty sat in Dr. Howell's cramped office listening to her describe the research on decision making. They had told her that they wanted to clone their best salespeople. She replied that this was a novel way of putting it but that the technology existed to do it—well, not for genetic cloning but for identifying the salient attributes of good salespeople and for formulating a policy for using those attributes in hiring or training salespeople. She explained that the technology had its weaknesses but that it could at least introduce order and reason to the selection decision process. Whatever its faults, the technology probably would lead to better overall results than the company's present methods were producing. By the time they left, Ralph and Betty knew the next step in solving their sales problem.

* * *

The purpose of this chapter is to examine the use of policy for decision making. This follows directly from our previous discussion of framing. When a situation is framed, the decision maker can make decisions about it in one of three ways. (1) Recognition: The situation is so similar to one that he or she has encountered before that behavior that worked before can be used again—or, at least, a variation of what worked before can be used. (2) Inference: The situation is familiar enough that the decision maker can make an educated guess about what to do. (3) Choice: The situation is sufficiently unique that neither recognition nor inference provide adequate guidance and the decision maker must explore his or her options and choose the most promising option. Recognition and inference both involve policy, the subject of this chapter and the one that follows.

Recognition

When a decision situation is encountered, the decision maker uses its salient features to probe his or her memory. If the probe locates a contextual memory that has features that are virtually the same as those of the current situation, the latter is said to be recognized. The advantage of recognition is that the decision maker can draw on his or her knowledge about the previously encountered situation to guide behavior in this one. In decision making, old behaviors that are used in new but similar situations are called *policies*. In the psychology of learning, these preformulated actions are called *habits*. In social psychology they are called *scripts*. In all cases, the point is to add efficiency to the process by using precedent rather than engaging in choice for every situation.

The most thorough exploration of policy use in decision situations has been done by Gary Klein and his associates (1993). Their studies have focused on nonlaboratory decision tasks, such as fire fighting, army tank platoon command, and design engineering. The key is that the decision makers are highly familiar with the situations in question and that they have extensive training and experience in dealing with those situations. Upon encountering a situation of the same type, they draw on their training and experience to act appropriately. Klein calls this "recognition-primed decision making," and his description of it is called the RPD model.

There are three levels in the RPD model. The most basic level is the simple match, in which the situation is recognized and what has been done in the past is done again. The second level involves more evaluation; the decision maker performs mental simulations of variations of past behaviors and what might happen if one or another variation was used here. The third level applies when there are flaws in the variations, requiring major modifications and more complex mental simulations. That is, recognition primes the decision about what to do, it does not wholly determine what to do.

The mental simulations are an important key to recognition-primed decision making. Klein (1989) has gathered descriptions of what decision makers think about when making decisions and shows that they imagine what might happen if they did this and what might be the result of doing that, in which both this and that are drawn from past experience. Past behaviors have not all been successful, and past failures inform current decision making as much as, or more than, past successes. Thus, when they think about whether some act might successfully deal with a situation, decision makers can use past failures to help them diagnose flaws in the action under consideration and to guide modifications (or rejection) of the action. The point is, recognition of situations does not necessarily result in blind application of a policy based on past experience; often, it prompts consideration of modifications and revisions while providing the strategy for approaching the decision.

Inference

The RPD model strikes a responsive chord in most people who hear about it. The lowest of the three levels is closely related to learning and memory research in psychology. The middle level allows for minor modification of learned behavior; it introduces a cognitive flavor and accounts for the fact that behavior seldom is exactly the same from one time to another, just as situations are never identical. Nevertheless, the RPD model's account of the highest level is too vague to be of much use in either studying decision behavior or helping decision makers do their jobs. For the necessary specificity, we must turn to an older model, the lens model (Brunswik, 1947). Whereas the lens model does not directly address all of the issues raised by the RPD model's third level, it provides a more systematic treatment of the processes involved when the course of action in a familiar situation is not wholly clear.

It all began with Egon Brunswik (1947), an Austrian psychologist who came to the United States just before the outbreak of World War II and specialized in studies of perception. Specifically, he studied how people use perceptual cues to make decisions (inferences) about the state of their surrounding environment. Let us take a moment to explore the underlying logic of Brunswik's position because that logic is the basis of all that follows in this chapter.

It is widely accepted by perceptual psychologists that one's mind does not directly experience the objects and events in the world around one. Instead, sensory information permits the mind to construct mental representations of those objects and events (e.g., Prinzmetal, 1995; Yantis, 1995). There are many phenomena that reveal that what seems to be direct experience of the external world actually is a mental representation built from sensory information, but let us concentrate on the following.

Consider a table that has a rectangular top. When you look at the top, what do you see—a square, a rectangle, a trapezoid? In fact the image of the table's rectangular top forms a trapezoid on the retina of your eye, but you perceive that tabletop to be rectangular. That is, to make the tabletop look realistic, an artist would have to draw it as a trapezoid; the nearer edge of the table would be longer than the farther edge and the two sides would form acute angles with the nearer edge and obtuse angles with the farther edge. When you look at the drawing, you would see a table with a rectangular top.

Look around you for a table. Then look at it analytically, as an artist would, and you will see that its rectangular top is, in fact, presented to your eye as a trapezoid. Moreover, if you walk around the table you will note that the trapezoid changes shape as you move. But your perceptual system is never tricked into thinking that the top changes shape as you walk around it. This is called "perceptual constancy," and it has been studied for 100 years (James, 1890/1983). For our purposes, it serves as evidence that what you experience (a solid rectangular tabletop that does not change as you move around) and what is presented to your senses (a trapezoid that changes shape as you move) are not identical. In fact, your perceptual system must use the dynamic sensory information about the table to make inferences that tell you

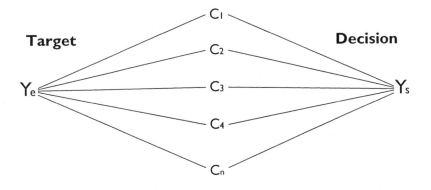

Figure 3.1. Brunswik's Lens Model

there is a stable object out there—otherwise the contents of your experience would be in constant flux.

Brunswik (1947) summarized his idea about perceptual inference in the form of the lens model, diagrammed in Figure 3.1. To make it simple, imagine that your perceptual system is called on to identify some target object (Y_e). Light and air surround the target and convey information to you through your vision, hearing, and other senses. These are cues ($C1, C2, C3$) that convey information about the target. On the basis of these cues, you must make a decision (Y_s) about the nature of the target.

Suppose the target's outline on your retina indicates that it is small. Your color receptors sense that it is white. And because of the way in which its surface reflects light you infer that it is covered with something soft, perhaps fur. You smell alfalfa on its breath, you can feel the radiance of its body heat, and your hearing tells you that it is nearly silent when it moves. You see that the pointy part of the target (its nose?) is constantly twitching and, even more telling, there are two long white appendages that project upward from just above and slightly behind the pointy part (ears?). And the round things between the pointy part and the (assumed) ears are pink (eyes?). This must be a rabbit!

Actually, all of this happens virtually instantaneously and with little effort on your part—your perceptual system is designed to make inferences and it does so without much help from your conscious mind. This is especially true if the situation is framed so that there is a limited number of possibilities to begin with. If I had told you that we were at a 4-H club, it would have limited the possibilities so much that the system would not have had to work very hard. Nevertheless, if I told you that we were in a pet store, you might have expected the target to be a dog or cat, which would have required your perceptual system to work a little harder to avoid error.

Identifying targets is but one function of the perceptual system. It also serves to make comparisons among targets. Suppose I framed the situation as a county fair and told you that your job was to judge the rabbits. Now we have lots of rabbits and your perceptual system is called on to make comparisons among them. This requires some additional effort and your conscious mind now will be called on to augment your automatic perceptual processes. Now you are more discriminating; again, the cues will be size, coloring, texture of the fur and so on, together with whatever else livestock judges use when judging rabbits. And this time, instead of merely inferring that the target is a rabbit (which you now take as given) you must use the cues consistently (a *policy*) when deciding about each of the rabbits so you can tell which are winners and which are not. In short, you must evaluate each rabbit's location on an underlying scale, with the best rabbits at the high end and the worst at the low end. Then you must select the winner based on the rabbits' locations on this scale— presumably you would select the one that was highest on the scale.

Applying the Lens Model

Enough about rabbits. The idea is that Brunswik's (1947) apparently simple description of how the perceptual system identifies targets has hidden within it a great deal of sophistication. It applies both to basic perceptual decisions and to higher order decisions that permit ordering of the targets on an underlying scale, usually related to preference. And it is here that we return to Ralph and Betty and their cloning problem.

When Betty and Ralph speak about cloning their good salespeople, they mean that they would like to know how to look at a job applicant (target) and make a good guess (decision) about whether he or she will turn out to be a successful salesperson. The first step is to turn the inference process around and find out what makes salespeople successful. The second step is to use this knowledge to devise a policy for using information about potential job applicants to decide how well they are going to do (not unlike judging which rabbits are at the winning end of the scale). The third step is getting the human resource (HR) folks to use this policy to select new salespeople or to design a program for retraining failing salespeople. Let us look at each of these steps in turn.

The Left Side of the Lens

To simplify things, let us assume that you have been hired to do the work for Betty's company. Let us assume further that the company has a pretty good performance evaluation scheme in place. The first step in discovering what makes a good salesperson (Y_e) would be to sit down and read the performance evaluations of both the good performers and the poor performers, concentrating on what differentiates them. What you learn should be augmented by discussions with supervisors and with the salespeople themselves. Eventually you should get a fair idea about some of the differences between the two groups.

Unfortunately, much of what you learn will not be very valuable. That is, much of what you learn will be about how good salespeople behave in the selling situation, but you seldom have direct information about selling behavior when you are judging the applicant's suitability for hiring. This is the crux of the problem. You usually have to make your evaluation on the basis of only tangential information—and this could have been one reason the HR people told Betty that hiring was hardly better than a crapshoot.

On the other hand, things may be better than they appear. For one thing, you know who are the good and bad salespeople. And you have their original job applications somewhere in their personnel folders. We can think of the information on job applications as potential cues for predicting whether an applicant will turn out to be successful or unsuccessful. But now you can turn things around—by knowing who are the good salespeople, who are the so-so salespeople, and who are the poor salespeople, you can look back at the cues on their applications and see which cues would have been the best predictors of later performance.

The procedure is fairly straightforward. First, you have supervisors rate each salesperson for performance, perhaps on a scale from 1 (*poor*) to 7 (*excellent*). Then you go to each person's original job application and code the answer to each question on the application so that it can be entered into a computer (i.e., you must convert qualitative information to quantitative information; coding yes or no answers as 1 or 0 and assigning numbers to different levels of more complicated answers).

For each salesperson, you now have a set of data consisting of his or her performance rating and one coded answer for each of the n questions in the application. Then, across all salespeople's data, you do a multiple regression analysis using the performance ratings as the dependent variable and the coded answers to each of the n questions on the application as the independent variables. This analysis will yield an equation that describes the structure of the relationship between the cues (the independent variables) and performance (the dependent variable) for the sales force as a whole:

[3.1] $$Y_e = a + B_1C_1 + B_2C_2 + B_3C_3 + \ldots + B_nC_n.$$

This regression equation is a statement of the optimal policy for using the cues to predict performance. Here, Y_e stands for the supervisors' ratings of performance, C stands for a coded answer to a question on the application (Questions 1, 2, 3 and so on up to n questions), and B stands for the standardized regression weight for each question, called the beta weight; a is merely a scaling constant that has no particular importance for us at the moment. A cue (question) that has a large beta weight can be regarded as contributing more information to predicting performance than a cue with a small weight.

In addition, the analysis yields an indication of how well this equation fits the data, expressed as the square of the multiple correlation coefficient, R^2. This coefficient can be interpreted as the degree to which the equation is capable of predicting the performance ratings. Of course, because the equation is derived from data across all salespeople, the ratings are made by different supervisors, and there is bound to be noise (error) in the data, the equation never can perfectly predict the performance ratings for every one of the salespeople. But if R^2 is large it means that the cues from the application permit reasonably accurate prediction across the group as a whole. If it is low, you must assume that the cues are not very discriminating—you have the wrong cues, they are not measured accurately, or it simply is not possible to predict performance in this situation. Let us consider what you might do when the R^2 is high and when it is low.

If R^2 is high, you should be very happy—at least Ralph and Betty should be very happy. This means that they can instruct the HR people to use the policy summarized by Equation 3.1 for selecting new salespeople. To do this, an applicant's coded answers should be substituted for each C in the equation. Then these numbers should be multiplied by their respective weights (using the nonstandardized form of the weights, which will be provided by your statistical package). The sum of these products should be added to the constant, a. The resulting number will lie between one and seven, which is on the same scale the supervisors used for rating the performance of your existing sales force. If the applicant's number is high on the scale, the bet is that he or she will turn out to be a good salesperson; if it is low, the bet is that he or she will turn out to be poor. Of course, it is still just a bet, but the odds probably are better than using the present system (although we do not know that yet), and in the long run, the quality of the sales force ought to improve.

If R^2 is low, it means that the information is not sufficient to predict performance. But you are not without hope. In fact, you have learned a lot. First, the whole point of the questions on the application is to predict performance, so any questions that have small beta weights can be taken off the application (unless there is some other reason for keeping them—but either way you omit them from performance prediction). This means you retain the cues with the largest beta weights, but the low R^2 tells you that you still have work to do.

Now is the time to return to what you learned when you reviewed the performance evaluations and conducted your interviews with supervisors and salespeople. Is there something there that you could turn into a cue that could be made available at the time a person applies for a sales job? For example, if enthusiasm seemed to be important you might find a test for enthusiasm that could be administered as part of the job application procedure. Or if motivation is crucial, you might add a question on the application about what the applicant aspires to make in commissions, which might reflect motivation. In short, you must be creative in changing the application information—omitting the nondiagnostic information and adding diagnostic information. Then, you add the new questions, obtain answers to these new questions, drop the useless questions from the application while retaining the good questions, and do the multiple regression analysis over again. If you were successful in spotting relevant information to add to the analysis, the new R^2 will be higher than the old one and the new equation will be a better way of evaluating new applicants than the old equation. If the R^2 still is too low, do not give up. Assuming it is at all possible to predict sales performance, it is worth it (or at least worth it to Betty and Ralph) to keep trying.

The Right Side of the Lens

The use of multiple regression in the way just described is pretty standard. Moreover, it does not have a lot to do with human decision making. So turning to the right side of the lens in Figure 3.1, let us consider the role of the HR people in the hiring process.

As noted earlier, the purpose of an application is to provide information for an HR employment officer (let us call him Hank) to make a decision about how well an applicant will perform. Use of Equation 3.1 might appear to eliminate Hank from the process; a clerk could merely obtain the required information and put it into the equation. However attractive (and inexpensive) this substitution might appear to Ralph and Betty, it is unlikely to work. The equation is mechanical and inflexible. It treats every applicant the same, acknowledging no mitigating circumstances and making no exceptions. As such, its blind application probably is an invitation to a lawsuit.

Clearly, human intellect has its limitations, but it excels in its ability to detect exceptions to rules (anomalies). Indeed, it tends to go to sleep when things are constant, but when something unique comes along it is quick to seize on it. Therefore, the intellect of the people in HR (Hank in particular) should be used, not subjugated to the inflexible application of Equation 3.1. You need the HR people to make sure the equation does not blindly commit injustices or do stupid things. For example, if you have no cue in the equation for some kind of diagnostic information, perhaps because it has never arisen before, you could overlook the best applicant you have ever had. Let us say that the applicant has owned his own highly successful company in the same field as Betty's company, but his physician told him that the stress of running it was going to kill him. Therefore, he decides to sell his company and to go to work as a salesman for a similar company—he knows the business inside and out, he was his own best salesman, and he wants to work for Betty. Because this has never happened before, there is no way to put this information in Equation 3.1, so somebody has to override the system and hire him before he goes to a competitor.

Even for more mundane cases, Hank has to be active in the hiring process—laws must be observed and information has to be interpreted. Equation 3.1 is merely a policy guide. So the question becomes one of helping Hank align his hiring policies with the policy described by Equation 3.1, while retaining his discretion in unique cases.

The first step is to find out what Hank is doing now—what policy characterizes his use of information about the applicant to evaluate acceptability. This involves returning to the lens model. Your evaluation of how the cues could be used to predict good sales performance involved the left side of the lens in Figure 3.1. Your evaluation of how the cues are used by Hank involves the right side. In the past, Hank read the applications, talked with the applicants, and made a decision about how acceptable was the person—that is, placed him or her on a scale of preference for hiring.

The question of interest is about Hank's policy for using the cues on the application to make his decisions. You can find this out by performing an analysis very like the one you did before, except that this time the resulting equation will describe Hank's policy (Equation 3.2) rather than the optimal policy (Equation 3.1). First, you present Hank with the applications for each of the people on the sales force (with identifying information blanked out). Do not tell him that these are people who have already been hired so he will treat them as new applicants and rate their acceptability (on a scale from 1 to 7). For each salesperson, you now have the coded answers on their original application (that you already coded for the earlier analysis) and Hank's acceptability rating. Once again you do a multiple regression analysis, this time using his rating as the dependent variable (Y_s) and the same coded cues (C) you used before. The analyses will yield an equation of the form

[3.2] $Y_s = a + B_1 C_1 + B_2 C_2 + B_3 C_3 + \ldots + B_n C_n.$

Note that the form is the same as Equation 3.1, but some of the components will be different. The things that are different are Y_s, which is Hank's acceptability rating; a, which again is an uninteresting relative influence (importance) of the cue to Hank's ratings. Notice that the coded cues, C, in Equation 3.2 are the same as in Equation 3.1. That is, you used the same information from the applications in the analysis for Equation 3.2 as you used for Equation 3.1. This means that if Hank's policy for using the cues (Equation 3.2) is different from the optimal policy (Equation 3.1), it will show up as differences between the beta weights in the two equations.

In addition, having Hank's acceptability ratings allows you to see how good a decision maker he is; you merely correlate his ratings with the ratings the supervisors made for the salespeople. This correlation is called the *achievement coefficient,* and it indicates how well Hank's judgments of acceptability (that presumably reflects his prediction of the applicant's performance) correspond to the supervisors' performance ratings. Nevertheless, a low achievement coefficient is not necessarily an indictment of Hank. Let us look more closely at this, and then let us look at how we might help Hank do a better job if he is not doing too well.

Consider Hank's dilemma. He has the answers to the questions on the application, which may not be very good predictors of performance in the first place. So if he does poorly, it could be for either of two reasons: (1) Nobody could do a good job with the information in the application, or (2) another person might do a good job but Hank cannot.

The difficulty of Hank's task is revealed by the R^2 for Equation 3.1. If it is low, the cues are not good predictors of rated performance, and we should not expect Hank to do very well either. The low R^2 puts an upper limit on Hank's achievement coefficient (actually on the square of his achievement coefficient) so he will be unable to do better than that no matter how hard he tries.

On the other hand, if the R^2 for Equation 3.1 is high, but Hank's achievement coefficient is low, there is only one place the problem can lie—he must be weighting the cues in a way that lowers his ability to predict accurately. As we observed earlier, this would be revealed by differences between the beta weights in his equation and the beta weights in Equation 3.1. The remedy is to train Hank to weight the information in the appropriate manner.

If Hank is a poor predictor of performance, it does not necessarily mean that the R^2 will be low for Equation 3.2. This is because the R^2 for Equation 3.2 indicates how well Equation 3.2 is able to account for *his* ratings on the 7-point scale, not how accurate these ratings are (that would be achievement). He may be using the cues incorrectly, but so long as he uses them in a consistent manner the equation will be able to account for his ratings and the R^2 will be high. To the degree that he is inconsistent in his use of the cues, it becomes more difficult to account for his ratings and, therefore, the R^2 is reduced.

What might it mean if the R^2 for Equation 3.1 was low, but Hank's achievement coefficient and the R^2 for Equation 3.2 were high? The answer is that Hank is using the information consistently (hence, the high R^2 for Equation 3.2), but he must know something that Equation 3.1 does not know (hence the high achievement coefficient even though the R^2 for Equation 3.1 says that highly accurate prediction is not possible). This might happen if Hank has access to information about the applicants that is not represented in Equation 3.1.

Making a Recommendation

Now you have equations for both the left and right sides of the lens model, and you know that you are not simply going to replace Hank with a clerk who knows how to use Equation 3.1 because you need Hank's intellect and experience to deal with unique cases.

What, then, might you recommend to Betty and Ralph about how to clone their best salespeople? One recommendation might be to go ahead and have a clerk code the data from each job seeker's application and enter it into a computer that is programmed to apply Equation 3.1 and yield a score (the predicted Y_e). Except, instead of replacing Hank with the equation, Hank could be given this score together with other information that is unique to the applicant and asked to make an overall decision about the qualifications of the applicant. This would mean that Hank would not have to learn to use the cues the way Equation 3.1 uses them, he merely would use the output of Equation 3.1 as information on which his decision could be based. This would leave him in control, but it also would make sure that the information on the application was presented to him in a form that was both concise and valid. Of course, you would have to do a follow-up study to see if this new arrangement improved the sales force, which, after all, is the point.

A Brief Review

Let us review the use of the lens model, referring back to Figure 3.1. The basic idea is that the decision maker must make inferences (Y_s) about some set of events (Y_e) on the basis of cues (C) that are not wholly reliable. The left side of the lens can be regarded as a description of what is going on in the environment, the events of interest and the cues that emanate from them. The right side can be regarded as a description of what is happening in the decision maker: reception of the cues and their use in deriving decisions (inferences) about the events on the left.

A little creativity in measuring the cues and the events (Y_e) permits the use of multiple regression to model the left side of the lens. This provides an equation that describes the optimal policy for weighting the cues in order to make the best possible predictions about the events. Use of the same cue measurements and a measure of the decision maker's decisions (Y_s) about the events permits use of multiple regression to obtain an equation that describes the decision maker's policy for weighting the cues in order to arrive at his or her decisions. Moreover, you can calculate how well the decision maker actually does by using the achievement coefficient, the correlation between the measures of Y_e and Y_s.

What you do with the two equations, the one for the optimal policy and the one for the decision maker's policy, depends on the question that motivated the study in the first place. If achievement is low, but the R^2 for the optimal policy (Equation 3.1) is high, you could simply replace the decision maker with the equation for the optimal policy, or you could train the decision maker to use the optimal policy. If both achievement and the R^2 for the optimal policy (Equation 3.1) are low, perhaps you should be sympathetic with the decision maker because he or she cannot be expected to do a very good job. If the R^2 for the decision maker's policy equation is low, it means that the decision maker is not using a consistent policy. This almost always results in lower achievement than could be achieved by consistent use of the optimal policy, even when the R^2 for the optimal policy is fairly low. That is, use of an inconsistent policy seldom buys the decision maker much of anything. Even when events are not particularly predictable using the available cues, the decision maker would do better to consistently use a marginally serviceable policy.

The Lens Model in Research

The lens model has been used in many studies of decision making. In one of the earliest, Frederick Todd (reported in Hammond, 1955) examined 10 clinical psychologists' ability to use patients' responses to Rorschach cards (ink blots) to predict the IQ of each of 78 patients. The IQ tests previously had been given to the patients, and their Rorschach responses previously had been coded using a standard coding system. The results of each patient's IQ test was Y_e and his or her coded Rorschach responses were the cues. Each clinician was given the coded Rorschach responses for each patient and asked to make a decision (Y_s) about each patient's IQ. Using multiple regression to obtain the optimal policy (across patients) yielded a R^2 of only .23, which means that it objectively is very difficult to predict IQ from Rorschach responses. The 10 clinicians' median achievement (squared) was .22, which indicates that their achievement was about as good as could be expected given that IQ cannot be reliably predicted from Rorschach responses. The median R^2 for their policy equations was .72, which means that even in the face of this unpredictability they tended to use the cues consistently—which probably accounts for their achievement being as high as it was.

Among the more interesting results of early policy research is, for example, Rorer, Hoffman, Dickman, and Slovic's (1967) finding of no consistency among the policies of the attendants in a mental hospital in judging whether patients should have weekend passes; imagine how confusing that must have been for the patients. Similarly, Slovic, Rorer, and Hoffman (1971) found four different policies being used by various radiologists for judging malignancy of ulcers. Dawes (1971) modeled the decision policies of the admission committee for a PhD program and found that replacing the committee with its own policy equation (called *bootstrapping*) resulted in better predictions of applicant success than using the committee itself, presumably because the committee's membership changed over time and therefore was not wholly consistent. Roose and Doherty (1976) studied how agency managers for an insurance company used application information to hire new agents and found that they relied too highly on a nondiagnostic cue; training them to use the optimal policy promised substantial increase in successful hires.

More recently, Dougherty, Ebert, and Callender (1986) studied how applicant information is used by employment interviewers in a large corporation; they had very consistent policies, but it was not clear that they were the best policies. Over the years there have been many studies done in the context of businesses or other organizations, but for proprietary reasons or because there is no payoff for the investigators to do so, little of this has been published in the scientific literature.

Social Judgment Theory

Since the 1970s, the point of view represented by the lens model and its applications has come to be known as social judgment theory (Hammond, Rohrbaugh, Mumpower, & Adelman, 1977; Hammond, Stewart, Brehmer, & Steinmann, 1975) with Kenneth Hammond generally regarded as its central figure. In addition to examining interesting practical problems, such as the selection of bullets by the Denver police department (Hammond & Adelman, 1976; see Brehmer & Joyce, 1988, for other applications), fundamental psychological issues also have been addressed. Among these is how people learn to use cues appropriately (Klayman, 1988). It is found that people learn most quickly when the cues have a simple, linear, relationship to events (Y_e) and when the task content gives rise to reasonable hypotheses about weighting, but often, learning is surprisingly slow. It turns out that having to learn by trial and error is very inefficient but that efficiency can be increased through provision of "cognitive feedback" (Hammond, 1971) consisting of information about the optimal policy. There also has been social judgment theory research on decision processes in small groups, focusing largely on conflicts resulting from differences among the group members' various decision policies and how these differences can be reconciled (Rohrbaugh, 1988). A recent article by Hammond, Harvey, and Hastie (1992) provides a social judgment theory analysis of social policy formation.

Summary

In this chapter, we have examined how the lens model can be used to study both the decision maker's policy and the optimal policy. Moreover, the degree to which these policies account for Y_e and Y_s, as well as the degree to which the latter are correlated (achievement), permits us to prescribe different courses of action—replacement of the decision maker with mechanical application of the optimal policy or training the decision maker to use the optimal policy. As it has been developed in social judgment theory, the logic of the lens model is applicable to a broad range of nonlaboratory, socially interesting areas of decision.

In the next chapter we will examine some of the problems that arise when the lens model approach is used and some alternative methods of formulating and examining policies.

4 Policy

———

PART 2

Ralph watched Betty try to calm Hank's rage. She was good at this sort of thing, but even her skills were sorely tested. He and Betty had been taken aback by Hank's reaction—they thought he would appreciate their efforts to help him with his job. Clearly, they had been wrong.

Hank was seething. He had never in his life been so insulted as when they showed him those absurd equations and told him that they revealed what he should be doing and what he actually was doing when he evaluated job applicants. Of all the nerve! Twenty-two years of experience in human resources, 10 of them as the employment officer for this company, and they reduce his accumulated knowledge to an equation.

The idea that a simple additive equation could ever capture the richness of his use of information about applicants! Didn't they realize that knowing the applicant's answer to one question on the application often changed the interpretation of other answers? Their equation simply didn't address this sort of thing, and therefore, it didn't come close to describing how he actually uses information.

And that was just the beginning—when considering applicants' past job experience, for example, too little or too much were bad signs. Too little experience meant that the company had to train them and too much meant that they probably were set in their ways and might not fit in with how things are done around here. Let's see that wimpy little equation take this sort of thing into account! Beyond even that, much of his reasoning had at least two or three levels to it, not just the cue-to-decision sort of thing implied by equations; after all, he wasn't simpleminded.

* * *

Hank's concerns are not uncommon. Whereas the logic of the lens model has its attractions, it is rather simplistic and the appropriateness of the multiple regression analyses can be questioned on many grounds.

The Charges

First, the equation presumes that the cues are additive—that the information provided by each simply piles on top of the other information and as the pile increases the applicant moves higher on the preference scale. Nevertheless, it does not take much imagination to understand that information conveyed by some cues sometimes amplifies what is conveyed by other cues, rather than just adding to it, so the applicant would move up the scale in ever-increasing steps. Amplification is described mathematically as a multiplicative combination of information instead of the additive combination assumed by the model. That is, the cues may not be independent (there may be an interaction between them), but the mathematics of multiple regression requires them to be independent if the equation is to make sense. The problem is important because even if the cues are not independent the analysis will blindly impose additivity on them, with the result that the optimal policy or the decision maker's policy will appear to be much simpler than they are really. It is possible to tinker with the equation to include interactions, but it is cumbersome and seldom works very well (Kort, 1968).

Second, the equation assumes that each cue is linearly related to the dependent variable. For example, the larger the cue value the higher the applicant will be on the preference scale for hiring. Nevertheless, as Hank observed, some cues have a curvilinear relationship to preference. For example, low and high values of the cue are associated with low preference and medium cue values are associated with high preference. Unless special steps are taken, the analysis will blindly impose linearity on the cues and the resulting equations will suggest a greater simplicity than actually exists.

Third, the lens model presumes a single level of inference, from the cues to the decision. Clearly, this is not the way things always are. Often, there are intermediate levels in which subsets of the cues are used to make intermediate decisions that, in turn, are used to make the final decision. For example, when considering investment opportunities, the decision maker will use some of the information to decide about the financial aspects of the opportunities, other parts of the information to decide about management capabilities, and yet other parts of it to decide about growth potential. These three decisions then serve as the basis for an overall decision about the preference of each opportunity. The lens model, as outlined in Figure 3.1, does not permit analysis of these intermediate decisions.

The Defense

Those who defend the multiple regression analysis point out that it is very robust. For example, it is possible to include nonindependence in the equation by combining coded cue values before they are included in the analysis (that will be described later). Nevertheless, they argue that from a practical standpoint, often by so doing there is little gained. As was demonstrated very early (Kort, 1968), unless cues are highly dependent (in which case, one or the other might best be eliminated as redundant) the R^2 for the equation that uses combined coding usually is not much different from the R^2 for the equation that treats the cues as independent.

The argument continues that the equations do not have to be absolutely accurate representations of the environment or of the decision maker's policy to be valuable. That is, they can get you in the ball park even though they might not be right on the mark. As such, it is usually less expensive and less laborious to assume independence (or drop one of those dependent cues or combine those dependent cues into a single measure), go with the simple equation, and temper its use with a little common sense.

These same defenders of multiple regression use a similar argument in regard to curvilinear cues. Unless the curvilinear relationship is especially crucial, the analysis's imposition of linearity may not do much damage. By recoding the cue (so now, both low and high values of the cue are recoded as low numbers to use in the equation and medium values are recoded as high numbers), it is possible to derive a more accurate equation, but it often does not buy much for the effort; the R^2 may stay pretty much the same. Of course, there are other forms of nonlinearity than curvilinearity, but much the same argument is made for them.

The third criticism of the lens model, that it fails to model the multilevel nature of decision making, is even more easily met. Very early on Hammond (see Beach, 1967) suggested that the intermediate decisions could be modeled as separate lenses, the output of which would serve as cues for another lens that culminated in the final decision. Today, that same objective is more easily attained using structural modeling, and the statistics is considerably more justifiable than it was for the multiple lenses. At any rate, by expanding the lens model to multiple levels and by replacing multiple regression with more complicated structural modeling techniques, the lens model can be modernized to take advantage of advances in statistical theory.

Some Cautions

Nevertheless, one must not overestimate the robustness of the multiple regression analyses. Profound nonindependence or nonlinearity can, in fact, undermine even the best efforts. Typically, a low R^2 is a tip-off that something is wrong, but it is difficult to know whether it is because the cues are inherently poor predictors of Y_e or Y_s, or whether it results from nonindependence or nonlinearity. The only way to tell is to look at the other statistics your program provides, particularly in the intercorrelation matrix, for the cues. In addition, if a cue that you think ought to have a large beta weight turns out to have a smaller one, it may mean that the cue is nonlinearly related to the dependent variable and the analysis cannot accommodate it. Similarly, if the decision maker's achievement coefficient seems too high given the R^2 for either the optimal equation or his or her own equation, it may mean that the decision maker knows about nonlinearities that are ignored in the equations.

Hank's outrage may be directed toward the lens model and its regression equations, but they may not be his real target. It is not insulting to suggest that a professional decision maker such as Hank is consistent in how he or she goes about the job. Neither is it insulting to say that careful study of that professional decision maker can allow us to understand the nature of that consistency and permit us to describe it in words or in an equation. What is perhaps insulting is an oversimplified description of that consistency, a trivialization of the decision maker's policy. The robustness of the regression equations may be a benefit if they are to be applied in a complicated task environment, but that very robustness may hide real and important subtleties. True, the equation may work quite well for predicting the great middle range of cases, but the test comes with the extreme cases.

So, what do we do about Hank and those like him who are uncomfortable with the lens model equations? One option simply is to drop the whole thing and go back to what was being done before—probably not a good idea. Another option is to ignore Hank and his colleagues and go ahead with implementation of the model and imposition of a training program to make them behave in accordance with the equation—again, not a good idea. The third and most reasonable option is to pay attention to these folks and build a model that more closely represents the richness of their decision policies.

Information Integration

The questions about how to combine information in the equation, additively or multiplicatively, and whether a cue is linearly or nonlinearly related to decisions have implications about how information is to be integrated in order to arrive at a decision regarding the person, object, or event of interest. When we are modeling the left side of the lens model, we can tinker around with the cue information to obtain the highest R^2—the left side of the lens model does not "get insulted" when we impose our model on it. The decision maker's side of the lens model is a different story. Here, we want to model what he or she is doing with the information, and we do not want to merely impose the most serviceable model—as with Hank, decision makers tend to be sensitive and, probably, rightly so. So, if we want to placate the decision maker and honestly create an accurate model of his or her policy, we must look beyond the lens model.

Cognitive Algebra

Norman Anderson (1970) provided the tools for examining whether cues are integrated additively or multiplicatively (additive includes averaging). The matrix on the left at the top of Figure 4.1 is defined by various levels of one cue dimension on the left side and various levels of another cue dimension along the top. The cells in the matrix represent combinations of the values on the side and top. A decision maker's evaluations of those cue combinations can be written in each cell. The goal is to infer from the pattern of the evaluations how the decision maker is integrating the cue values on the margins of the matrix, additively or multiplicatively. An additional goal is to discover the decision maker's subjective scales (i.e., his or her perceptions of the relative magnitudes of the various levels of the cue dimensions), but we will come to that in a moment.

Let us assume that Hank thinks that experience and training interact (multiply) to make applicants increasingly acceptable. To test this, we can do a little experiment. We create simulated applicants by pairing each level of experience with each level of training, resulting in one simulated applicant for each of the 25 cells in the matrix on the left in Figure 4.1. We present Hank with the 25 combinations of cue values and ask him to rate the acceptability of each as though it were a job applicant who had that combination of cues. His ratings on a scale of 1 to 100, are placed in the matrix cells.

Now comes the part about perception of cue values. The convenient thing about Anderson's method is that the different cue levels do not have to be presented as quantities, they can be qualitative. Thus, we need not specify how much training or how much experience each applicant had. Instead, we can have different *kinds* of training and different *kinds* of experience. Of interest is how Hank lines up the different kinds of training and experience to form levels of training and levels of experience. In other words, what is Hank's *subjective quantitative scaling* of the qualitative kinds of training and experience?

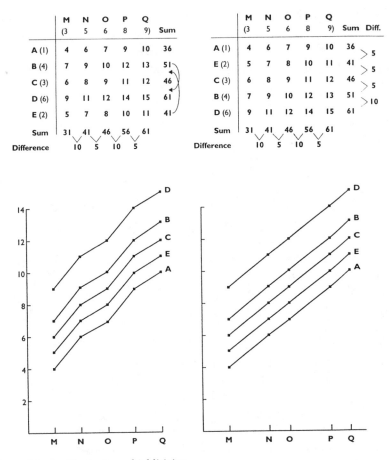

Figure 4.1. An Illustration of Additivity

Additivity

Consider Figure 4.1 first. We graph the rows in the matrix, as is done on the bottom left, by plotting the decisions (Hank's ratings) in the cells for each level of experience (A-D) against each level of training (M-Q). Note that the lines are a little jagged, but they are parallel with one another. In fact, they can be made into nice straight lines by adjusting the locations of M through Q on the bottom axis of the graph (graph on the right). This adjustment is permissible because the levels of training are not quantitative anyway, so their locations in the graph on the left (equally spaced on the bottom axis) are wholly arbitrary. But as soon as we adjust them so the curves become straight lines, their positions on the bottom axis become meaningful. Now the spaces between the levels of training indicate the degree to which Hank equates them with more experience, in terms of the acceptability of candidates. Thus, Training Programs N and O and Training Programs P and Q are both seen by Hank as contributing pretty much the same amount to acceptability, but there is a big difference between how much is contributed by M and N and by O and P. In short, the adjusted scale represents Hank's subjective scale (quantitative levels) of the different kinds of training (qualitative).

Just as the spacing of the levels of training is informative, so, too, is the spacing of the levels of experience—the further one line in the body of the graph is above the line below it, the more Hank thinks that level of experience contributes to acceptability. Note, too, that the levels of experience are not in the same order in the two matrices. The order in the matrix on the left is A, B, C, D, E, but the matrix on the right reveals that Hank sees the proper order as A, E, C, B, D. That is, he sees level A as the least experienced, E as next, C next, and so on. And he sees the steps between A to E to C to B as pretty much equal, but then it is a big step up to D—indicating that D represents a considerable jump in experience.

So parallel lines result when the decisions result from an additive integration of cue information, and the spacing of the cue values on the bottom axis as well as the spacing of the lines in the graph reveal the decision maker's subjective scales for the various levels of the two cues.

Multiplicativity

Now assume that Hank's integration was multiplicative. This would yield the data in the matrices in Figure 4.2. Plotting the rows as we did before, at the bottom of Figure 4.2, yields very different results from what we got for additivity. This time the lines are a fan rather than parallel. The fan reflects the amplification that results from multiplicative integration. Again, adjusting the values on the bottom axis reveals Hank's subjective scale for training and the spacing of the lines in the graph reveals his subjective scale for experience. Notice that the subjective scales are the same for the graphs of Figures 4.1 and 4.2.

	M (3	N 5	O 6	P 8	Q 9)	Sum
A (1)	3	5	6	8	9	31
B (4)	12	20	24	32	36	124
C (3)	9	15	18	24	27	93
D (6)	18	30	36	48	54	186
E (2)	6	10	12	16	18	62
Sum	48	80	96	128	144	
Difference		32	16	32	16	

	M (3	N 5	O 6	P 8	Q 9)	Sum	Diff.
A (1)	3	5	6	8	9	31	>31
E (2)	6	10	12	16	18	62	>31
C (3)	9	15	18	24	27	93	>31
B (4)	12	20	24	32	36	124	>62
D (6)	18	30	36	48	54	186	
Sum	48	80	96	128	144		
Difference		32	16	32	16		

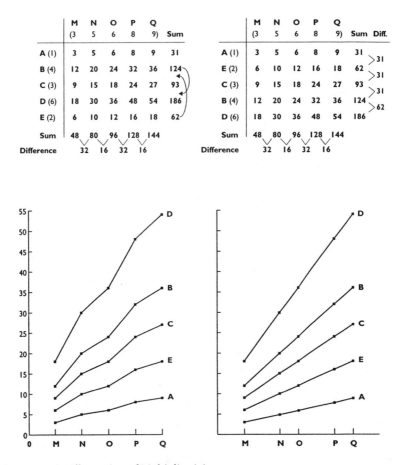

Figure 4.2. An Illustration of Multiplicativity

Of course, the numbers in the matrices in Figures 4.1 and 4.2 were rigged so I could give you clear examples of what data look like for additive and multiplicative integration. Seldom are real data so orderly—often, it is difficult to tell by looking whether the lines are truly parallel or truly fans. It is better to subject them to statistical analysis to make sure. We do this by performing a two-way analysis of variance on the matrix of decisions. If Hank's policy is to integrate additively, we will get significant main effects and no interaction. If his policy is to integrate multiplicatively, the interaction between effects of training and experience will be significant.

Using the Results

Returning to the lens model, the information integration analysis that we just completed helps us adjust the regression equation so it more accurately represents the decision maker's policy. We now have quantitative scale values for the qualitative training and experience cues; the numbers reflect the decision maker's perceptions and they can be used in the mathematics of the regression analysis. Moreover, we know whether training and experience should be entered into the equation as separate (additive) cues or whether they should be integrated (multiplicatively) to form a new cue, perhaps called *knowledge*, that will be entered as a single cue. Both modifications of the lens model equation improve its descriptive adequacy and, one would hope, improve Hank's attitude.

A second use of the results in Figure 4.2 is to determine trade-offs between the cues that will result in the same levels of acceptability. Suppose that you were an outsider who was planning to apply to Hank for a job sometime soon. You know that to have a shot at a job you must be rated at or above some specific level of acceptability by Hank, and somebody slips you a copy of the bottom left graph in Figure 4.1. You think that you might be able to compensate for your lack of experience by getting additional training before applying. So you draw a line on the graph, parallel to the bottom axis, at the level of minimum acceptability that will give you a shot at a job. Note that every point on that line describes a different mix of training and experience that will result in Hank assigning the same level of acceptability. If you trace upward from your level of experience, it will tell you the least amount of training you must have to be at least minimally acceptable; more training will give you more acceptability and, one presumes, give you increasingly better chances of getting a job. The same trade-off logic holds for the multiplicative graph.

Using graphs such as those in Figures 4.1 and 4.2 to figure trade-offs is a common tactic in marketing and manufacturing. If you know that customers will buy a product that has at least X level of acceptability, you can figure out the combinations of features (cues) that will produce that level. If some features are more expensive to produce than others, knowing about the permissible trade-offs allows you to reduce cost while retaining sales.

A few years ago (Van, 1983), an instructive example of product research appeared in the newspaper. I cannot vouch that the research actually was done in the way I am going to describe, but it must have been something like this. Two researchers, A. Drewnowski and M. C. R. Greenwood examined people's preferences for various combinations of sugar and fat. It is known that most people do not like sugar in concentrations greater than 8% to 9% but that they eat junk foods with far higher concentrations (Van, 1983). The suspicion was that when mixed with fat, greater concentrations of sugar become more attractive.

The researchers gave people combinations of various concentrations of sugar and various concentrations of fat (safflower oil in skim milk) and asked them to rate each combination for its preferability. The results showed that the effect of sugar and fat concentrations combine multiplicatively to determine preference. The most preferred combination was 10% sugar (that nobody likes by itself) and 52% fat (that alone would be like eating a candle). In short, the perfect candy bar is composed of concentrations of sugar and fat that, alone, would be shunned by most people. Because the graph of the results would look a good deal like Figure 4.2, a manufacturer could determine the trade-offs between sugar and fat in order to reduce use of the more expensive ingredient while maintaining a given level of preferability.

Obtaining Importance Weights

Having addressed the question of how cue information is integrated, we can turn to the question of the importance of the different cue dimensions. The spacing in the graphs in Figure 4.2 indicates that the various values of training and experience that we selected for our experiment were not equally spaced along their respective dimensions. But this does not say anything about the relative importance of the training dimension or the experience dimension per se to decisions about applicants' preference. Multiple regression infers the differential importance of the cue dimensions from the decision maker's decisions and represents them as beta weights in the equation for the decision maker's policy. This assumes that a cue that has a large impact on the decision is more important to the decision maker than one that has a smaller impact.

There are other ways of ascertaining the relative importance of cue dimensions, and in some sorts of decision tasks, they are more suitable than multiple regression. For one thing, multiple regression requires you to go to a considerable amount of trouble: creating a set of objects (i.e., job applications) for the decision maker to make decisions about, quantification of the cues so the mathematics can be done, checking the independence and linearity assumptions, and all the rest. It is far easier to ask the decision maker merely to tell you the importance he or she attaches to the cues. But does the decision maker actually know? And if the decision maker thinks that he or she knows, how accurate is what he or she reports?

The early work on the accuracy of reported cue importance was done in the context of lens model studies. Each decision maker was asked to tell the experimenter how important he or she thought the various cues were for his or her decisions and then these reports were compared to the beta weights in the regression equation derived from his or her decisions. Invariably, the reported weights were different from the inferred weights. Often, it was found that one or two cues got pretty large beta weights and all the rest got small ones. In contrast decision makers thought that many of the cues were important for their decisions (e.g., Hoffman, 1960). This result was interpreted by most researchers to mean that decision makers had little insight into their own policies, that their reports about the importance of the cues did not reflect how they actually used those cues when making decisions (Nisbett & Wilson, 1977).

This conclusion has been called into question, however. The problem is that beta weights can vary substantially without producing much change in how things are ordered on the preference scale. That is, the ordering tends to be rather *insensitive* to variations in the weights. In fact, it is known that the output of linear equations in general, of which the regression equation is one example, is surprisingly insensitive to weights (e.g., Dawes, 1979; Dawes & Corrigan, 1974). This suggests that differences between decision makers' reported weights and the beta weights in their equations may not always mean much. That is, if we were to substitute the decision maker's apparently inaccurate reported weights for the beta weights in the regression equation, the predictions might not change much. If this were the case, it would suggest that decision makers know as much about how important the cues are to their decisions as they need to know. More accuracy in their reports would not produce more precise predictions.

Srivastava, Connolly, and Beach (1995) conducted the study implied by the foregoing arguments. Five methods of eliciting reported weights were drawn from those commonly used in decision research. For example, participants reported the importance of the cue dimensions by rating them on a 7-point scale or by dividing 100 points among the dimensions to indicate the relative importance of each dimension or by rank ordering them in terms of their importance. The analysis consisted of computing correlations between the orderings resulting from each of the five methods and between each method's ordering and the ordering produced by a multiple regression equation.

The correlations among the orderings ranged from the high .70s to the low .90s, indicating that by and large all of the methods yielded fairly much the same orderings. The differences in orderings often involved disagreements about the top two or three, which were usually very close together. Interestingly, as part of the experimental controls the multiple regression method was done twice, and the correlation between the two equations' orderings was only .83. In fact, it looked as though the variance attributable to unreliability in the decisions or in the reports may have been larger than the variance produced by using different methods.

As with all research results, care must be taken in interpreting these results, but they suggest that there may be many ways to elicit cue dimension weights (importance) and good sense and a sensitivity to what is appropriate in different tasks must dictate which is used.

An Example

Jefferies (personal communication, January 1983) has described a particularly creative use of reported cue weights to solve a practical problem for which multiple regression would not be appropriate. His example is representative of many practical applications of a cue elicitation technique. Jefferies was employed by an advertising agency that had produced five TV commercials for a well-known soft drink company. Two weeks before the commercials were to air, the agency was notified that a sixth would be needed—in just 2 weeks. Jefferies was assigned the task of auditioning the actors to be in the sixth

Acting	Singing	Movement
1. Characterization	5. Tone	9. Dance
2. Style Energy	6. Volume	10. Agility
3. Energy	7. Quality	11. Control
4. Imagination	8. Range	12. Entry-Exit

Figure 4.3. Performance Categories Used by Jefferies

commercial. Nevertheless, no script had yet been written; he was merely told that it would require 20 high school students. Because the other five commercials had involved singing and dancing, Jefferies assumed the sixth would too.

Because of the time constraint, Jefferies had to have the right actors available as soon as the script was ready. But he did not know how to do this because he did not know precisely what the script would require. To solve this problem, he came up with a method that would warm the heart of any decision theorist. Referring to the works of Stanislavski, a famous acting teacher, Jefferies identified three relevant categories of performance (acting, singing, and movement) and four cue dimensions within each of them. Figure 4.3 contains these categories and their constituent cue dimensions.

Next, Jefferies prepared index cards with the 12 cue dimensions written down the side. A "cast call" was sent to the city's high schools and a card was prepared for each student who came to audition. The student's name, address, phone number, and so on, were written on the top of the card and then his or her audition was rated on a 1 to 10 scale for each of the 12 cue dimensions.

When the script finally was written, Jefferies read it carefully and for each role he prepared a set of cue weights. He knew that he could not assign weights directly to the 12 cues because there were too many and because some of them were difficult to compare with each other. (How can you decide on the relative importance of the role of, say, imagination and agility?) So he broke up his task into simpler tasks that were easy to do. Using a diagram like that in Figure 4.3, he divided 10 points among the three categories to indicate the relative importance of acting, singing, and movement to the role in question. Then, within each of these categories he divided another 10 points among the four cue dimensions to indicate their relative importance to the role. Finally, he multiplied the points assigned to each cue dimension by the points assigned to its category. This resulted in a set of 12 weights, one for each dimension.

To determine the best student for each role, Jefferies went back to the index cards for the auditions. For each person who auditioned, he multiplied the rating the person received on each cue dimension during the audition by the dimension's weight for the role. Then he summed the products across the 12 cue dimensions to arrive at an overall score for each student. The student who received the highest sum for each role was offered the role in the sixth commercial.

Jefferies' method is, in fact, one of the methods examined in the study described above (Srivastava et al., 1995), where it stood up reasonably well against other methods (its ordering correlated .82 with the multiple regression ordering). In fact, nearly all of the methods commonly used to elicit reported cue weights involve breaking the overall task into manageable pieces so the decision maker can make simple comparisons. Then the results of the simple comparisons are combined in some way, often by multiplying and summing as Jefferies did, to arrive at some sort of overall evaluation. Rigorous versions of this, called *multi-attribute utility assessment,* can be quite time-consuming, but as demonstrated by Srivastava et al. (1995), simpler methods can produce results that are accurate enough for practical applications.

Summary

In this and the previous chapter we have discussed the use of policy to make decisions. We have also examined, in this chapter, some of the shortcomings of the lens model and how they might be overcome. Information integration techniques help us understand whether decision makers' policies treat cues as additive or multiplicative as well as providing us with subjective scales of the variables. The implications for correcting the lens model and for making trade-offs between the cue variables were reviewed. Alternatives to regression, for determining the importance of cue dimensions to decision makers, often produce results that are sufficiently similar to beta weights to be useful. We ended with a practical application of one of these alternative methods.

The focus in this and the previous chapter has been on policies for sets of persons, objects or events that permit the decision maker to order them on some dimension, in our example the dimension was acceptability for a job. Note that there has been no mention of riskiness, doubt, or uncertainty, all of which are crucial and ominous features of most decisions. In the next chapter, we will examine choice, in which riskiness, doubt, and uncertainty are central concepts.

5 Choice

Ralph, Betty, and Hank sat at the large conference table in Betty's office, a stack of application folders looming over them. Although the stack contained only a small proportion of all the applications they had received, it was still daunting. Their task this morning was to select three new salespeople, which had seemed simple enough until they sat down to do it. They waited for the coffee pot to brew its magic, hoping that caffeine would show the way.

Ralph was thinking about how far they had come. Guided by his sister-in-law, Professor Karma Howell, they had used the lens model to evaluate their good salespeople, and, in turn, to evaluate applicants. It was a lot of work, and Hank hadn't been very comfortable at first.

Now they had before them the application information for 50 applicants identified by the lens model analysis as more or less clones of their best salespeople. None was a perfect clone, of course. Each had a different constellation of characteristics that made him or her unique. The lens model identified all 50 of them as equally satisfactory, which isn't much help when you have only three jobs to offer.

So here they sat—ready to make decisions, having no idea how to go about it. Ralph thought it was comical that they had invested in all that analytic stuff up front only to be faced with having to use their intuition to do the hardest part. He cleared his throat to indicate that official business was about to begin and stated the obvious: They had all read the 50 applications and now it was time to choose 3. There was a long pause. Finally, Betty proposed that they start at the top of the stack and work their way down, discussing the pros and cons of each applicant. Then each of them would rate the acceptability of the applicant on a scale from 1 to 5, with 5 meaning *outstanding*. They would average their ratings of each applicant and select the three who have the highest averages. Nobody else had a better idea, so they agreed.

Twelve hours later, after endless discussions and too much coffee, displays of temper and attempts at conciliation, and wandering in a shared maze of confusion and uncertainty, they finally began to average their ratings. There was good news and bad news. In the course of their discussions, it was clear that they agreed on the best applicant, and indeed, she had an average rating of 5. Unfortunately, 7 other applicants also had averages of 5, and 14 more candidates had an average of 4; for every high rating someone gave one of these folks, someone else gave a low rating.

It was awful. They had long ago stopped focusing on the applicants and now were wholly engrossed in resolving their differences. Betty swore that she was going to put all the names on a list, pin it to the wall, and throw darts to select the new people. Hank was pouting because neither Ralph nor Betty were inclined to let his opinions prevail—after all, he had been doing this sort of thing for years. Ralph simply was tired and had long ago lost confidence in his own ability to make reasonable decisions. He tried to console himself with the thought that all over the world there were managers faced with this same problem, but it didn't help much. All three felt that they had shirked their duty, that because they were managers they ought to be able to be more decisive, but they were so sick of the whole thing they simply wanted resolution.

* * *

Decision making can be relatively easy when it boils down to the application of policy. But when policy fails to resolve matters, the decision maker has to make reasoned choices in the face of uncertainty and of questions about what he or she really wants. In short, when one moves beyond policy for decision making, things can become quite difficult. Decision making by groups can be even more difficult, if only because you now have the uncertainty and desires of other people to consider. In fact, often, the whole process is so messy, complicated, overweighed with information, full of uncertainty and differing wants and needs, and hemmed in by social expectations, it is a wonder anything ever gets decided.

Researchers have approached choice in two ways. One is to ignore the confusion and complexity and assume that the process has an underlying orderliness to it. The resulting description trades realism for simplicity. Nevertheless, within the limits imposed by this trade-off, it provides concrete methods for determining what decision to make. The other way is to focus on the confusion and complexity and to assume that they are integral to the process. The resulting description trades simplicity for realism. It captures more of what actually goes on in decision making, but it does not provide much concrete help to the decision maker faced with a problem (March & Shapira, 1982). In this chapter, we will examine the first of these two ways of describing decision making, the one that trades realism for simplicity. Then, in the following two chapters (Chapters 6 and 7) we will examine the research on the two central concepts that make up this description in an attempt to evaluate its validity. Following that (Chapter 8), we will examine the second of the two ways of describing decision making, the one that trades simplicity for realism.

Normative Decision Theory

The primary approach to imposing order on decision making is through the use of normative decision theory. Normative theory has its roots in the reasonable assumption that decision makers strive to do what is best for themselves or for the organizations for which they are making decisions. "Doing best" usually is interpreted as deciding on the option that offers the most desirable payoff, be that maximum benefit or minimal loss. Note that this requires two guesses: a guess about what the payoffs (i.e., the consequences or results) will be if the option in question is chosen and a guess about how valuable those payoffs will be when they actually accrue to the decision maker (March & Shapira, 1982). In a perfect world, the decision maker would always know the payoffs and their future values. Good sense then would dictate that the decision maker choose the options that offer the payoffs that would be most valuable when he or she receives them.

But the world is not perfect and decision makers seldom can be sure of the consequences of their decisions. Even if they could be sure about what would happen, they could not know that those consequences will turn out to be as good or as bad as they thought they would be when the decision was made. Indeed, as Ralph and Betty and Hank found out, decisions are steeped in doubt and uncertainty and mired in riskiness. In fact, one can think of most decisions as gambles. Each option is a potential bet and the decision maker has to choose which bet to make. Each bet can be characterized by its potential gains if things turn out one way and its potential losses if they turn out another way, because often the way things will turn out is beyond the decision maker's control.

This gamble analogy has a long history. The 17th century philosopher and mathematician Blaise Pascal is credited with having put the issue most clearly when addressing the question of whether or not one should believe in the Christian God. Let us assume that the decision maker will not know for sure about the existence of God until judgment day. The decision is to believe (Option 1) or not to believe (Option 2). If the decision maker chooses Option 1, belief, and it turns out that God exists, then the outcome will be a blissful eternity in heaven. Alternatively, if the decision maker chooses Option 1 and it turns out that God does not exist, the decision maker is out whatever time and effort he or she has invested in worship and other religious observances. Weighing the enormous benefits of eternity in heaven against the relatively small costs of religious behavior makes Option 1 very attractive.

Option 2, disbelief, is a very different story. If it turns out that God exists, failure to believe will result in eternity in hell. If God does not exist, the disbelieving decision maker really has lost nothing because he or she invested nothing in religious observances. Weighing the enormous costs of being in hell against the trivial benefits of not having invested in religious behavior makes Option 2 very unattractive. Pascal argued that the choice between Option 1 and Option 2 is very easy; the decision maker should choose to believe in God.

About 100 years later, Daniel Bernoulli (1738) was asked by a group of young noblemen to prescribe a rational method of gambling. His prescription was much the same as Pascal's, if a bit more formal. He noted that in most gambles, the objective (money) payoffs for winning and losing are fairly clear and that in many cases, the probabilities of winning and losing are known (and if not known, can be guessed). He prescribed that for each bet the payoff for winning should be multiplied by the probability of winning and the payoff for losing should be multiplied by the probability of losing. Then these two products should be added together (note that, often, the payoff for losing is a negative number because you lose money, so its product with the probability is a negative number, and adding it actually turns out to be subtracting it). If the sum is negative, if the *expected value* is negative, one should refuse the bet. If there are two or more bets, the gambler should select the one with the largest sum, the largest expected value.

Now, why would you play only positive expected value bets and bets with the larger expected value? After all, on any bet you will not receive the expected value, you will receive the payoff for winning or lose the payoff for losing. So what does the expected value have to do with anything? The answer is that if you play a bet repeatedly, the expected value represents the amount that you will most likely end up with in the long run. But what about a one time, unique bet? Well, that is controversial. Some people claim that the expected value characterization of a bet is irrelevant for unique bets, others claim that it still serves as a handy guide for evaluating the bets and that maximization always is the best strategy.

Bernoulli (1738) did two other important things. He noted that the value of winning or losing a dollar is less for a rich person than for a poor person. Therefore, the dollar amount of the payoffs really does not accurately describe the attractiveness of those payoffs to the two people. Hence, the dollar amounts should be replaced by their subjective worth, which is called *utility*. This accounts, for example, for why a rich man might be willing to accept a bet that a poor man might turn down—the loss would be of minimal importance to the former and devastating to the latter.

Bernoulli (1738) also outlined the logic for insurance. Suppose a merchant was shipping products to the New World, how much should he pay to have someone else assume the financial risk if the ship was to sink or be captured by pirates? (The flip side of this question is how much should the other person demand for assuming the risk?) Bernoulli suggested that when the merchant sends out the ship he is taking a gamble; winning means the ship gets to the New World and back and the payoff is the profit. Losing means the ship is lost either coming or going and the merchandise and profit are lost with it. If, say, 6 ships of 10 generally make it, Bernoulli assumed that the probability of this particular ship returning safely is .60 and the probability of this ship failing to return is .40. If the utility of the profit is X, the utility of the ship itself is Y, and the utility of the cargo's wholesale value is Z, the utility of winning is X and the disutility of losing is the sum of losing the profit $(-X)$, losing the ship $(-Y)$, and losing the cargo $(-Z)$.

That is to say, the worth of the bet (sending the ship and its cargo to the New World), its *expected utility,* is the product of the probability of the ship returning (.6) multiplied by utility of winning (X) added to the probability of the ship being lost (.4) multiplied by the disutility of losing (the sum of $-X$, $-Y$, and $-Z$). If, after the computations are done, the expected cost of losing is greater than the expected benefit of winning (the expected value is negative) the merchant should be willing to pay someone to insure his possible loss. Of course, if the insurance costs more than the potential profit, then the merchant ought to keep the ship at home.

Insurance is interesting in light of the question about the applicability of expected value to unique gambles. An insurance company makes many bets against its policy holders—the company bets the policy holders will not have losses and the policy holders bet they will. So maximization of expectation makes sense for the company. But does it make sense for the individual policy holder? After all, insuring your life or house or ship probably is a unique bet for you. Clearly, there is risk; clearly, you want someone else to assume it; clearly, a loss would be a financial blow. But is expected value (utility) the best way of reasoning about whether to insure and how much to pay? Do people actually make such calculations, or do they merely buy the most coverage for the lowest price, if they bother even to shop around? That is, maybe insurance companies are betting, but policy holders are merely buying a product that will reduce their anxiety.

After several hundred years of muddling along, the expected value approach to gamble evaluation received a thorough analysis by von Neumann and Morgenstern (1947). They called gambles *games,* and two kinds were identified: games against nature and games against persons. The two examples given above are games against nature— God either exists or does not and the ship will either make it or not; there is no opponent actively playing against the decision maker. Games against persons, on the other hand, pit the wiliness of the decision maker against the wiliness of an opponent or coalition of opponents.

von Neumann and Morgenstern's (1947) work gave rise to modern microeconomics, as well as to the psychological study of decision making. It is, of course, the latter that is of interest here, and that interest will focus on how gambles (decision options) can be analyzed so that their worth to the decision maker can be evaluated. This brings us to the art of decision analysis, using decision matrices, expectation calculations, and decision trees, all three of which are related methods for characterizing gambles and evaluating their worth.

Decision Analysis: Games Against Nature

Decision Matrices

Consider the matrix at the top of Figure 5.1. This is called a decision matrix, and it is for a game against nature. For simplicity, only two decision options occupy the left axis and only two states of nature occupy the top axis; outcomes occupy the cells. To add life to this, put yourself in the place of an executive for a timber company in 1980 when Mount St. Helens, in the state of Washington, began to belch steam and ashes. You have logging crews and expensive equipment on the mountain when you hear from the geologists that the mountain might erupt. Because volcanology is a relatively new science, the geologists cannot say for sure that an eruption will take place, nor can they tell you when it might happen. All they can say is that it is likely, is getting more likely, and could happen at any time—then again, it might not happen at all.

The manager has two options: to evacuate the crews and equipment (Option 1) or to leave them on the mountain (Option 2). Nature has

Matrix

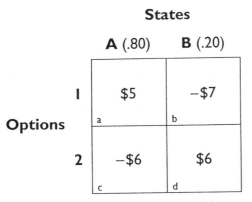

Equations

$$EV_1 = PU_{1A} + (1 - P)U_{1B} = .80\,(\$5) + .20\,(-\$7) = \$2.60$$

$$EV_2 = PU_{2A} + (1 - P)U_{2B} = .80\,(-\$6) + .20\,(\$6) = -\$3.60$$

Figure 5.1. A Decision Matrix

two states, eruption or failure to erupt; the manager thinks the probabilities are .80 for eruption and .20 for failure to erupt.

If the manager chooses Option 1 and the volcano in fact erupts, the crews and equipment will be saved and the manager will be a hero, but if it does not erupt, the company will sustain both the costs of evacuation, the loss of productivity while the crews and equipment are elsewhere, and the manager will be judged a fool. If he or she chooses Option 2 and the volcano erupts, the crews are likely to be killed and the equipment is likely to be lost and the manager will be blamed, but if it does not erupt, productivity will continue and the manager will be judged to be competent. What to do?

Which option is most attractive depends on how the manager (organization) values the safety of the crews, the replacement costs of the equipment, continued productivity, and being judged a hero or a fool. Not all of these are readily assessed in dollars—crew safety or being a hero, for example. But the manager has to balance them out somehow, even if he or she does not explicitly assign numbers to them or do calculations for each of the two options. In fact, what the lumber company actually did was evacuate its crews (which cost very little) and take the loss in productivity (which cost a lot) but left its equipment there so productivity could be easily resumed if the volcano calmed down. Of course, it did not calm down, its massive eruption flattened most of the forest and destroyed all of the equipment. So the final result was a mix of good and bad; the crews were safe, productivity would have been lost whether the crews stayed or not, and the equipment had to be replaced.

Expectation Computations

To evaluate the relative attractiveness of two options, we must calculate the expected value for each. The process is the same as for Bernoulli's ship gamble. Suppose we have the matrix in Figure 5.1, and that the amounts in the cells are the payoffs. Again let us assume that the probabilities for the two states of nature are $P(A) = .80$ and $P(B) = .20$.

Now we can construct the two equations in Figure 5.1, one for each option.

Comparing the calculated expected value ($2.60) for Option 1 with the calculated expected value (−$3.60) for Option 2 and applying the principle of maximization, the analysis prescribes the choice of Option 1.

Decision Trees

Note that the matrix in Figure 5.1 is two dimensional, options and states of nature, and that each dimension is divided into two, Options 1 and 2 and states A and B. Of course, decisions can be much more complicated than this, more dimensions divided into more parts. But it is difficult to comprehend more complex matrices. Equations are better able to handle increased complexity, but they, too, lack intuitive clarity for most of us. As a way of drawing a clear picture of a decision, decision trees are far superior to either matrices or equations.

The tree in Figure 5.2 describes the decision in the matrix in Figure 5.1. A tree usually starts with a box that indicates an action on the part of the decision maker. Events that are outside the control of the

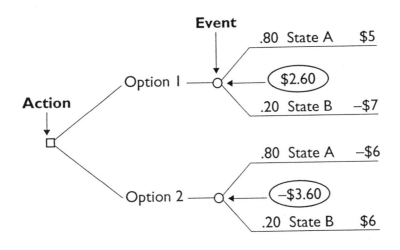

Figure 5.2. A Decision Tree

decision maker are indicated with a small circle. So beginning on the left, we see a box indicating that the decision maker has two options, 1 and 2. The circle indicates that an event occurs—which means that nature takes on State A or State B. The numbers on the branches from the circle indicate the probabilities of the states, and the numbers at the ends of the branches indicate the payoffs. Each path through the tree from left to right is a possible scenario. The top path says that Option 1 is chosen and State A occurs and the payoff of $5 accrues to the decision maker. The next path says that Option 1 is chosen, State B occurs, and the payoff of –$7 accrues to the decision maker. And so on for the other paths.

The rub, of course, is that the decision maker does not know which state will occur, so the paths through the tree actually are scenarios about gambles. The gamble aspect, the uncertainty, is injected by including the probabilities in the scenarios. To do this, we begin on the right and "fold back" (Raiffa, 1968) the payoffs, which means that we discount them by multiplying them by the probabilities. Then we sum the discounted payoffs across all of the branches to the right of the circle, thus deriving the overall expectation for that option. This sum is written in the oval near the event circle. Note that all of these numbers are the same numbers we used in the equations in Figure 5.1, and the calculated expected values (in the oval) also are the same as above. Again, because the expected value ($2.60) for Option 1 is greater than the expected value (–$3.60) for Option 2, maximization prescribes the choice of Option 1.

Decision Analysis: Games Against Persons

The general logic of games against persons is the same as for games against nature, so all that has been said earlier still applies. The complication is that whereas nature may not be wholly predictable, it is not actively trying to compete with the decision maker. von Neumann and Morgenstern (1947) viewed games against persons as analogous in structure to the interactions of firms. In some cases (called zero-sum games), the payoffs are symmetrical in that anything that is a gain for the opponent is a loss for the decision maker and vice versa. Thus, if one firm gains a market share as a result of a decision, the other firm loses that market share. In other cases (called non-zero-sum games), the payoffs to the two players are contingent on their respective decisions but are not symmetrical. The most famous, if somewhat depressing, example of a non-zero-sum game is called the "prisoner's dilemma."

The Prisoner's Dilemma

Suppose that you and a friend have been arrested for a major theft. You are taken to separate rooms in the police station and subjected to questioning. The officer explains your dilemma to you and you, being a good decision analyst, draw the matrix in Figure 5.3. Your options are to confess (Option 1) or not to confess (Option 2). Similarly, your friend's options are to confess or not to confess.

If you both confess, you both will get 5 years in jail. If you confess and your friend refuses to confess, the prosecutor will throw the book at your friend, giving him 10 years in jail, while you go free. Similarly, if your friend confesses and you do not, they will throw the book at you, giving you 10 years, while your partner goes free. If neither of you confesses, the prosecutor will get you both on lesser charges with the guarantee of a year in jail for each of you. Your dilemma is to decide whether to confess given that you and your friend are in separate rooms and you do not know if he will confess.

Other Person Confesses

		Yes	**No**
You Confess	**Yes**	him: 5yrs you: 5yrs	him: 10yrs you: 0yrs
	No	him: 0 you: 10yrs	him: 1yr you: 1yr

Figure 5.3. The Prisoner's Dilemma

In one sense, the prisoner's dilemma is not actually a dilemma because, clearly, the optimal choice for you is to betray your friend, to confess no matter what he does. This way you get off completely if your friend does not confess and you get only 5 years if he does. Your friend's best choice is precisely the same, not knowing what you are going to do, he should confess. Thus, instead of getting off free or getting only 1 year, you both ensure yourselves of 5 years in jail. Moreover, confession is the optimal choice if you think there is any chance at all that your friend will confess, and the same is true for him. That is, the expected values for your two options will be better for Option 1 no matter what probabilities (other than zero) are used to describe your uncertainty about whether your friend will confess.

But the prisoner's dilemma is, in fact, a dilemma because most people are very uncomfortable with the prescription to confess no matter what. They think that if the other person is a friend, they ought to behave honorably (as in "Honor among thieves"?), trust their friend, and refuse to confess. Nevertheless, honor is not part of the normative analysis of the dilemma, which presumes people always look out for their own best interests.

The prisoner's dilemma has real-life counterparts in things such as OPEC (Organization of Petroleum Exporting Countries) members' decisions about whether to undersell their fellow oil producers and liquor producers' decisions about whether to break the agreement not to advertise on television. OPEC was founded so that oil producing nations could present a united front to the oil consuming nations. Its members agree on a price that all will charge for their oil, but it is in the interest of any single member to charge less than the agreed-on price because its sales volume would be immense. Nevertheless, doing so would encourage other members to lower their prices, thereby reducing the profit for all OPEC members. The only way for OPEC to operate successfully is for all of its members to abide by the agreement, which has not always happened.

Similarly, liquor producers had agreed not to advertise their products on television, thereby avoiding government oversight of their advertising practices. If they each behaved honorably, all would be well. Nevertheless, it is in the interest of any single producer to break the agreement, thereby increasing its sales. Now that some have succumbed to the temptation, the other producers must follow suit until the government decides to intervene, perhaps imposing limits on all forms of liquor advertising.

A particularly salient example of the prisoner's dilemma is provided by the Cold War between the West and the USSR. The actions available to each side were to escalate weapon production or not. If neither side escalated, the payoff for both was saved resources and reduced chances of going to war. If one side escalated and the other did not, the side that escalated could attain military superiority while the other became endangered (and its politicians lost their jobs). If both sides escalated, at best they might ruin their respective economies and at worst they could stumble into war. Because neither side was willing to trust the other, the only thing that saved them both was the existence of nuclear weapons. The possibility of mutual annihilation kept both sides from chancing disproportionate escalation.

Change Versus the Status Quo

Speaking of dilemmas, the same word is used to describe another kind of situation, but this time, the prescribed decision can be more satisfying. The situation is one in which an opportunity arises that, if it works out, can make your life better than it is now but if it does not work out can make your life worse. That is, the opportunity is a gamble, and the status quo is more or less a sure thing; you have a pretty good idea what the future will look like if you stick with the

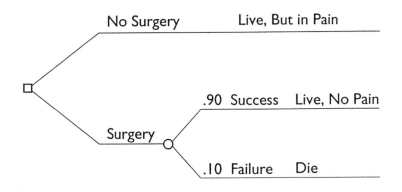

Figure 5.4. Basic Decision Dilemma

status quo, but you do not know for sure what will happen if you abandon the status quo for the opportunity.

Behn and Vaupel (1982) call this problem the "basic decision dilemma," an example of which is a heart bypass decision: Assume that you are a 59-year old businessperson who has had angina pain for a year. Your physician says that an artery is 90% blocked. Medical therapy has proved to be inadequate. You can have surgery or endure the pain. The physician tells you that, given your age and physical condition (too many hot dogs and not enough exercise), there is a 10% chance you will die on the operating table, but there is a 90% chance you will survive the surgery and be free of angina pain for a good long time. Your dilemma is whether to stick with the status quo and endure the pain or to have the surgery, which can either result in death or leave you free of pain. Figure 5.4 shows the decision tree for this kind of decision.

As before, the box on the left indicates the act of making a decision (have surgery, forego surgery). The lower branch represents the opportunity (surgery), which is called the risky alternative because it is a gamble. An event, the small circle, will occur that will determine whether the gamble leads to success, with probability p, or failure, with probability q, in which $p + q = 1.00$. Success will bring the best payoff (absence of pain); things will be better than they will be if you stick with the status quo. Failure will bring the worst payoff (death); things will be worse than they will be if you stick with the status quo. The upper branch represents the status quo (forego surgery), which is called the riskless alternative, and its payoff is somewhere between the best and worst payoffs offered by the risky alternative (you will not be free of pain, but you will not be dead).

This kind of decision is, of course, very common for both individuals and organizations, and from a normative viewpoint, its resolution is rather simple. The decision maker should calculate the expected value of the risky alternative and compare this to his or her value for the payoff for the riskless alternative. If the expected value for the risky alternative is greater, he or she should abandon the status quo and pursue the opportunity. If it is less, he or she should stick with the status quo.

Decisions of this kind may look simple from the normative viewpoint, but they are wretched in real life. Doubtless, candidates for bypass surgery consider the possible consequences and the chances that things will go wrong, but how does one assign values to things such as death? In addition to this problem, there is also the question of applying expected value to a unique decision. If you have the surgery, you will be either well or dead, and you will not play the gamble repeatedly. So although the tree certainly lays out the dilemma, it is not wholly clear that maximization of expectation is the best way of making the decision.

Individuals and Organizations

In all of the above, we have talked as though the decision maker is a single individual. Part of the beauty of the normative analysis, made clear by von Neumann and Morgenstern's (1947) discussions of coalitions, is that the decision maker can be either an individual or a group. The analysis is not about the decision maker *per se* but about the structure of the decision. True, the decision maker's utilities and probabilities may be used in the analysis, but whether these are for an individual or a group is of no relevance to the analysis.

Behavioral Decision Theory

In contrast to normative decision theory, behavioral decision theory has a rather short history. It builds on the order-imposing nature of normative theory to study how people actually make decisions rather than how they ought to make them.

Note that only two variables contribute to the computation of an option's expected value, payoffs and probabilities. In most normative analyses, the payoffs are assumed to be known to the player. Sometimes the probabilities also are assumed to be known, but frequently they are not. Nevertheless, even when everything is known things are not very straightforward. It has been clear for over 200 years (Bernoulli, 1738) that a payoff of a given magnitude will be valued to different degrees by different people—that is, each level of payoff has a corresponding psychological value to each person, which is called the *utility* of the payoff to the person. When probabilities are known to the player, it is assumed that he or she uses them in determining the option's expected value. When the probabilities are not known, the player must rely on hunches about the likelihood of winning or losing—that is, probability belongs to the player, which is called the player's *subjective probability* of winning or losing.

In 1954, Edwards introduced behavioral researchers to the thinking of von Neumann and Morgenstern (1947) and related ideas from economics. He pointed out that many decisions are made under conditions of uncertainty and therefore they can be viewed as gambles. As a result, von Neumann and Morgenstern's logic could be used as a starting point for studying human decision behavior as it actually occurs rather than as it is prescribed by decision models. Starting with Edwards's 1954 paper and extending until the present, much of the behavioral research has focused on the subjective counterparts of "objective probability" and "objective value," called subjective probability and utility.

In 1955, Edwards identified the four variations of the expected value model contained in Figure 5.5. Cell 1: When the player knows the objective probabilities and his or her utility is isomorphic with the objective value of the payoffs, the computations described earlier constitute the *expected value (EV) model.* Cell 2: When the player knows the objective probabilities but has nonisomorphic utility, the computations constitute the *expected utility (EU) model.* Cell 3: When the player has only his or her subjective probabilities but has isomorphic utility, the computations constitute the *subjective expected value (SEV) model.* Cell 4: When the player has only his or her subjective probabilities and his or her utility is not isomorphic with the objective

Probability

	Objective	Subjective
Isomorphic	Cell 1: EV	Cell 3: SEV
Non-isomorphic	Cell 2: EU	Cell 4: SEU

Utility

Figure 5.5. Edwards's Four Variations on the Expected Value Model

value of the payoffs, the computations constitute the *subjective expected utility (SEU) model.* The SEU model is a wholly psychological model, which makes it very interesting to behavioral researchers.

Since its inception, the agenda for behavioral decision research has been to study the degree to which unaided human decision making resembles the processes and prescriptions of normative theory. Until recently the driving assumption has been that decision performance will be best if the decision maker's cognitive processes correspond to the dictates of utility theory and probability theory, the attractiveness of an option is summarized as the sum of the probability-discounted utilities corresponding to its potential payoffs, and the decision maker chooses the option that offers the greatest sum. If performance falls short of what a theorist could achieve by following these prescriptions, the fault must lie in the failure of the decision maker to behave according to these assumptions. Therefore, by examining the noncorrespondence between what the decision maker *should* do and what he or she actually does, one ought to be able to (1) better understand human decision processes and (2) find ways of helping the decision maker perform better. In choice research, utility theory, probability theory, and expected value maximization all are referred to as *normative models* because they are seen as defining the norms for correct processing of relevant information. Systematic differences between the prescriptions of the normative models and what decision makers actually do are interpreted as reflections of people's cognitive shortcomings and their systematic processing errors. Techniques for helping decision makers overcome these shortcomings and avoid these errors are called *decision aids*.

Summary

We began our discussion by examining the normative model of decision making. The underlying assumption is that people strive to do what is best for themselves, choosing the option that offers the most desirable consequences. This is, of course, complicated by the fact that consequences will occur in the future, so the decision maker cannot be completely certain that he or she actually will receive them or that they will be all that is anticipated if they are received. This uncertainty makes decision making analogous to gambling; the decision maker bets on the most promising alternative and waits to see how things turn out.

Over the years, a technology for analyzing decisions has developed, based on the gamble analogy. Thus, decisions can be cast in decision matrices, subjected to expected value computations, or analyzed with decision trees. In all cases, the goal is to make the structure of the decision as clear as possible, to clarify the decision maker's thinking.

The gamble analogy also prompts characterization of decisions as games. Games can be against nature or an opponent, the most famous of which is the prisoner's dilemma.

Behavioral decision theory and research uses the prescriptions of the normative model to study how people actually make decisions rather than how they ought to make them. The emphasis has been on people's preferences, utility, and how people deal with uncertainty, subjective probability. For a long time, the driving assumption has been that decisions will be better if the decision maker's thinking corresponds to probability theory and utility theory and if he or she combines them according to the dictates of expected utility theory. Recently, however, the focus of behavioral decision theory has changed, as we will see in later chapters.

6   Subjective Probability

Hank was feeling a little introspective. He, Betty, and Ralph had spent more time than any of them could afford trying to choose the best applicants from the pile. He had tried to behave as rationally as possible, reading each application, thinking about the applicant's strengths and weaknesses, and rating the person as best he could. The problem was that the information on the applications always left him in doubt—he never felt that he was as well-informed as he should be.

Earlier, he had told Betty that selecting new employees was a crapshoot. Apparently she thought he meant it was sheer chance. What he really meant was that there was a lot of uncertainty involved—he was never very sure how the applicant was going to do, and he was never very sure he was making the right decision. The more he thought about it, the more he was convinced that his uncertainty was fundamental to the whole process for him.

*   *   *

In decision research riskiness, doubt, and uncertainty are captured by probability. Recall from Chapter 5 that two (EV and EU) of the four versions of the normative theory of choice use objective probability to represent the decision maker's uncertainty about whether the various outcomes actually will be attained if the option is chosen, and two (SEV and SEU) use subjective probability to represent this uncertainty. All four versions assume that the probabilities have the mathematical properties required by probability theory—that is, they are "real" probabilities and not just any old decimal numbers. This is equivalent to saying that uncertainty is appropriately represented as a probability.

Whereas this assumption is not difficult to accept for objective probabilities, it seems rather shaky for subjective probabilities; who knows where they come from? On the other hand, if subjective probabilities are not "real" probabilities, the SEV and SEU models lose their claims to normative (prescriptive) status. Because of this, a good deal of research in the 1960s through the early 1980s centered on whether those claims were valid by examining how well subjective probability conforms to probability theory. To understand this research, we must briefly review the rudiments of probability theory.

A Brief Review of Probability

Probability theory is an abstract, axiomatic mathematical system of rules for assigning numbers to sets of hypothetical elements (Kolmogorov, 1933/1950). As such, it has nothing to say about events in the real world—that comes later when the user of the theory ties its concepts to specific events of interest.

Mathematical probability theory begins with a set of hypothetical elements, consisting of individual elements (A, B, etc.), unions of elements (A∪B), intersects of elements (A∩B), and complements of elements (A − B).[1] A number can be assigned to each of these elements. The number assigned to an empty set of elements is .00 (which defines the lower limit of the range of acceptable numbers). The number assigned to a subset of elements is equal to the sum of the numbers assigned to each of its constituent elements (which defines additivity). The number assigned to the set of all elements is 1.00 (which defines the upper limit of the range of acceptable numbers). Thus, the numbers assigned to the elements in question must lie between .00 and 1.00, and the system is additive.

Assignment of numbers to individual elements occurs when we attempt to use probability theory for real-world applications. To do this, we use one of three definitions.

The first definition is *necessary probability,* exemplified by the probability that a three will be observed on a roll of a single die equals to $1/6 = .17$. That is, because a die (one of a pair of dice) has six sides, only one of which has three spots on it, and if we assume the die is unbiased and the roll is fair, the probability of .17 is necessary given the physical structure of the die. If we were speaking of a deck of cards, the probability of drawing a three would be $4/52 = .08$, because there are four cards with threes on them in the deck of 52 cards.

A second definition is *frequentistic probability,* exemplified by actuarial tables used in the insurance industry. For example, by knowing the past relative frequency of thefts of the kind of car you want to insure, your insurance company can judge the probability that your car will be stolen: "The probability (past relative frequency) of theft of this kind of car is X." Then they can set the premium high enough to make it worth taking the risk of insuring you. Similarly, when a particular weather pattern is observed, the weather service can use the past relative frequency of rain under these conditions as the probability that it will rain this time: "The probability (past relative frequency) of rain under these conditions is X." Note the conceptual leap in going from the relative frequencies of past events to the probabilities of future events. It depends heavily on the assumption that however the processes operated in the past, it will continue to operate in the same way in the future—thieves will continue to have the same taste in cars and climatic systems will continue to operate as they have before. Moreover, it assumes that the relative frequency for a collective of past events is applicable to a single future event (theft of your car or occurrence of rain today).

The third definition is *subjective (personal) probability,* exemplified by my statement that, "I think the probability is about .75 that Senator Smog will run for president." This is a statement about my certainty (uncertainty) about future events. It is not at all clear where these probabilities come from, but they are quite distinct from necessary and frequentistic probability. There is no necessity for Senator Smog to run for president (except perhaps in his own mind), and it is not at all clear how relative frequency would apply. If he had never run before, the relative frequency would be undefined (because you would have to divide by zero), so does that mean there is no way of assessing a probability that he will run in the future? If he ran in the last election, would it mean the probability of his running this time is 1.00? But even then, he only ran one time out of the something like 50 U.S. presidential elections, so does that make the probability that he will run again 1/50 = .02? Neither necessary nor frequentistic probability make any sense in this kind of situation.

Probability theory is deceptive in its simplicity. Exploring the logical implications of those few rules for assigning numbers to elements has permitted mathematicians to derive the useful tools of modern statistics. One aspect of these logical implications, *conditional probability*, has been of particular interest in behavioral research on probability judgment. To understand conditional probability, let us begin with an intuitive description, move to a formal statement, and then explore its importance to research on subjective probability.

Conditionality and Bayes's Theorem

A conditional event is one in which the probability of one event is modified by the fact that some other event already has occurred. Thus, Hank may think that the probability of a new job seeker being successful is .50, if only because he does not know anything to sway his opinion one way or another. Then he reads the answer to the first question in the person's application. The information in that answer modifies Hank's certainty—making him less certain or more certain about success. The new probability of success is correspondingly lower or higher than the beginning probability, let us say that it goes up to .65. Then Hank reads the second answer and modifies the .65 either upward or downward and so on until he has read the answers to all the questions on the application or until he becomes sufficiently certain about success to hire the person or sufficiently uncertain about success to turn the person down. That is, Hank's subjective probability (uncertainty) is conditional on the answers in the application.

Formally, conditional probability is an algebraic consequence of the axioms we described above (Bayes, 1763/1958). Let us consider two events that, for reasons that will be clear in a moment, we will call H and D rather than A and B. The numbers (probabilities) assigned to elements H and D will be written as $P(H)$ and $P(D)$. Conditional probability, written $P(H|D)$, is defined in terms of the intersect of H and D, written $P(H \cap D)$ as well as $P(H)$ and $P(D)$. Thus, the conditional probability of H given that D has occurred is defined as $P(H|D) = P(H \cap D) \div P(D)$, which is read as "the conditional probability of H given D is equal to the probability of the intersection of H and D divided by the probability of D." Conversely, the conditional probability of D given that H has occurred is defined as $P(D|H) = P(H \cap D) \div P(H)$, which is read as "the conditional probability of D given H is equal to the probability of the intersection of H and D divided by the probability of H." Multiplying both sides of the two equations by $P(D)$ or $P(H)$, respectively, and rearranging terms, yields the following:

$$P(H \cap D) \, P(D) = P(H|D) \, P(D),$$

and

$$P(H \cap D) = P(D|H) \, P(H).$$

Because the left sides of both of these equation are the same, the right sides must be equal to one another:

$$P(H|D) \, P(D) = P(D|H) \, P(H),$$

and, dividing both sides by $P(D)$,

[6.1] $$P(H|D) = [P(D|H) \div P(D)] \, P(H).$$

Equation 6.1 is called Bayes's theorem, after the Reverend Thomas Bayes (1763/1958) who first recognized its primary implication. To make that implication clear, let us say that H stands for *hypothesis* and D stands for *data*. Starting on the right, we begin with the probability that a hypothesis is true before we procure data about it, $P(H)$, called the *prior probability*. Then we gather some data (D), compute the probability that these data would have been obtained if the hypothesis is indeed true, $P(D|H)$, and divide it by the probability that these data would have been obtained whether or not this hypothesis is true, $P(D)$, called the *likelihood*. Then we multiply the prior probability by the likelihood, arriving at $P(H|D)$, the *posterior probability* that hypothesis, H, is true in light of the observed data, D.

Recalling Hank and the new job seeker, Hank's prior probability of .50 for the success was revised in light of the job seeker's answer to the first question on the application to .65, indicating that the answer had a large impact—called the *diagnosticity* of the data, which is reflected in the likelihood. In effect, Hank had to ask himself, "How probable is it that this applicant would have given this particular answer if he were going to succeed relative to the probability that he would have given it whether or not he were going to succeed?"

Subjective Probability, Bayes's Theorem, and Decision Research

Because the normative legitimacy of the SEV and SEU models rest on the legitimacy of subjective probability, for 20 years or more the agenda for many behavioral decision researchers was set by the question of how closely subjective probability conforms to probability theory. This work addressed three issues: measurement of subjective probability, subjective probabilities for simple events, and the revision of subjective probabilities in light of data.

Measurement Issues

Before you can do reasonable research on how closely subjective probability conforms to probability theory, you have to decide how to measure subjective probability. Clearly, if different measurement methods yield different results it is going to be difficult to evaluate conformity. This is not the place for a tutorial on methodology; suffice it is to say that many methods have been tried (direct assessment, psychophysical measurement, inferences from bets, confidence ratings, and verbal statements such as "sure thing" or "toss up"). Early on, comparisons were made among these (e.g., Beach, 1974; Beach & Phillips, 1967; Beach & Wise, 1969; Galanter, 1962; Wise, 1970). Of course, the measurement technique one uses is going to be dictated in part by the demands of the research setting and task, but based on the research and judging from the frequency with which researchers use it, direct assessment appears about as good as any other method (von Winterfeldt & Edwards, 1986). That is, simply asking people to give a number to represent their opinion about the probability of an event appears to produce data that are not markedly different from data produced by the other methods, and the procedure is simpler than for most other methods. The least attractive method involves verbal statements—individuals may be consistent in what they mean when they use statements such as "sure thing," "very likely," or "unlikely," but there is very little agreement across individuals about the level of probability represented by such statements (Lichtenstein & Newman, 1967). The irony of this is that many experiments, both in behavioral-decision research and in other areas, rely on rating scales anchored with verbal statements of this kind.

Direct assessment can be done in two ways. One way is to ask people to state the probability. The other way is to ask them to state the relative frequency (or proportion) with which an event might be expected to occur: ("The probability of a given person having characteristic X is .10" versus "Ten people out of 100 can be expected to have characteristic X" or "Ten percent of these people have characteristic X"). For a long time, it was assumed that all direct assessments were equivalent, but as we shall see later, this may not be true, and what one concludes about the nature of subjective probability depends on which kind of assessment, probability or relative frequency (proportion), one asks participants to report.

Accuracy and Coherence for Simple Events

One way of evaluating the conformity of subjective probability to probability theory is to study areas in which it is possible to calculate objective probabilities (necessary or frequentistic) and then compare decision makers' assessments with them. This is called *accuracy*. Frequently it is found that people tend to give assessments that are a bit too high for objectively low probability events and a bit too low for objectively high probabilities (e.g., Preston & Baratta, 1948). This generalization ignores many exceptions, but as a summary, it is roughly correct.

Sometimes people's assessments bear almost no discernible relationship to objective probabilities, but that does not mean that they do not conform to probability theory. It is quite possible for a person's probabilities to be *coherent* (i.e., interrelated in ways demanded by probability theory) even if they are inaccurate—it merely means that the person is not well-informed about the necessary probabilities or the relative frequencies for the domain in question. Ignorance is not the same as incoherence.

Coherence among subjective probabilities that are inaccurate or for which there are no objective counterparts can be measured by having participants assess the probabilities of each of the events and each of the compounds (unions, intercepts, or conditionals) in a set. Then the experimenter analyzes the degree to which the assessments are coherent. For example, Peterson, Ulehla, Miller, Bourne, and Stilson (1965) presented participants with a list of personality traits and for each asked a question of the form, How many people in 100 are witty, brave, and so on, for $P(A)$, $P(B)$, and so on. Then they asked for conditional probabilities with questions of the form, "One hundred persons are known to be brave, how many would you expect to be witty?" for $P(A|B)$ and "One hundred persons are known to be witty, how many would you expect to be brave?" for $P(B|A)$. Recall from our previous definition of conditionality that $P(A|B) P(B) = P(B|A) P(A)$. Therefore the product of the participants' assessments of $P(A|B)$ multiplied by their assessments of $P(B)$ ought to be equal to the product of their assessments of $P(B|A)$ multiplied by their assessments of $P(A)$. To test this, Peterson and his colleagues merely correlated the two products across participants; the mean correlation was .67. This may not seem very high, but the experimenters recognized that asking people to do a strange task such as this is unlikely to produce very stable assessments, so they measured the reliability of the assessments: The mean reliability correlation was .72. Because response reliability (.72) places an upper limit on coherence, the correlation of .67 for the latter is not too discouraging. Even higher coherence for assessments of familiar, concrete events was obtained in other studies. For example, Barclay and Beach (1972) obtained correlations in the high .70s, .80s, and .90s for both group data and for individual subjects.

Accuracy and Coherence in Probability Revision

Recall that Bayes's theorem follows directly from the definition of conditional probability, and it can be interpreted as a mechanism for revising probabilities in light of data. As a result, it affords a way of examining the accuracy and coherence of subjective probabilities in a more dynamic situation than for single events. Edwards (1955) and his colleagues were the first to do "Bayesian" studies of accuracy and coherence. They used variations on what was called "the bookbag-and-poker-chips task." This consisted of showing participants two or more cloth bags (bookbags were the forerunners of backpacks as the conveyance of choice for students' textbooks). Each bag contained a mixture of blue and red poker chips. The proportion of blue chips differed from one bag to another and the participants were told the proportions for each bag.

Out of the participants' view, the experimenter randomly selected one of the bags, drew a sample of chips from it, and told the participants the proportion of blue chips in the sample. Then for each of the bags of chips, the participants assessed the probability that that bag was the one that had been selected.

Because the bag to be sampled was randomly selected, the number of bags determined the prior probability of each being the selected bag; if there were two bags, the prior probability of each was .50; if there were three the prior probability of each was .33, and so on. The proportion of blue chips in the bag determined the likelihood; if a bag's proportion was high and the sample had lots of blue chips in it, the likelihood was high that the bag was the one that had been selected—if the proportion was low but the sample had lots of blue chips in it, the likelihood was low that the bag had been selected. Thus, the posterior probability (each bag's probability of having been selected in light of the composition of the sample of chips) was jointly determined by the prior probability and the likelihood, and this should have been reflected in the probability assessments given by the participants for each of the bags.

There were two major findings (Phillips & Edwards, 1966). First, participants tended to treat the prior probabilities of the bags as if they were more equal than they were actually. Second, participants tended to be less influenced by the data (the blue chips in the sample) than they should have been. As a result, their posterior probability assessments were *conservative* relative to the posterior probabilities that a statistician would arrive at using Bayes's theorem. Close examination of the data showed that participants' posterior probabilities after the first data were moderately accurate but that successive draws from the same bag (the posterior after one observation of data becomes the prior for the next observation of data) led to increasingly severe conservatism (Peterson, Schneider, & Miller, 1965).

Conservatism was robust in that it was obtained in many replications of, and variations on, the bookbags-and-poker-chip experiments and in even more realistic tasks of comparable logical structure. Although training sometimes reduced conservatism in a specific task (e.g., Christensen-Szalanski & Beach, 1982; Peterson, DuCharme, & Edwards, 1968; Wheeler & Beach, 1968) the general conclusion remains that, compared to Bayes' Theorem, decision makers' revised subjective probabilities are neither accurate nor coherent.

Heuristics and Biases

Research on the underestimation or overestimation of probabilities for simple events and conservatism in the revision of subjective probabilities started a landslide of studies. Indeed, because it was so easy to do, demonstrating the failure of subjective probabilities to conform to the demands of probability theory became something of a cottage industry.

In the early 1970s, Daniel Kahneman and Amos Tversky (both of whom had been at the University of Michigan in the 1960s when Edwards was doing his research on conservatism) went beyond conservatism in a series of experiments (Kahneman, Slovic, & Tversky, 1982) that demonstrated widespread inconsistencies in subjective probabilities. They conjectured that these "biases" were the result of decision makers using cognitive shortcuts, called heuristics, when they performed probability assessment tasks. Furthermore, these heuristics often served decision makers well because they produced answers that were moderately accurate while reducing the cognitive effort required to make them. But in some circumstances the heuristics produced serious systematic bias.[2]

Tversky and Kahneman's (1974) list of biases can be grouped under the three heuristics that are presumed to give rise to them. When using the first heuristic, *representativeness,* decision makers assess the probability of an event on the basis of how closely it resembles some other event or set of events. In the bookbags-and-poker-chip task, the more the sample resembles the proportion of blue chips in one of the bags, the more probable the decision maker thinks it is that the sample came from that bag. In general, this is a pretty good rule because it produces fairly accurate answers for the first draw from the bag, and it does not require the mental mathematics that Bayes's theorem requires. Nevertheless, after a couple of draws it leads to severe conservatism, and of course, it results in insensitivity to prior probabilities and to sample size (indeed, subjects sometimes put more faith in a small sample than a large one if the former is similar to the proportion of chips in the bag).

When the *availability* heuristic is used, decision makers assess probabilities on the basis of how easily instances of the events in question can be brought to mind. This means that familiar events will be judged to be more probable than unfamiliar events—which, in fact, is often correct, but it sometimes fails to produce assessments that conform to probability theory. Similarly, events that are easy to imagine are judged to be more probable than those that are not.

When using the *anchoring and adjustment* heuristic, decision makers start from some initial value (the anchor) and then adjust their assessment upward or downward in light of whatever considerations seem appropriate. As in the case of conservatism, the usual finding is that decision makers do not adjust enough.

There has been a long, acrimonious debate (e.g., Cohen, 1993; Jungermann, 1983) about heuristic and biases. The least controversial criticism is that the heuristics have no theoretical substance; they do not relate to, follow from, or lead to any other major concepts in cognitive science. They are often treated as explanations, but they are shallow explanations because there is nothing to which they refer at a more basic level. As a result, they remain merely hypothetical processes and not very well defined processes at that. What is worse, because they are so ill defined, they are easily used for post hoc accounts of decision makers' behavior and therefore appear able to "explain" almost anything. Concepts that explain everything explain nothing.

As it turns out, these criticisms of the heuristics and biases research are almost beside the point because research has demonstrated that there are all sorts of influences on probability assessments that have no counterparts in formal or applied (statistics) probability theory at all. Thus, for example, Tversky and Kahneman (1982) demonstrated that inferences about causality influence assessments—and causality simply is foreign to probability theory (why else do you think your statistics teacher insisted that correlation could not be interpreted as causality?). Indeed, as the research results have piled up it has become clear that, instead of doing probability calculations badly, decision makers usually are doing something else entirely.

It is only in very specific circumstances that subjects attempt to behave like intuitive statisticians (Barnes, 1984). More frequently, they attempt to understand the causal forces at work in a situation—they formulate causal models rather than statistical models and base their judgments on what they see as the logical consequences of these causal forces (Pennington & Hastie, 1986, 1988, 1992). They can state their judgments in the form of a probability if asked to do so, but that does not mean that the judgment is, or should be, regarded as a probability in the probability theory sense (Beach, Christensen-Szalanski, & Barnes, 1987). In short, participants seem to be more aptly described as causal modelers than as intuitive statisticians.

Strangely enough, some researchers concluded that failure to think like a statistician in every task to which statistical logic reasonably can be applied shows that decision makers are irrational "mental cripples." However, two arguments caution against this indictment. The first is that in some situations decision makers, in fact, seem to behave like statisticians, albeit not always rigorous ones. How can you broadly indict people's rationality if they sometimes behave in the way you have chosen to define as rational? The second argument is that even when it is applicable, probability theory may not be the only rational way of thinking about some of these tasks—causal logic or some other knowledge-based logic may be equally reasonable, if not more so. It depends on how the problem is framed.

Consider the following (Beach, 1990): Suppose that an experimenter was to *randomly* select a church in the United States and visit it one Sunday afternoon in June, the traditional month for weddings. He stands outside and waits for the wedding party to emerge. Then he approaches the best man and asks, "If I were to randomly select a couple that is getting married this afternoon somewhere in America, what is the probability that they will still be married to each other 10 years from now?" Assuming that he knows the divorce rate, the best man would probably give it, in probability form, because that was what he was asked for.

Now, what if the experimenter instead asked, "What is the probability that the couple for whom you were just best man will still be married to each other 10 years from now?" For the experimenter, the change in question does not change the problem—he randomly selected this couple and he knows absolutely nothing about them as individuals; for him, they are interchangeable with any other American couple getting married on that or any other day. But for the best man, the change of question reflects a substantial change in the framing of the task. The divorce rate for the population at large may influence his answer but only if he is particularly cynical. (Indeed, if he really thought the probability of his friends' marriage working was only about .50, he might well have declined to be their best man on the grounds that it would be a poor investment of his time.) Rather, his answer to the second question, the one that is specific to his friends as individuals, is properly based on his knowledge about them and his theories about what causes successful and unsuccessful marriages. It is perhaps presumptuous to condemn the best man as irrational for not using statistical reasoning when answering the second question. That is, it is unreasonable to insist that the frame that is appropriate from the experimenter's point of view is the only admissible frame and the use of any alternative is an instance of irrationality.

Reexamination of Subjective Probability

By the late 1980s, it was generally agreed that probability theory does not adequately describe subjective probability. Nevertheless, most investigators persisted in their belief that the four variants of the expected value model were descriptive of choice, and subjective probability is a component of two of those variants. One might think, therefore, that these researchers would move from testing the fit with probability theory to investigating the nature of subjective probability itself, in the hope of salvaging the SEV and SEU models. This is not what happened. For the most part, interest in subjective probability simply evaporated. It disappeared from the agendas of conferences, both here and abroad. It was as though everyone simply was bored with the topic and anxious to move on to something else. And then a new voice, with new data, was heard calling for a reexamination of our conclusions about subjective probability judgments.

The new voice belongs to Gerd Gigerenzer. In the late 1980s, he and his colleagues undertook a reexamination of the literature on subjective probability, particularly the studies of heuristics and biases. Their conclusion was that it is necessary to differentiate between decision makers' assessments of relative frequency, which implies long-run probabilities of events, and assessments of the probabilities of unique events (Gigerenzer, 1991). This echoes the best man example given above.

It has long been known that people are very good at assessing proportions (Peterson & Beach, 1967), and Gigerenzer's studies show that when decision makers make assessments in the form of relative frequencies or proportions, many of the celebrated biases disappear. Nevertheless, when asked for probabilities for unique events, the biases are strongly in evidence. Gigerenzer's conclusion is that frequentistic judgments made by people who are reasonably familiar with the domain of interest are apt to conform reasonably well to the demands of probability theory. Probability assessments for unique events are not very apt to conform to probability theory. This conclusion makes sense in light of many statisticians' strong opinions that applied probability theory only addresses long-run relative frequencies and has no meaning for single events (e.g., von Mises, 1928/1957).

In fact, it has been clear for quite a long time that it is necessary to differentiate between judgments for long-range and unique events (Lopes, 1981). Beach, Barnes, and Christensen-Szalanski (1986) proposed that decision makers use different *judgment strategies* for different *judgment tasks* encountered in different *judgment environments*, and that the final judgment is contingent on all three. The strategies fall into two categories, aleatory and epistemic. (An aleator is a dice player; hence, *aleatory* refers to necessary and frequentistic probability; epistemology means knowledge; hence, *epistemic* refers to the use of knowledge to derive subjective probabilities.) The general idea is that the decision maker selects one or the other strategy depending on the demands of the judgment task (whether chance appears to be an important component, repeated versus unique events are involved, or statistical or causal logic is the norm for the domain in question). He or she then applies the selected strategy with more or less rigor depending on the demands of the judgment environment (the payoff for accuracy, whether the judgment can be revised later, the degree to which the decision maker's credibility is on the line, the quality of the information with which he or she must work). More recently, Gigerenzer, Hoffrage, and Kleinbolting (1991) proposed a process model for both aleatory and epistemic judgment based on work by Egon Brunswik. Thus, things have come full circle; we began with Brunswik and we seem to have come back to Brunswik.

Hank Revisited

So where does this leave Hank the HR man? When all is said and done, he does not much care whether his uncertainty conforms to probability theory or not. The fact remains that his judgments about the preferability of job applicants are influenced by his increasing and decreasing uncertainty as he learns more about them. He is not interested in relative frequencies so much as he is in the chances (in the everyday sense) that one or another applicant will succeed at this particular job. He is going to use his uncertainty to make his decision no matter what decision researchers conclude about the nature of uncertainty. So it would seem that decision researchers ought to recognize this fact and turn their attention to what he is doing with his uncertainty—whether it conforms to probability theory or not.

Summary

We have been examining one of the two components of the expected utility model, subjective probability. We began with the mathematical formulation of probability and then moved on to examine Bayes' theorem, which is a consequence of the definition of conditionality. Behavioral studies comparing subjective probability with the demands of formal probability theory show that some similarity is often found for simple events but that there is consistent error for more complex events and for the revision of subjective probability, called conservatism.

The conservatism findings prompted widespread investigation of the failures of subjective probability to conform to the requirements of probability theory. The result is a series of well-known studies that attribute observed failures (biases) to habitual modes of thinking (heuristics) on the part of decision makers. While there is controversy about the interpretation of the results of these studies, they have had a profound effect on how decision making is studied.

We closed with an examination of a new line of work by Gigerenzer (1991) that claims to refute many of the conclusion reached in the heuristics and biases research, and then we looked at a theory that suggests decision makers use different strategies for assessing subjective probabilities depending on the demands of the problem and the environment in which the problem is encountered.

Notes

1. Recall that the union of elements is *both* A *and* B, the intersect is *either* A *or* B, and the complement is what remains when B is subtracted from A (or vice versa).

2. The list of biases has lengthened over the years (hindsight bias, overconfidence bias, etc.). Many of the newer additions are conceptually quite different from the ones originally described by Kahneman and Tversky, which reflect deviations of subjective probability judgments from probability and statistical theory. Many of the others deal with some other aspect of problem solving (Kahneman, Slovic, & Tversky, 1982).

7 Utility

Hank looked across the table at Betty and Ralph, who were deep in a heated discussion about procedure. He tuned them out as he thought about how he usually went about making the choices they were trying to make as a group. True, uncertainty was a key to his decision making, but it also was true that he tried to anticipate the outcomes that might result from hiring a particular applicant. It wasn't all that difficult. He merely tried to imagine the applicant in various situations that might arise and how he or she would handle them. Of course, he had very strong views about what was the right thing to do in those hypothetical problem situations. If it seemed as though applicants would do what he preferred, he liked them; otherwise he didn't.

*　*　*

We saw in Chapter 6 that subjective probability may not conform to probability theory in other than rather special circumstances. In this chapter, we want to examine the fit between subjective value for outcomes and utility theory. Unfortunately, the research on utility does not provide as clear a test of its fit with theory as the research on subjective probability provides; the evidence is more indirect.

As we have seen, the methods for comparing decisions with normative prescriptions are inherent in the nature of the normative theory itself. Because normative theory views choices as gambles and the usual prescription is to maximize expectation, it follows that studying choice means studying how people deal with gambles. As in Bernoulli's example in Chapter 5 of the decision about sending a ship to the New World, this can consist of deciding to take or not to take a gamble (send the ship) or deciding on a fair price for a gamble (insurance). Or as in the example of the lumber executive and Mount St. Helens, it can consist of choosing the best from among two (or more) bets. In the laboratory, subjects might be presented with a pair of gambles for which the expected value of gamble M is greater than that of gamble N, in which case they are predicted to choose M. In successive presentations, the payoffs can be systematically changed so that at some point the expected value for gamble M becomes less than that of gamble N. Of interest is the point at which subjects switch from preferring gamble M to preferring gamble N, from which, with a little algebra, one can infer the utilities underlying their choice of one bet over the other.

Utility Theory

Just as formal probability theory is a way of assigning numbers to events and not a theory about decision makers' uncertainty, utility theory is another way of assigning numbers to events and not a theory about what is valuable to decision makers. In application, however, utility theory is used to represent preferences, and the question is how usefully it does its job.

As Yates (1990) has pointed out, there are two ways of relating preference to the "objective" value of outcomes. The first is called a *value function,* which represents the increase in the strength of the decision maker's preferences as a function of the outcomes' objective value. It is as if there was a scale in the decision maker's head on which the various *outcomes* are placed such that the ordering of their locations are consistent (higher scale values mean higher preference) and the distances between the ordered outcomes on the scale represent meaningful differences in preference for the outcomes. This first kind of scale is the most common view of utility; the relative preference of various outcomes.

The second way of relating preference to the objective value of outcomes is called a *utility function*. Here the assumption is that preference reflects both the value of the outcome to the decision maker *and* his or her feelings about risk—that is, uncertainty about whether the outcome will or will not occur. Using conventional expected value logic, this means that preference is for gambles rather than merely for the outcomes. Hence, it is as if there was a scale in the decision maker's head on which the various *gambles* are placed such that the ordering of their locations is consistent and the distances between them are meaningful. This second kind of scale is the one used in most discussions of utility in decision theory and research.

There are numerous versions of utility theory (von Winterfeldt & Edwards, 1986), but they all make three fundamental assumptions:

- *Connectivity:* They assume that the decision maker can judge his or her preferences (or indifference) when faced with two gambles.
- *Transitivity:* They assume that preferences among gambles are consistent such that if gamble M is preferred to gamble N and gamble N is preferred to gamble O, gamble M is preferred to gamble O.
- *Summation:* They assume that the preference for a gamble is greater than the preferences for any of its component parts. For example, the preference for a gamble that offers a payoff of $50 and a movie ticket must be greater than the preference for the $50 alone or for the movie ticket alone. That is, the preference for a compound outcome of a gamble is a combination (usually the sum) of the preferences for the component outcomes.

If these and some ancillary enabling assumptions are met it can be formally shown that gambles can be arrayed according to preference on an underlying scale of utility.

Because utility theory is an abstract method of attaching numbers to events, it is not altogether meaningful to talk of testing it. Nevertheless, it is meaningful to talk of testing the degree to which decision makers' preferences conform to its assumptions and implications, and it is here that the behavioral decision research has focused, but—to repeat—the tests, which are far fewer than one might expect, have been less direct than in similar research on probability theory.

Research

- If the connectivity assumption holds, decision makers' preferences ought to be robust because connectivity means that they know what they prefer. Instead, it is found that preferences change depending on task characteristics, measurement methods, and context (e.g., Fischhoff, Slovic, & Lichtenstein, 1980; Fryback, Goodman, & Edwards, 1973; Schoemaker, 1980; Slovic & Lichtenstein, 1983).
- If the transitivity assumption holds, the order of decision makers' preferences should be reliable. Research shows that frequently this is not the case and that intransitivity is easily induced (e.g., Tversky, 1969).
- If the summation assumption holds, preferences for compound gambles ought to be a function of the sum of their component gambles. Again, research finds that this is not always the case (e.g., Shanteau & Anderson, 1969).

To convey the flavor of the research that led to these conclusions, consider a study by Tversky (1967). Using inmates in a federal prison as subjects, Tversky asked each inmate to state the price he would ask to sell his right to play a particular gamble. Everyone in the room was given the same gamble and the idea was that each inmate should ask a price lower than anyone else's so he and not someone else could sell the gamble to the experimenter. (Because the experiment was set up so that the inmates might not get the opportunity to play their gamble, in which case it became worthless, it was better to sell it and make at least the sale price.) On the other hand, they should not sell the gamble for less than the worth of the gamble—that is, not for less than its expected utility.

The gamble's probabilities were presented as a two-sectioned pie diagram with a spinner attached to the center. If the spinner landed on one section of the pie, the inmate who got to play would win some stated amount, and if it landed on the other section, he would win nothing. Thus, the expected utility of the bet was the product of the probability of winning, from the pie diagram, and the inmate's value for the payoff. The payoffs were in cigarettes and candy, which were used as currency within the prison. There were simple gambles and compound gambles—the latter had compounds of the payoffs that had been offered for some of the simple gambles and were designed to test the summation assumption described above.

The presumption was that the competition to sell the bet would drive down the inmates' selling prices until the lowest price asked would be equal to the subjective expected utility of the gamble. That is, $\$_s = (P \times V)$, in which $\$_s$ is the lowest price any inmate in the group asked for the bet (in cigarettes or candy), P is the probability of winning (from the pie diagram), and V is the inmate's private value for winning whatever has been offered as the payoff. Because Tversky (1967) knew the probability of winning and the price asked by the inmate who under-priced everyone else, he could figure out what that inmate's value must have been for the payoff:

$$\$_s = P \times V,$$

$$V = \$_s / P.$$

This says the price divided by the probability reveals the inmate's value for the payoff.

To state the complex results rather simply, Tversky (1967) found that inmates' asking prices suggested that they in fact evaluated the gambles in terms of the product of the probability and their value for the payoff, and that value appeared to be additive, both of which are congruent with utility theory. Nevertheless, the inmates consistently set selling prices higher than the expected value of the gambles. In any strict sense, utility theory does not allow for what appears to be the inmates' desire for a profit margin, or interpreted another way, their value for retaining the gamble (a value for gambling). On the other hand, common sense finds both of these explanations reasonable.

Utility theory generally assumes that the value for a payoff must be the same whether it is a "sure thing" or part of a gamble. To test this, in one condition of the experiment Tversky's (1967) inmates simply set a price on each of the payoffs. Later, when these same payoffs were included in gambles, the inferred value for them (using the equation) was not the same as the simple prices. This result contradicts the utility theory assumption and implies that value is not independent of risk, which means that the simple expectation equation is not an adequate description of the determinants of individuals' utility for the gamble.

This is but one of a number of studies that obtained data suggesting that utility theory is not a very good description of human preferences, even in well-controlled experimental conditions.

Prospect Theory

Despite all the evidence that probability theory does not describe decision makers' uncertainty and that utility theory does not describe their preferences, it remains clear that uncertainty and preferences influence choices. It is also clear that while the variants of the expected value model (EV, EU, SEV, SEU) are not wholly successful in describing choice, they sometimes come close. Understandably, researchers who have invested heavily in the expected value approach have been reluctant to throw out everything and start all over.

Kahneman and Tversky's (1979) prospect theory was an attempt to retain the general structure of normative expected value theory and the notion of options as gambles, while "psychologizing" it in order to produce a theory that more accurately and precisely describes human choice behavior. First of all, *value, V,* which in utility theory is understood to be relative to the decision maker's total assets (winning a dollar means less to a rich person than a poor person), is reinterpreted as gains or losses relative to a specified reference point. The reference point may be one's total assets, but more frequently, it is some other amount defined by the situation (for example, the value of a shirt may be defined by the difference between its price at one store and its price at another store). Similarly, subjective probabilities are reinterpreted as *decision weights,* π, which reflect the decision maker's uncertainty and are represented as a transformation on probabilities, with the weights being slightly higher than low probabilities and slightly lower than medium and high probabilities. The weights are decimal numbers.

As with expected value (and its variants), prospect theory evaluates the attractiveness of gambles by computing the sum of products for each gamble. In this case, the products are the values of the various payoffs offered by an option multiplied by the decision weights (uncertainty) for each payoff, πV, and the sum is across payoffs for each option. As in utility theory, prospects (gambles) are ordered on a scale in terms of the magnitude of their respective sums of products and the prescribed choice is the option having the highest sum of products.

A particularly interesting feature of prospect theory is that the decrease in V for losses relative to the reference point is considerably more precipitous than the increase in V for gains. That is, the theory assumes that the negative value of losses is greater than the positive value of gains (the loss of $500 causes more pain than the gain of $500 causes happiness) and it retains the utility theory assumption that marginal increases (decreases) in value decrease as the amounts to be won or lost become bigger. Much of the research on the theory has focused on working out the implications of these assumptions.

Prospect theory, both in its original and expanded versions (Tversky & Kahneman, 1992), is an impressive work. Although it is similar in form, it is not merely a modified version of normative theory. It is in fact a psychological and behavioral theory. For example, it posits that decision makers "edit" gambles before they evaluate them for comparison and choice. The editing process consists of coding payoffs as gains or losses relative to the reference point on V, segregating risky payoffs from riskless ones (if you will receive some amount no matter whether you win or lose, you can regard this payoff as riskless), simplifying the bet by rounding amounts up or down to make calculations easier, and so on. The editing part of the theory is a substantial contribution to cognitive theory on problem solving in general, but cognitive researchers have not given it as much attention as it deserves.

Whatever its strengths, prospect theory, as a result of its retention of the gambling metaphor for choice, has its critics. True, it appears to be immune to criticisms that focus on its use for unique decisions, because decision weights are not supposed to be probabilities; thus, the question of whether probability makes sense for unique events does not apply. Nevertheless, decision weights are viewed as a transformation on probability (presumably objective probability), so in some sense, they may merely beg the question. The theory's use of deviations from a reference point as the determinant of value also has its attraction. But critics (e.g., March, 1978) point out that even this change in the normative formulation does not address the problem that value of outcomes at the moment of choice has to reflect future value, the value the outcomes will have when they occur, and that decision makers very frequently do not know what that future value will be. Including a mechanism in the theory for evaluating future value, given the vagaries of the world, might well overburden it. As Tversky (1967) pointed out about expected value theory, every time you add a mechanism to account for some anomaly, you make the theory that much more flexible and impervious to falsification.

In general, prospect theory does a fine job in the realm in which it has been most frequently applied, choices among laboratory gambles. Perhaps the argument is not with the theory but with the realm. As we will see in subsequent chapters, when you leave the laboratory to observe decision making in its natural habitat, you quickly discover that it seldom is about gambles. Gambling requires you to make your decision, to place your bet, and then await the verdict of some outside event (a spinner, a roulette wheel, a throw of the dice, the turn of a card). But outside the laboratory, in government and commerce for example, decision makers seldom are forced to passively await their fate. Instead, they actively work to influence events in order to make their choice the right choice. Indeed, passivity is scorned and situations that might require it are avoided—most of us strive to control events, and to the degree that we do so, the gamble metaphor is inappropriate. To the degree that the metaphor is inappropriate, theories and methods that assume that it accurately characterizes choice also are inappropriate. It can be argued that this includes both normative theory and prospect theory.

In support of criticisms of the aptness of the gamble analogy in particular and the normative theory in general, consider the following: If the gamble metaphor actually is valid, at the very minimum you would expect real gamblers in real casinos to behave normatively, or at least in the way prospect theory predicts. Keren and Wagenaar (Keren & Wagenaar, 1985; Wagenaar, 1988; Wagenaar, Keren, & Pleit-Kuiper, 1984) studied the customers in casinos in the Netherlands. Interviews revealed that gamblers do not think of gambles in terms of maximization of expected value. Indeed, most casino games have a negative expected value for the player, so if gamblers were attending to expected value, they would not even go to casinos. Instead, gamblers attend to a variable that is not even part of the normative or prospect theory formulations—*luck*. Someone who is lucky will win irrespective of the probabilities involved. Players do not believe that they can influence the turn of the roulette wheel or fall of the dice, but luck influences their choice of what to bet on (hunches), and if "their luck is running," their choices will be the correct ones. That is, a gamble favors no one, but luck favors some. This, of course, is what keeps casinos and lotteries in business; the odds are low for any single player, but there is no statistical law actually preventing that player from winning. In the course of events, someone eventually will win, and in the view of most gamblers, that someone is the person who is lucky.

As Wagenaar and Keren (1988) point out, the concept of luck does not run counter to a purely physical (necessary) explanation of probability for roulette wheels, dice, cards, and so on, it merely makes such an explanation irrelevant to the behavior of the gambler. In short, gamblers' conceptions of gambles do not much resemble either the normative or prospect theory conception.

There is probably little interest in incorporating luck into normative models, although it might be worked into decision weights in prospect theory. But the point is, if even casino patrons do not think of their choices among real gambles in the way prescribed by normative theory and prospect theory, how can one possibly think that decision makers outside casinos think of their choices as gambles—or at least as gambles of the kind described by the theories?

More evidence for the criticism of gambles and normative theory is provided by the observation that few people regard expected value as a valid way of evaluating unique gambles, and it can be argued that most decisions are unique—otherwise the decision maker would use his or her preestablished policies to deal with them. Lola Lopes (1981) has been the most visible and compelling of the critics of expectation for unique gambles. In the course of her critique, she includes a telling quotation from a paper by the celebrated economist Paul Samuelson (1963). Samuelson recounts offering to bet a colleague $200 to $100 that the side of a coin he specified would not appear on the first toss. The colleague replied:

> I won't bet because I would feel the $100 loss more than the $200 gain. But I'll take you on if you promise to let me make 100 such bets. . . . One toss is not enough to make it reasonably sure that the law of averages will turn out in my favor. But in a hundred tosses of the coin, the law of large numbers will make it a darn good bet. I am, so to speak, virtually sure to come out ahead in such a sequence, and that is why I accept the sequence while rejecting the single toss. (p. 109)

According to Lopes, Samuelson is interested in this answer because he considers it "irrational."

Samuelson's point is that the expected value of the single bet favors the colleague 2:1. Therefore, the rational decision maker should be willing to accept the bet. By being unwilling to do so, Samuelson's colleague had shown himself to be irrational. Moreover, Samuelson goes on to prove that in these circumstances anyone who wants to maximize expected value cannot accept a sequence of bets if each of the single bets is unacceptable. Samuelson must conclude, therefore, that his colleague did not want to maximize expected value. The reader is invited to decide whether that actually makes the colleague irrational, as Samuelson claimed.

Keren and Wagenaar (1987) took this argument one more step, showing that experimental participants agreed with Lopes and with Samuelson's colleague and not with Samuelson. They presented pairs of gambles to individuals and asked them to choose the one they would prefer to play. In one condition, the gambles were unique in that the chosen gamble would be played only once. In the other condition, the chosen gamble would be played 10 times. The gambles were designed so that the one with the highest expected value had the lower probability of winning. If the participants were operating like Samuelson's colleague, they should prefer the lower expected value gamble (which had the highest probability of winning) when the gamble is to be played only once, but they should prefer the higher expected value gamble (which had a lower probability of winning) when the gamble was to be played repeatedly. The results were as you might expect: When the gamble was unique, 68% of the participants choose the *lower* expected value gamble, and when the gamble was to be played repeatedly, 67% choose the *higher* expected value gamble. If people tend to see their decisions as unique, it is doubtful that they think that expected value maximization is a good rule for making them.

Fungibility

It is assumed by most economic theories that payoffs can be described by their "objective" market value, which is stated in terms of money. In this view, money is money, its source is unimportant and one's present asset value is the sum of all of one's different forms of wealth as well as one's expectations for future income. Even presuming decreasing marginal utility for additional money, it is convenient to assume that a dollar is a dollar. This is called "fungibility" of money.

A little reflection reveals that for most of us money is not fungible. Consider the person with $20,000 in the bank earning 4% interest who takes out a 7% loan to buy an $18,000 car. Or the person who refuses to purchase a pair of pants for $32 because they are too expensive but who then pays $40 for a pair of comparable quality because they are marked down from $50. Clearly, the $20,000 in the bank and the money borrowed for the car are different kinds of money to the car buyer, and money "saved" by buying on sale is not the same as money "squandered" by buying at full price. The point is, people value different categories of money differently, and this means that utility is a far more complicated concept than it may at first appear.

von Winterfeldt and Edwards (1986) introspected about the different categories in their own personal finances and came up with four categories:

- *Quick cash:* The money in one's wallet, credit card, checking account
- *Capital assets:* Money in one's house, car, investments, retirement fund
- *Income and fixed expenditures:* Salary, taxes, house payments, utility payments, insurance, and so on
- *Play money:* Money reserved for extravagances such as vacations, household extras, risky investments, sports cars

Thaler (1985, 1992) refers to categories such as these as "mental accounts." He suggests that we exercise self-control over spending by treating different parts of our assets in different ways. Thus, we might force ourselves to save by putting money in a Christmas club (which usually pays no interest) even though the money could be more profitably used to pay off a credit card account (on which, often, the interest approaches 20%). We allow ourselves to spend pocket money for fun but would never touch the grocery money for anything but food. Windfalls, such as winning $50 at a charity raffle, may not be regarded as real money and therefore can be spent frivolously.

Thaler has attempted to integrate the idea of mental accounting into prospect theory and in so doing has added to the breadth of the scope of the theory. Nevertheless, even with this increase in breadth, the theory remains a theory of gambling, with all the faults described above.

Summary

We have examined some of the basic assumptions of utility theory and described the general results of attempts to evaluate its adequacy as a description of human preferences. In fact, it does not come off too well. Together with the failure of probability theory to adequately describe human uncertainty, the failure of utility theory makes the expected value approach to choice highly questionable.

Prospect theory is an attempt to take the experimental results into account while retaining the flavor of the expected value approach. It is, however, a radical departure from expected value and, therefore, can be thought of as a major step away from the classical view and toward a new, descriptive approach to decision theory. As such, it sets the course for others to follow in revision of, or total abandonment of, the expected value model of choice. In doing this, prospect theory and any renegade theories it prompts (which will be discussed later) give up their claim to normativeness. They are descriptive theories, not prescriptive theories. Indeed, it is no longer clear what would constitute a normative theory—few contemporary theorists are willing to suggest that there is only one way to characterize decisions and make choices.

 **8** Interpersonal Decisions

Recall that we left Betty, Ralph, and Hank trying to decide which job candidates to hire. Betty looked around the table. They weren't fighting among themselves, but something was odd. They were competing, as though by getting his or her way one somehow won something from the others; but they weren't talking about it; they were just doing it. It was a game or an emotion-charged negotiation, each of them trying to influence the other's decisions, each trying to impose his or her idea of fairness, each trying to get the others to cooperate but without relinquishing anything themselves. Very confusing and very unpleasant!

* * *

In previous chapters, we spoke as though decision makers operated pretty much alone. Nevertheless, this is clearly not the case; nearly every decision involves other people in one way or another. We are social creatures, and even when we make decisions alone, we take into account the views and potential reactions of others. More to the point, most of us spend the majority of our time with other people: our spouses, children, friends, and colleagues at work. Therefore, it is realistic to think of decision making as a social activity as much as it is an individual's cognitive activity.

When decision making is approached in this way, two things immediately become clear. First, one must consider the possible effects of one's decisions on others, partly out of a sense of fairness and partly to anticipate how they might react so the decisions can be tempered accordingly. Second, and this follows from the first, one must cooperate with others to reach one's own ends; often, success is contingent on the actions of others, and only through cooperation can all parties attain the outcomes they desire.

Our discussion of interpersonal decisions will focus on two areas of behavioral research that examine the descriptive adequacy of normative game theory and normative negotiation theory. Like normative decision theory, these normative theories grew out of economic thought and view decision makers as thoroughly rational, strictly self-interested beings who seek optimal ways to behave in a fairly well-defined world.

Behavioral Game Research

Recall our description of the prisoner's dilemma in Chapter 5. Two prisoners are kept in separate rooms. Each is offered freedom from punishment if he confesses and implicates the other person or very heavy punishment if he keeps quiet but the other person confesses and implicates him, as opposed to moderate punishment if they both confess or very light punishment if neither confesses. Note that for this game to be interesting there must be a possibility that both players care about what happens to the other and both try to forecast what the other will decide to do. If neither of these conditions holds, each player's optimal course is to be ruthless and betray the other by confessing.

There are many variations of the prisoner's dilemma and similar games, all of which require the players to make decisions in light of their assumptions about what the other player(s) will decide. It is this, perhaps most of all, that distinguishes games from the sorts of individual decisions that we have discussed in previous chapters. Game theory specifically acknowledges that decision making takes place in a social environment, but in its most rigorous form, it regards the

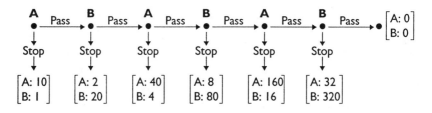

Figure 8.1. Structure of the Centipede Game

players much as expected value theory does—as thoroughly rational, strictly self-interested beings whose behavior is determined solely by the payoffs, although tempered by judgments about what the other player(s) might do (Luce & Raiffa, 1957).

Given this viewpoint, game theory attempts to identify the players' optimal strategies, called "solution concepts." Many solution concepts have been offered, the best known of which is the "equilibrium solution" (Nash, 1951) for games in which players are not allowed to negotiate with each other. The equilibrium solution is self-enforcing in that if all the players adhere to it, it behooves no player to change his or her strategy (hence, it is an equilibrium). There may be multiple Nash equilibria, which has led to attempts to identify a subset of them as the appropriate solutions, attempts known as "refinements" of the Nash solution. For different kinds of games, there are different solution concepts, depending on the particulars of the game.

The "centipede" game is fairly typical of the kind of research game theorists study. The diagram in Figure 8.1 is presented to the subjects. The letters along the line at the top (the As and Bs) designate the two players' turns. Player A starts. She can choose either to stop the game and give herself 10 points and Player B 1 point, or she simply can pass the play to Player B. Similarly, Player B can stop the game and give Player A 2 points and himself 20 points, or he can pass the play back to Player A. The game proceeds until one or the other player stops it or until they reach the right-hand end of the centipede, where Player B must stop the game and give Player A 32 points and himself 320 points; if he does not stop, both players receive 0 points and the game ends anyway.

Because they are seated right in front of the centipede diagram, Player A can anticipate that Player B is bound to stop on the last leg of the centipede, so she is inclined to stop on the next-to-last leg rather than give the last leg to Player A. Similarly, Player B can anticipate Player A's anticipation of his strategy for the last leg and can presume that Player A will stop on the next-to-last leg, so he may decide to stop on the third-to-last leg. Of course, Player A can anticipate Player B's anticipation of her anticipation of his anticipation . . . well, you get the idea.

The upshot is the solution concept dictates that Player A stop on the first leg. Nevertheless, participants generally do not stop early; they are more likely to play a turn or two, trusting their opponent to stay in the game (McKelvey & Palfrey, 1992). On the other hand, as the game progresses both players begin to worry and trust wears thin. The tricky part is to trust your opponent long enough to build up the payoffs but not so long that he or she gets to stop first.

Insofar as it is possible to identify a solution concept for a game, or to delineate a set of appropriate solutions (strategies), game theory is a normative theory in the sense discussed in previous chapters. And as stated above, just as behavioral decision research examines the degree to which normative decision theory is an adequate description of decision makers' actual behavior, behavioral game research examines the adequacy of normative game theory as a description of players' actual behavior. Of particular interest are two noneconomic factors ("externalities") that influence players' strategy selections, fairness and cooperation.

Fairness

Numerous studies have shown that players' decisions reflect a preference for fairness in the distribution of payoffs, which indicates that the game theory assumption of strict self-interest is incorrect. This does not necessarily mean that game theory is wholly wrong, because fairness can be interpreted as a determiner of utility by incorporating the player's concerns about the outcome to be received by the other player(s).

One paradigm for studies of fairness involves one player, A, who chooses one of several possible distributions of money to be divided between himself or herself and another player, B. For example, the experimenter might present A with the distributions (4, 10), (5, 5), or (12, 0), in which A would get the first amount and B would get the second. A chooses one of the distributions and negotiates with B, who must agree to it or neither player receives anything.

The theoretical solution is for A to choose the distribution that offers the largest total payoff and, in addition, demand a side payment from B that will end up giving A most of the payoff. With the distributions given above, A should choose (4, 10) and then demand a side payment of 8 or more to make her total at least 12, which is what A would get in the (12, 0) distribution if it had been chosen and agreed to by B. The idea is that B should agree to this deal because even a little something for agreeing to A's demands is better than nothing, which is what B would get for refusing A's demands. In theory, even if B stands to gain as little as one penny, he should agree to A's offer.

In fact, however, people who play A in these experiments seldom demand anything like the theoretically prescribed deal. Most often, they split the payoffs equally between themselves and B, going for what they perceive to be the "fair distribution." The A players can, however, be induced to offer deals that favor themselves if they believe that they have the right to play the role of A or if they have won that right in some preceding game of skill (Hoffman & Spitzer, 1985). As Camerer (1990) observes, unequal division can be acceptable if people think that the right to the larger share somehow has been earned. Apparently, earning the right allows unequal division of the payoffs to be regarded as fair, and fairness seems to be the dominant factor in the player's decisions.

Fairness also arises in what are called "ultimatum games." These are not unlike the game described above, but they lack the negotiation of a side payment—A merely offers the division of payoffs to B who must take it or leave it. Again, if B fails to take the offer, neither player gets anything. (The situation is analogous to buying something from a monopoly; you pay the price or go without.) As before, the theoretical prescription is for A to keep the largest share and offer B a pittance; B should accept anything because it is better than nothing.

Again, fairness reigns. People who play the role of A seldom offer B less than 40% of the total payoff—not exactly a .50-.50 split but not .99-.01 either. Moreover, people who play the role of B often refuse offers that give them less than about 20% of the payoff, contrary to the theoretical prescription that they should be grateful for any amount greater than zero. In short, people who play A tend to give fairer offers than they have to and people who play B would rather receive nothing than accept an offer they see as grossly unfair.

Just as earning the right to an unequal distribution of payoffs seems to qualify the distribution as fair, demonstration of a true need for a disproportionate share of the payoff, as opposed to merely wanting it, also seems to qualify as fair. Of course, both earning and true need are externalities—not strictly part of the normative game theory model.

Cooperation

The question of cooperation most often arises in the context of what is called "social dilemmas" and the issue of "free riding." The classical example of a social dilemma is the "dilemma of the commons" (Hardin, 1968). Imagine a village that has a common pasture on which each of n households can place one cow. The pasture can support only n cows; any more leads to a reduction in food for the herd and a consequent reduction in the health of all the cows. Thus, it is in the best interest of the village as a whole to limit the number of cows to n, but it is in the best interest of any individual household to place a second cow on the pasture. The $n + 1$ cow would lead to a slight decrease in the health of all the cows, including the extra one, but the free riding household still would be ahead by having two slightly unhealthy cows rather than one very healthy cow. The hitch is, of course, that if every household behaves this way the ever-growing herd will become increasingly unhealthy and everyone will be ruined. Only when each player forgoes the opportunity to increase his or her own advantage can the group as a whole prosper.

A similar dilemma arises in the case of what is called "collective goods," for example, a public park or a public beach. Someone must fund the collective good in order for it to be provided. From a strictly self-interested viewpoint, an individual ought to elect to be a free rider— to use the collective good but resist contributing to its provision.

There have been numerous studies of social dilemmas and of contributions to the collective good. The major finding is that people tend to be cooperative even when they could do better by not being so. That is, they contribute more to the collective than they would if they were being guided strictly by self-interest. Indeed, people who value the collective good highly or who have more resources contribute even more (Rapoport, 1988). Moreover, if the players can discuss the game or if the experimenter "preaches" about cooperation, contributions increase, especially if they benefit the player's own colleagues (Camerer, 1990). In short, people tend to avoid taking the self-interested position of becoming a free rider.

The foregoing is merely the tip of the iceberg for behavioral game research. There are games of such wonderful complexity that one doubts that the players can comprehend them (indeed, players often simplify complex games by ignoring parts of them and making them into more tractable games). It is beyond the scope of our presentation to discuss them, but the results presented above give you the theme: By and large, unbridled self-interest is uncommon; people are sensitive to the economic factors embodied in the games, but they impose their own standards of fairness and cooperation. The resulting picture is of decision makers who are less ruthless and less selfish than game theory assumes.

Behavioral Negotiation Research

Negotiation is a process in which two or more players decide what each will give and take in an exchange between them (Rubin & Brown, 1975). Negotiations are games, in the sense discussed above, but the rules of play are slightly different. As with games, negotiators presume that they have conflicting interests, but (1) communication is possible, (2) compromise is possible, (3) players may make provisional offers and counteroffers, and (4) offers and counteroffers do not result in outcomes until accepted by the players (Thompson, 1990). Here, too, the normative model for negotiation derives from economics and classical decision theory (Raiffa, 1982; Rapoport, 1966). The basic idea is that the players (and, for simplicity, we will assume that there are only two—although they may represent constituencies) arrive on the scene with "reservation prices," which represent the least they will settle for without walking away from the negotiation, and "targets," which represent what they really want. The difference between the two players' reservation prices is called the "zone of agreement," the range of outcomes within which negotiation can take place.

Negotiations can be about dividing some fixed amount of a resource (distributive bargaining) or about adding to the resource (integrative bargaining). Negotiations in which the players do not have compatible interests involve distributive bargaining, and the normative prescription is to maximize one's gains at the expense of the other player. When there is at least some compatibility of interests, the negotiation calls for integrative bargaining, and the normative prescription is to seek the agreement that maximizes the players' joint profit. Integrative agreements allow both parties to do better than they would if they merely negotiated about the distribution of a fixed amount of a resource because the essence of integrative agreement is that it expands the resource so each player gets more than he or she otherwise would receive. An integrative agreement is said to be "Pareto optimal" if no other agreement would improve the utility of one or both players while not hurting either player (Nash, 1950).

But, do negotiators seek integrative solutions? Neale and Northcraft (1986) had both novice (students) and professional negotiators participate in a negotiation simulation. Actually, the experiment was done separately on the novices and the professionals. Half of each group was assigned the role of buyer (retail stores) and the other half assigned the role of seller (manufacturers of refrigerators). They were told that the issues for negotiation involved delivery, discount, and financial terms. Then they were given information about profits as a function of different levels and combinations of these three issues and asked to negotiate as many deals as they could in 25 minutes. The profits were set up so that integrative solutions were Pareto optimal, and the question was whether participants would seek integrative solutions. The answer was that they did; they were not perfect at it, but they improved as they made more deals. Moreover, whereas the expert negotiators moved more quickly to integrative solutions and always did a better job, the novices improved with time and ended up performing nearly as well as the experts.

Just to help you think about integrative solutions, Follett (1940) provided the most frequently cited example: Two people negotiating over the distribution of a basket of oranges discover that one wants the juice and the other wants the peels. Because of the discovery, conflict over distribution ceases and an integrative agreement results in one player taking all of the juice and the other taking all of the peels. This agreement provides both players with more than they would have obtained had they merely divided the oranges, no matter what distribution they agreed on. In general, differences between the players in terms of how they value the various characteristics of the resource of interest provide opportunities for integrative agreements.

Fairness and Cooperation

Distributive and integrative agreements almost automatically evoke the two concepts we discussed when examining behavioral game research, fairness, and cooperation. Fairness is of particular concern when the negotiation involves division of some fixed set of resources, and clearly, it influences how players feel about the offers they make and receive and the final agreement they reach. Cooperation is necessary if resource is to be expanded, if a suitable integrative agreement is to be reached. When players ignore fairness or cooperation and look out only for their own interests, negotiations often reach an impasse and nobody profits. Players seem particularly sensitive to exploitative behavior on the part of opponents, particularly opponents who misrepresent their reservation price (Gruder, 1971). Similarly, when players try to control rather than cooperate, they are less likely to reach an integrative agreement (Tjosvold, 1978).

Of course, fairness and cooperation are tempered by the conditions under which negotiation takes place. In the first place, players' views about what is fair are often self-serving. For example, Messick and Sentis (1979) asked players to specify a fair rate of pay for themselves when they had worked 10 hours and another person had been paid $25 for working 7 hours and a fair rate for the other person when they had been paid $25 for working 7 hours and the other person had worked 10 hours. In the first case, they awarded themselves an average of $35.24 for the 10 hours they worked, and in the second case, they awarded the other person only $30.29 for the 10 hours they worked. That hardly seems like perfect fairness.

On the good side, however, players tend to behave more generously when negotiation takes place face-to-face rather than through the mail or over the phone and they are more generous when they expect to have to negotiate with the opponent in the future (Ben-Yoav & Pruitt, 1984a, 1984b). Understandably, they are less generous when the constituencies they represent pressure them to "win" (Neale, 1984; Tjosvold, 1977).

Strategies

Much of the research on negotiation behavior has focused on the strategies players adopt. Indeed, a catalogue of strategies has evolved, each of which can be commonly observed but not all of which yield outcomes that can in any way be regarded as optimal. There are four categories of observed strategies: (1) yielding, (2) compromising, (3) contending, and (4) problem solving.

Yielding Strategies. Here the player simply gives in before the negotiation seriously gets underway. One strategy is for the player to preempt the negotiation by stating his or her reservation point. If the opponent accepts, agreement is reached immediately. If the opponent does not accept, the player simply walks out and neither party gains or loses resources. An alternative is for the player to keep quiet about his or her reservation point and simply accept the first offer that exceeds it. Both of these strategies serve to reduce the conflict the player must experience in reaching an agreement, but they both ensure that he or she will receive, at worst, nothing at all or, at best, only the minimum he or she will settle for, which may be considerably less than he or she might otherwise get. That is, use of yielding strategies often results in one's opponents gaining more than his or her reservation and more than his or her target.

Compromising Strategies. Here the player seeks the middle ground. One strategy is for the player to assess the difference between his or her target and reservation point and to offer the midpoint to the opponent. A second strategy is for the player to make an offer and ask the opponent to make an offer and then suggest that they compromise at the midpoint between the two offers. Like the yielding strategies, compromising strategies reduce conflict and have the advantage of being simple, cutting the negotiation short. Nevertheless, they seldom produce a very satisfactory solution for the player. In the first compromise strategy, he or she gets more than the reservation point, which is nice, but less than the target, which is disappointing—although the opponent may be very happy to agree to the offer. In the second compromise strategy, neither the player nor the opponent have reason to be very happy; it is likely that the proposed compromise will fall short of both players' target points. Although many people feel that it is the epitome of fairness, "splitting the difference" seldom is a good strategy for either player because both fall short of their aspirations.

Contending Strategies. Here the player tries to impose his or her position on the opponent, sometimes escalating the pressure by applying the strategies successively. One strategy, persistence, is simply to state a position and hold firm, repeating the same offer over and over until the opponent is worn down or walks out. A second strategy, persuasion, is to hold firm but to manipulate the opponent with arguments centered on equity, need, or desires. A third strategy, promises, is to hold firm and make promises about future favors that justify the opponent accepting the player's offer. Finally, the fourth strategy, threat, is to hold firm and make promises about dire consequences for the opponent if he or she does not accept the offer—walking out, saying bad things to others about the opponent, getting revenge.

Problem-Solving Strategies. Here the player has a firm target but is willing to take advantage of the fact that he or she and the opponent are interested in different aspects of the resource in question or are willing to give up some of the resource for others of which they have a need. The first strategy, expanding the pie, requires the player to identify additional resources that can be shared with the opponent in such a way that each of their needs can be met. The second strategy, side payment, requires that one player be granted his or her target for which the other is compensated by a resource of some other kind. The third strategy, logrolling, requires trade-offs such that each player makes concessions on issues that are less important to him or her and receives large rewards on issues that are more important to him or her. This presumes that what is important to one player is less important to the other player and vice versa. The fourth strategy, cost cutting, requires the player to grant the opponent's demands with the understanding that the opponent will collect those demands in a way that furthers the player's goals. For example, management agrees to raise workers' pay if they agree to accept the increase in salary in stocks, instead of cash, so that management can publicize the deal as an innovation in employee participation rather than as having given in to labor's demands. Finally, the fifth strategy, bridging, requires creative, cooperative rethinking of the situation faced by the players. This involves reformulating issues in terms of mutual needs, desires and priorities and seeking an agreement that will further both players' interests—that is, an integrative agreement.

Some Practical Conclusions

Behavioral negotiation research always has had one eye on practical applications. The results are best summarized in a slim book about how to move negotiations from distributive strategies toward integrative strategies. Since its publication in 1981, *Getting to Yes: Negotiating Agreement Without Giving In,* by Roger Fisher and William Ury, has constantly been a best-seller among business books. Its message is simple:

1. *Separate the people from the problem.* This guideline is aimed at helping players keep a clear head and avoid poisoning the waters for future negotiations. It is easy to demonize the opponent; after all, he or she is contending for the things we want. The emotional baggage this brings to the table tends to get in the way of clear thinking about the issues and prompts us to want to win at any cost rather than to reach an acceptable agreement.

2. *Focus on interests, not positions.* The positions taken by the players are merely reflections of their broader interests and focusing on the narrow position obscures what really is important. In businesses, for example, the broader interests involve the health of the organization, and the question is how the outcome of this particular negotiation can contribute to it, rather than whether the negotiator wins or loses some specific amount of a resource. In a marriage, the broader interests involve the health of the relationship, rather than who wins this or that argument. This is not to say that negotiations are never about momentous turning points in the history of an organization or relationship, but most are not, although they are treated as though they were. As a result, the players tend to lock themselves into positions and refuse to budge, usually leading to an impasse and jeopardizing future negotiations.

Focusing on interests means that an offer that fails to satisfy the opponent's stated position but that contributes as much or more to his or her broader interests may prevent an impasse. It is the search for offers such as this that leads the players away from a narrow, divisive distributive conception of the negotiation toward broader, cooperative integrative conception. With that movement comes the possibility of a mutually satisfactory agreement that leaves the road clear for future negotiations (and that establishes a model for those future negotiations).

3. *Invent options for mutual gain.* Once the negotiation is seen as integrative, the task becomes one of finding ways of increasing the pie rather than merely dividing it. As we saw in the problem-solving strategies described above, this may include increasing the pool of resources, side payments, logrolling, cost-cutting, or complete reformulation of the negotiation. However it is done, the goal is to allow both parties to come out of the negotiation with more than they went in with and with the feeling that they have been treated fairly.

4. *Insist on using objective criteria.* Part of any workable agreement is the definition of just what constitutes the outcomes for each player. If part of the settlement is that one player will do something for the other some time in the future, that something and that sometime must not be left vague or neither party will know how the debt is to be paid and when. Present satisfaction with the agreement is increased and the possibility of future misunderstanding is decreased if everything is made clear so everyone will know when obligations have been met and all parties to the agreement have behaved fairly and cooperatively.

Summary

Previous chapters have viewed decision making as a rather solitary activity. This chapter departs from that view by recognizing the interpersonal nature of decision making and by recognizing the competitive context in which many of those decisions arise. The normative theories of interpersonal decisions have the same roots in economic thought as the normative theories of individual decision making. The behavior research agenda also has been the same, assessing the adequacy of the normative theories as descriptions of actual decision making. The results of the research are much the same too. Behavior seldom conforms to the prescriptions of the theories, in part because decision makers take into consideration factors that are not strictly part of the normative theories. The two factors that repeatedly appear in interpersonal decisions are fairness and cooperation.

Games differ from negotiations, primarily in terms of communication. The most heavily researched games do not allow players to communicate about their strategies or reach an agreement that will coordinate their decisions. Negotiation, on the other hand, is largely about communication—offers and counteroffers, side payments, and cooperative attempts to augment the pie. In neither, however, do players strive to behave in ways the theories would describe as rational. Their aim appears to be somewhat less vigorous and certainly less selfish. Players appear to recognize that interpersonal decision making is just that, interpersonal; both parties must gain and both must leave without hard feelings, particularly if they are going to interact in the future. This strikes many people as a reasonable viewpoint and provides a glimmer of hope in what is often characterized as a overly competitive and selfish world.

9 Organizational and Group Decisions

They were done! Offers had been made and accepted, and now it was time to think about how to reshape the sales force, to take advantage of these talented new people. Reorganization always causes turmoil, so they wouldn't know whether their "cloning" strategy was working until the dust settled. It was going to be rough, but then these are the kinds of decisions and actions Betty signed on for when she became president of the company. Actually, she was optimistic. She and her department heads understood each other and shared a vision about where the company was headed and how it was going to get there. In fact, Betty was struck by how well the organization was working these days; there was a sense of cooperation that was absent before Ralph came aboard and before they identified the sales problem. It was amazing how a vivid threat to the organization brought people together and showed them how much they had in common.

* * *

The Decisional Nature of Organizations

The first thing we must understand about organizations is that their members work together, however haphazardly, to construct socially shared interpretations of events. This means that there is a common core of understanding throughout the organization, or at least in parts of it. It is this commonality that allows people to work together and to communicate about the events that occur and the goals they share. Without this shared understanding, there would be no organization in any real sense.

Shared understanding is never perfect. It is frequently the case that nobody knows all that is to be known about an issue, and different people often know different things about it. This means that to one degree or another they all conceive of the problem differently. That is, they tend to frame things differently, meaning that they are all starting from different assumptions and are trying to tackle different problems— often, the differences are small, but sometimes they are large. The upshot is that, in the aggregate, most decision problems are very ill defined and the decision options are not at all clear.

Most of the effort in organizational decision making is not directed at reaching a decision. As is true of individuals, too, the real work is in trying to understand the problem and to conceive of options for dealing with it. In organizations, this is complicated by the differing frames that different people begin with. Indeed, decision making is a decidedly disorderly process in which the search for a good definition of the problem engenders ideas about possible solutions that, in turn, influence the problem definition and further thinking about options. Clearly, it is a very complicated, convoluted, involved process that, to the outside observer, often looks like total chaos.

On top of all this, add coalitions and the differential power of the participants, and things get really complex. Seldom are major decisions made by everyone who has a stake in what is decided, especially in large organizations. More often, decisions are made by representatives of the various units in the organization, each of which has its own interests, or representatives of various powerful coalitions in the organization, each of which has its own turf to guard and power to protect. The result is a form of negotiation, sometimes covert sometimes overt, in which various representatives attempt to advance the interests of their sponsors by influencing problem definition and option formulation as well as by having an impact on the final decision. Of course, if your power allows you to define the problem and delineate the options, you can constrain things so much that the decision is a foregone conclusion.

Organizational Models

One way of attempting to impose order on the apparent chaos is to classify the various models of organizational decision making that guide both research and applied prescriptions and to see what each contributes to a larger picture. Work on this began with Koopman and Pool (1991) and it is their outline that we will follow here.

The Rational Model

Most of the early descriptions of decision making in organizations were guided by the normative viewpoint described in previous chapters. The model usually presumes that there is only one paramount goal and that the members of the organization, individually and collectively, strive to achieve that goal. It presumes that the decision makers have unlimited information and possess the cognitive ability to use it efficiently; they know all of the opportunities open to them and all of the consequences of pursuing one or another of those opportunities. Finally, it presumes that the optimal course of action can be revealed by applying the appropriate normative analysis and that choice of that course of action will, if only in the long run, prove to be more profitable than choice of any other course of action. The key concepts are rationality, analysis, orderliness, and maximization. Because, like normative theory in general, this description is so patently wrong, both conceptually and empirically, it often serves as a foil for contrasting descriptions.

The Information Model

The apparent shortcomings of the rational model led to revisions, primarily in regard to assumptions about the cognitive abilities of decision makers. Simon (1947, 1957) and March and Simon (1958) pointed out that decision makers use only part of the information that potentially is available, both because they are cognitively limited and can handle only so much information and because there are resource constraints on acquiring complete information even if it is available. Often, decisions are made when a sufficient option is encountered (called "satisficing") rather than after a prolonged search for the best option. Moreover, even when search is undertaken it usually is limited—starting with options that have worked in the past and moving to new options only when old ones are demonstrably unsuitable. Indeed, only about 20% of the time are new options sought or considered.

The Structural Model

March and Simon (1958) suggested that the limited information processing and analysis capacities of individuals can be compensated for by properly structuring the organization—breaking it into appropriate units and apportioning various parts of the process to the units that have the corresponding capability. Whereas this may be a wise strategy, there are still problems with agreement about the organization's goals and adequate communication of those goals to the units. Even more telling is the lack of concentrated control over implementation of an option or part of it—so if things do not go as planned changes cannot quickly be made. The result is that decisions progress step-by-step rather than being made and committed to. This process, called "incrementalism" (Lindblom, 1959) allows the decision maker or decision-making unit to proceed cautiously in a general direction, changing things in light of feedback about the success of what is being done. In the course of this, wholly new options may evolve, options that were not obvious at the time the original decision was being considered. This process has been criticized as unduly conservative (Etzioni, 1967), but it has its defenders (Quinn, 1980).

Structural differentiation often proves to be inadequate because it promotes a limited view of the overall decision problem in favor of emphasis on the part for which a unit is responsible. Conflict often arises from a diversity of interests, from settling for local benefits at the expense of benefits for the organization as a whole, from an unwillingness of units to take risks for fear of losing out to other units, and from a resulting tendency to pass off hard problems to weaker units that are the least able to deal with them adequately. It is in this context that issues of power arise, how units (and individuals) derive power from their ability to control parts of the organization's environment, how difficult it is to replace them, how central they are to the organization's key activities, and so on (Hickson, Hinnings, Lee, Schneck, & Pennings, 1971). Certainly, exertion of power, struggles for power, and internal politics all heavily influence how decisions are made and how successfully they are implemented.

Often, structural differentiation is coupled with top-down managerial control, sometimes called a machine or bureaucratic organizational structure. Decision making can proceed rather efficiently in such organizations if top management lays out the guidelines for how decisions are to be handled by the units and how those different decisions are to be brought together to form a plan of action for the organization as a whole. Mintzberg, Raisinghani, and Theoret (1976) referred to this form of decision control as "metadecision making," decisions about how decisions will be made. Combined with structural differentiation, metadecision making can be a powerful way of confronting the limitations highlighted by the information model discussed above and is fundamental to the notion of strategic management.

The Garbage Can Model

Consideration of the apparent chaos in organizations led Cohen, March, and Olsen (1972) to propose the garbage can model of managerial decision making, an evocative name that has afforded the model more attention than it perhaps deserves. Here, organizations are seen as "organized anarchies," with unclear or inconsistent goals, using technologies that are not well understood by the organization's members and relying on decisions in which the members are inconsistent participants.

The basic premise is that organizations are collections of problems, solutions, participants, and choice opportunities in which participants must link problems and solutions—that is, make decisions. These elements are randomly mixed together in a garbage can, which means that solutions can precede problems, that both solutions and problems may await a choice opportunity, or that they all may come together when a particular set of participants convenes. In short, combinations of elements are intrinsically unpredictable—which is the attempt to mimic the apparent chaos in organizations. The model is an assault on the rationalistic description of decision making as identification of a problem, identification of options, evaluation of options, selection of an optimal option, solution to the problem. It more closely resembles the idea of "a solution in search of a problem," and similar clichés characterizing decision making as it is often observed in organizations.

The garbage can model does not necessarily imply that organizations are wholly irrational. It merely suggests that the attention of participants is divided and that decisions do not derive from the unidirectional, linear processes prescribed by a more rationalistic approach. Indeed, the garbage can model says almost nothing about decision processes per se. Its description is similar to what might be given by the legendary man from Mars who happens to land on a university campus. He hears the many different opinions, watches the different governance bodies, notes that nobody attends every meeting or understands every nuance of the problems under discussion, and observes that from this chaos some kind of direction emerges, even though no single person may be able to articulate it clearly. Despite everything, the university appears to soldier on, meet its obligations, and survive. Convinced that some sort of miracle has taken place, our martian e-mails a description of what he has observed to the folks back home. The description might look a lot like the garbage can model.

The Participation Model

Both the structural model and the garbage can model emphasize the roles of groups of participants in decision making. The participation model carries this further by examining the advantages and disadvantages of member participation as well as the conditions under which participation is warranted.

It is argued that involvement of an organization's members in group decision making contributes to better decisions and greater satisfaction with, and greater confidence in, the decisions on the part of the participants. The advantage of better decisions seems obvious, although it is really not clear whether it means decisions that are made better, in the sense of more thoroughness, or that the decisions produce better results; decision researchers favor the first definition and decision makers prefer the second. The advantage of increased satisfaction with whatever is decided supposedly lies in a greater commitment on the part of the participants to implementation of the decision.

Because groups are composed of people who do not all have the same viewpoints and prior experience, it can be argued that the pool of resources is greater for groups than for individuals trying to make the same decisions. Nevertheless, studies show that group discussion tends to focus on what is known by everyone and relevant information possessed by individual members either goes unmentioned or tends to be ignored when it is brought up (Sniezek, Paese, & Furiya, 1990; Stasser & Titus, 1985).

An experiment by Heath and Gonzalez (1995) demonstrates how studies are done in this area and provides interesting results. The experimenters were testing the hypothesis that an advantage of group interaction is that participants share information and therefore make better decisions. Pairs of subjects were specially selected for their knowledge about football. Each week, each subject predicted the outcome of 14 football games by choosing the winner of each game and stating the probability that that team would win. Then they each met with a partner to "share information and opinions," after which they individually made new predictions. It was found that choices were not more accurate after the opportunity to exchange information about the teams but that subjects were significantly more confident in their postdiscussion choices than in their earlier choices. The experimenters suggest that interaction in groups acts primarily to increase the members' confidence in whatever they subsequently decide as individuals rather than improving the quality of their decisions. Of course, the danger is that interaction will lead to confidence in what will in fact prove to be a poor decision (Janis, 1972, 1982; Sniezek, 1992).

Other research suggests that participation often decreases productivity (e.g., Locke & Schweiger, 1979; Wagner & Gooding, 1987). After all, group meetings and group discussions take up a lot of time that might otherwise be spent working, and the quality of the group decisions is not always very high. Detailed examination shows that participation is most useful if it can take advantage of expertise or if the reason for using it is to promote acceptance on the part of participants (Heller, Drenth, Koopman, & Rus, 1988; Koopman, 1980). Much the same conclusions are reached in studies of teamwork and team building (Katzenbach & Smith, 1993).

The spotty record of the participation model has prompted a great deal of research, some of which we will examine in the next section of this chapter. Nevertheless, the research has proved to be largely irrelevant to real-world practice. For most people, common sense dictates that participation is a good thing in and of itself and that it somehow ought to result in better decisions. The operative concepts appear to be fairness and cooperation, once again. It is only fair that an organization's members have a say in what goes on, and cooperation is a desirable thing that can be relied on to produce desirable results. In the face of such obvious "truths," data are not regarded as necessary.

This taxonomy of organizational models is valuable because it highlights the differences in how both researchers and practicing members may interpret what they regard as objective observations of a functioning organization and explain the very different prescriptions they may offer for the problems they identify. Characterizing an organization as rational leads to an emphasis on problems arising from insufficient or faulty analysis and prescription of support systems based on normative theory. The latter often take the form of computer systems designed around utility elicitation and maximization of expected value. At the other end of the spectrum, characterizing an organization in terms of participation leads to an emphasis on interpersonal processes and prescriptions for increasing member involvement decision making. At their best, these prescriptions can reduce conflict and increase participant satisfaction and commitment, and under the right circumstances, they may result in better decisions. At their worst, they can lead to touchy-feely triviality—what might be called the "Kumbiya model" in which the goal is to make everyone comfortable, never mind that stress and discomfort are the normal price for anything worthwhile.

Group Decisions

The participation model has had immense influence on small group research. The scope of this research extends well beyond our immediate interests, but there are three areas that are particularly pertinent to decision research: the conditions that call for group participation in decision making, the conditions that promote group generation of an increased range of decision options, and the conditions that lead to group consensus about one of those options and confidence in the correctness of that option.

Participation

One of the focal points for thinking about participation has been the Vroom and Yetton (1973) model of managerial decision making. Building on a store of earlier work on participation, the model holds that an organization's members can participate to different degrees in managerial decision making and that the leader's task is to select the right level of member involvement in light of the characteristics of the decision problem. The lowest level excludes them altogether; the leader makes the decision. The second level merely invites them to contribute information; the leader makes the decision, which may or may not reflect the input. The third level provides them with information about the problem and solicits each individual's ideas and suggestions; the leader makes the decision, which may or may not reflect the input. The fourth level provides them with information and solicits their collective ideas and recommendations; the leader makes the decision, which may or may not reflect the input. The fifth level provides them with information about the problem and convenes them as a group to arrive at a consensus that becomes the organization's final decision.

The problem characteristics that determine which of these five levels of participation is appropriate are the following: (1) the extent to which the quality of the decision is important, (2) the extent to which the leader possesses the expertise and information necessary to make the decision alone, (3) the extent to which the problem is clearly structured, (4) the extent to which member acceptance and commitment is critical to successful implementation of the decision, (5) the extent to which an autocratic decision by the leader will be accepted by members, (6) the extent to which members are motivated by the organization's goals rather than their own agendas, and (7) the extent to which members are likely to be able to reach consensus. The idea is that a leader can use these characteristics to make a metadecision about which level to use for making a specific decision.

There have been numerous attempts to test the Vroom and Yetton (1973) model. Many of them have found that self-reports by managers about the level of participation used for various successful and unsuccessful decisions indicate greater success when the level conformed to the prescriptions of the model (Thomas, 1990; Vroom & Jago, 1978; Zimmer, 1978).

On the other hand, persistent criticisms of the model prompted Vroom and Jago (1988) to add five more situational characteristics to the seven listed above. These characteristics are (8) the extent to which members have sufficient information to make a quality decision, (9) the extent to which time constraints preclude involvement of members in the decision, (10) the extent to which it is prohibitive to bring together geographically dispersed members for group participation, (11) the extent to which the decision must be made quickly, and (12) the extent to which it is important to foster member development through participation.

With the addition of situational characteristics, the model was formulated in terms of structural equations, the solution of which provides an overall effectiveness score for each of the five levels of participation, with the appropriate level presumably being the one with the highest score.

Brown and Finstuen (1993) used the self-report method used in earlier research to examine the new version of the model. The results did not support the contention that the highest scoring level of participation was necessarily the best, but the model was successful in identifying the relative effectiveness of the five levels. Although the researchers interpret their results as providing strong support for the revised version of the model, they point out that the computational complexity of the structural equations raises questions about their practical usefulness for managers. On the other hand, the model provides a major service for managers and researchers alike by identifying the situational factors that influence the effectiveness of member participation in managerial decision making.

Option Generation

Since 1957, when A. F. Osborn, an advertising executive, published his book about "brainstorming," there has been ongoing controversy about the value of group participation in option generation for decision making. Brainstorming is aimed at enhancing the group's creativity by encouraging free discussion and free exchange of ideas. It claims to work by separating idea generation and idea evaluation, on the premise that premature evaluation causes participants to become more cautious and less imaginative. Premature evaluation results in fewer new and potentially valuable ideas being available to the group during their deliberations, leading to conservative, familiar solutions to problems being chosen when the solutions might require more adventurous approaches. The four rules of brainstorming are (1) criticism must be withheld during the generation stage so participants are not discouraged from contributing novel ideas, (2) odd, even crazy, ideas are encouraged so that unique, unapparent options can be discovered, (3) the more ideas the better because quantity increases the chances that a good option will appear, and (4) using others' suggestions as a source of ideas about options is acceptable—sometimes called "piggybacking."

The usual measure of the effectiveness of brainstorming is the number and creativity of the ideas that are generated by a group compared to an equal number of people working independently. Unfortunately, an extensive body of research shows that for both quality and creativity, brainstorming groups seldom are more effective, and certainly less efficient, than individuals—even when redundant ideas by individuals are not counted (Davis, 1992; Diehl & Stroebe, 1987; McGrath, 1984). Indeed, some research finds that, in direct contradiction to assumptions underlying brainstorming, evaluative groups are *more* productive than supportive groups (Connolly, Jessup, & Valacich, 1990).

There is reason to believe that groups produce fewer ideas than individuals because of "production blocking" (Diehl & Stroebe, 1987). That is, as group size increases members must wait longer and longer before they can speak. Those who are waiting to speak may forget their ideas or suppress them because they seem less relevant as the discussion progresses. Moreover, while waiting, members' attention is focused on trying to remember their ideas, listening to others' ideas, and trying to find an opportunity to speak; they cannot pay attention to generating new ideas.

The growth of computer technology has led to the development of an electronic brainstorming system (EBS) that gets around some of the shortcomings of traditional face-to-face group meetings (Valacich, Dennis, & Nunamaker, 1991). Participants work at individual computer stations, typing ideas into a central pool that is displayed on their monitors. Thus, participants are working much like individuals, but the display permits piggybacking of ideas and the elimination of redundancy. Most important, however, there is no wait to contribute ideas to the pool, so production blocking is reduced. In an empirical study by Valacich, Dennis, and Connolly (1994), participants from a business school were asked to identify all individuals, groups, and organizations that would be affected by a proposed policy requiring all business students to own or have access to a personal microcomputer. Some students worked alone and others were assigned to groups of 3, 9, or 18 students. All of them worked at computers, recording their ideas as they thought of them. The difference was that the computers were linked to facilitate EBS for the groups, whereas the computers of the individuals who worked alone were isolated. The data were analyzed by randomly selecting 3, 9, or 18 individuals from those who worked alone, pooling their data (removing redundant ideas and scoring the survivors for uniqueness) and counting the number of ideas in the pool. This total was compared to the number of ideas generated by a real group of 3, 9, or 18 participants. The results were quite clear: EBS resulted in more ideas being generated by groups than by comparable numbers of independent individuals, the number of unique ideas increased as group size increased, and this happened without penalty to participant satisfaction. The experimenters conclude that a significant proportion of the increase in unique ideas results from the elimination of production blocking when the EBS is used.

Research continues on EBS (and related systems), particularly because a large number of firms throughout the world have installed facilities that permit its convenient use for a wide range of group decision problems. As people become increasingly comfortable using computers in decision making, EBS and related technologies hold immense promise for decision aiding.

Consensus and Confidence

Beginning with the classic Asch (1956) experiments on conformity, small-group research has explored how the members of groups are influenced by group processes. Of this work there are two areas of particular interest to us, the risky shift phenomenon and procedural effects.

In the 1960s, it was reported that groups tend to be more extreme than individuals in their willingness or unwillingness to endorse risky decisions (Nordhoy, 1962; Stoner, 1961; Wallach, Kogan, & Bem, 1962). This difference can be viewed as a shift when one moves from individuals to groups, called the risky shift (or more appropriately, the choice shift).

There has been an enormous amount of interest in the risky shift because it implies that group members end up agreeing with decisions that they would not make as individuals. One explanation is that group members can endorse a more risky alternative because responsibility is diffused across all of the members, but this fails to explain shifts in the conservative direction. Another explanation is that some decisions evoke members' social values for risk taking and when, during the group discussion, they find that they are less extreme than some of the others in the group they take an even more extreme position. Similarly, some problems evoke social values for conservatism and the same mechanism comes into play during discussion of the problem, resulting in less extreme positions. However, shifts in both directions have been observed for problems that have no social content and thus could not evoke values favoring risk or conservatism.

The explanation that appears to have the most going for it is that shifts reflect the emergence of a dominant faction during discussions and because participants assume that the majority has a right to have its decision be the group decision, opposition members subordinate their views (while not necessarily changing them) to the dominant one (Davis, 1992). This explanation is particularly plausible because the majority view usually becomes obvious either in the course of the discussion or because procedures permit it to be emphasized. For example, it is common procedure for the group leader to summarize "the sense of the meeting," or for straw votes to be taken prior to a final vote. Straw votes, at least, have been shown to have a sizable impact on the opinions of members who hold other than the dominant view (Davis, Stasson, Ono, & Zimmerman, 1988).

Majority rule is but one convention that may influence the outcomes of group decision making. Others involve use of an explicit agenda for meetings, rules for speaking (recognition by the chair, taking turns), voting procedures (secret ballot, show of hands), and criteria for arriving at a decision (majority, plurality, averaging). Each of these constrains how the discussion will proceed, how information is presented and persuasion is attempted, and how the final outcome will be determined. As an example of agenda effects, Davis, Tindale, Nagao, Hinsz, and Robertson (1984) showed that when charges against a defendant were considered in decreasing order of seriousness juries were more inclined to convict on a serious charge than when the charges were considered in an ascending order. In another example, Plott and Levine (1976) influenced the decisions of a recreational organization by manipulating the agenda such that successive decisions narrowed down the options until only the one favored by the researchers remained.

Perhaps the most famous examination of group consensus in decision making was done by Irving Janis (1972), resulting in what he called "groupthink"—an overemphasis on consensus and a consequent failure to critically evaluate assumptions and options when the group is highly cohesive. Janis illustrated his ideas using six major decisions by groups acting for the American government. The theory involves three categories of necessary conditions: cohesiveness of the group, characteristics of the organization, and characteristics of the situation. When these conditions are right, groupthink occurs, resulting in defective decision making and inferior outcomes. Symptoms of groupthink are illusions of invulnerability, unanimity, and group morality; stereotyping of oppositions as "the enemy," weak, evil, or stupid; self-censorship in which members fail to bring up counterarguments or concerns; censorship of others so that counterarguments do not reach influential members of the group; and direct pressure to keep errant members in line.

Like the garbage can model discussed above, the groupthink theory has an evocative label that perhaps gives the underlying ideas the appearance of more solidity than they have. In fact, the surprisingly sparse research literature on groupthink shows that support from experimental investigations is mixed at best; most of the support comes from case studies, in which both the selection of the particular case and the investigator's expectations can more easily influence the reported results (Park, 1990). Meta-analyses of experimental studies are not particularly encouraging either. For example, on the basis of nine research reports (17 experimental conditions) Mullen, Anthony, Salas, and Driskell (1994) conclude that group cohesiveness, a major theoretical variable, does not itself impair decision quality; interpersonal attraction may have a deleterious effect, but apparently even it can be compensated for by commitment to the task. Until there is more and better research, the jury is out. Groupthink may well be a good theory, but as things stand, one simply does not know.

Consensus is one thing, a group member may vote with the majority for any number of reasons, but actually believing in the correctness of the decision is another thing. Belief, usually studied as confidence in the group's decision, is important because subsequent support of the decision implementation probably is dependent on it. Actually there are two ways of looking at confidence: the confidence of individual decision makers in their group's decision and the whole group's confidence in that decision. Comparison of the two shows that the group's confidence tends to be higher than for individuals (Sniezek & Henry, 1989, 1990). Sniezek (1992) suggests that the higher group confidence may be the result of explicit or implicit pressure to achieve consensus and that consensus is treated as a cue to accuracy, thereby justifying higher group confidence. Indeed, Boje and Murnighan (1982) found that members of groups that reached consensus were satisfied with and accepting of the decisions and wanted to continue working together, even though, often, the decisions were not as good as those of groups with lower consensus. As Sniezek (1992) reminds us, high confidence is not a good thing if the decision is not a good decision.

Again, it is interesting to note that one of the pervasive arguments for using groups in organizational decision making is that it permits pooling of information held by the group's members and thus contributes to more informed and presumably better decisions. This suggests that, because they are better informed, groups are correct in being confident about their decisions. Unfortunately, examinations of information sharing in groups show that members do far less of it than this argument assumes; group discussion tends to focus on what is known by everyone and uniquely held information tends to be ignored (Sniezek et al., 1990; Stasser & Titus, 1985).

Summary

We have briefly examined the major models that drive thinking about decision making in organizations. Clearly, the rational model fares as badly for organizations as it does for individuals, and although each of the alternative models has its strengths, each also has its weaknesses. The participation model has been the main focus for much of the behavioral research on organizational decision making. The Vroom and Yetton (1973) and Vroom and Jago (1978) examination of conditions that call for member participation in managerial decisions have had a major impact on academic research and exerted some influence on managerial practice, if only as a conceptual framework within which to consider participation.

Brainstorming is popularly believed to be an effective way of increasing the set of decision options considered by a group. Unfortunately, the preponderance of evidence is that it seldom is more effective, and is certainty less efficient, than a comparable group of individuals each working alone. Nevertheless, in conjunction with computer-aided methods that reduce production blocking, there may be a renaissance of interest in brainstorming.

Group consensus is consistently interesting to researchers and practitioners alike. The so-called risky shift phenomenon and groupthink are included in virtually every management textbook and are broadly accepted as persistent dangers when groups make decisions. Researchers appear to be making progress on understanding choice shifts, but the jury is still out on groupthink.

Studies suggest that group interaction and group consensus may lead to overconfidence in group decisions, but the implications of this are dependent on how that confidence influences commitment and investment in implementation of those decisions. This is an area of research that shows a great deal of promise from both a theoretical and a practical standpoint.

This brings us to the end of our necessarily brief overview of interpersonal (Chapter 8) and organizational (this chapter) decision making. There is a wealth of possibilities for profitable research in all of this, possibilities that appear to have received far less attention than they deserve. Certainly it is more difficult to do research on multiperson decision making than it is to study individuals, but the fact is that most decisions involve more than one person—or at least reflect our knowledge about other people's criteria (Keysar, Ginzel, & Bazerman, 1995). On the other hand, the area seems to be dominated by flashy theories, like groupthink, which are more conceptually compelling than empirically justified. Of necessity the research is more pedestrian, with the result that its findings are slow to emerge and have less impact on practice than they deserve. This always is true in the behavioral sciences, but it is particularly unfortunate here because multiperson decision making is so important and such a large part of most of our lives.

10 Naturalistic Decision Theory

PART 1

◆

The newly hired salespeople were settling into their jobs and already things were looking better. Ralph sat back in his chair and pondered what had happened, determined to learn something useful. He recalled his misdiagnosis of the original problem as a production problem and how his views of things changed when he reframed it as a sales problem. He went over the conversations with Dr. Karma Howell and how he, Betty and Hank had used multiple regression (he hadn't even known the term 3 months ago) to establish criteria for hiring new people. He thought about the process of going through the files of all the applicants for sales jobs and the utter hopelessness they had felt as they bogged down in the details. He recalled the conflicting agendas they each brought to the table as they tried to agree on whom to hire. It had been long and hard, but somehow they had muddled through.

He was surprised by how much he wanted to understand what had gone on—to identify the various things they had done that produced progress as well as the things that had led them down blind alleys. Perhaps it was time to talk with Dr. Howell again to put all this in perspective. Perhaps someone already had thought this stuff through; no use reinventing the wheel. He called Dr. Howell for an appointment.

*　*　*

This chapter and the next are markedly different from what came before. In them, we will trace the beginnings of a radical departure from the established way of studying decision making based on axiomatic, normative theory. This departure is motivated both by the work of organizational researchers, who have found the normative approach inadequate, and the willingness of behavioral decision researchers to begin with observations of what decision makers actually do ("naturally") rather than with theories about what they should do. The result is a series of small descriptive theories and astute observations (that will be described in the present chapter) that give guidance in the construction of a more comprehensive descriptive theory (that will be described in the next chapter). Most of this naturalistic way of approaching the study of decision making is still in its infancy, but it is in fact the wave of the future.

In this chapter, we will examine some of the newest (and if not always the newest, at least the most persistent) ideas about how decision making takes place naturally. None of the ideas actually constitutes a full-blown theory, but each highlights one or more issues that a more comprehensive theory must address. Moreover, each of them offers an analysis of these issues in the form of a descriptive model. As promised, in the chapter following this one we will examine a theory that has pretensions of comprehensiveness and that attempts to address the issues raised by the ideas and models presented in this and previous chapters.

Our discussion of naturalistic models will flow more easily if we impose some order. Let us divide them into four categories: recognition models, narrative models, incremental models, and moral or ethical models.

Recognition Models

Policy

The role of recognition in decision making has two facets. First, no matter how it is conceived, decision making requires that the context be taken into account, and this means that the decision maker must be able to interpret ongoing events in terms of his or her past experience and existing store of knowledge. That is, much of the information that informs decision making derives from the decision maker's understanding about how the current situation came to be, relates to other situations that are occurring elsewhere at the same time, and relates to situations that will occur in the future. A decision maker armed with all the decision technology in the world would be completely stalled if he or she could not call on past experience and knowledge about ongoing events. In this sense, recognition is implicit in any theory of decision making.

The second facet of recognition, however, is the one that has received the most attention from decision researchers. In the context of organizations, Simon (1979) described the role of standard operating procedures and programmed responses to specified situations as a form of decision making. Standard operating procedures usually are very specific: "When situation X arises, do Y." This requires the decision maker to recognize situations that fit the description of situation X. To the degree that situation X is specified in detail, recognition is merely a process of matching features of the present situation to the prototype, situation X. Of course, real situations seldom are an exact fit to the prototype, so some discretion is required, and it is this that qualifies the matching process as a decision; how close is close enough and what do the points of mismatch mean?

When only general guidelines are given about situation X, the prescription for responding usually is called a "policy." That is, when situation X is a broad class of situations that cannot be defined in sufficient detail to permit feature-by-feature matching, the policy gives the decision maker only a general idea about the appropriate response. In this case, decision making is not so much "preprogrammed" as it is "constrained," in which the constraints are imposed by the policy. Of course, here too recognition of the situation as an example of situation X involves decision making. So there are two decisions: "Is this a situation to which the policy is applicable and, within the constraints of the policy, what should be done?"

From an organization's viewpoint, standard operating procedures and policies have the advantage that an important decision can be made once and then used on subsequent occasions for the same or similar situations. This is very efficient, but it also tends to be rather inflexible. It makes the behavior of members of the organization fairly predictable, but it also encourages stereotyped responses to situations that might profit from more creative and individualized decisions.

The Recognition-Primed Decision Model

As stated in Chapter 3, the most extensive examination of recognition-based decision making has been undertaken by Klein (1993) and his associates. This resulted in a detailed model, called the recognition-primed decision (RPD) model.

Klein (1989) stresses that situational conditions often diminish the applicability of problem analyses of the sorts prescribed by normative expected value theory. In such conditions, the decision maker must rely on previously tried decision solutions, tempering them in light of the unique features of the present situation. Thus, time pressure, prior experience, rapidly changing conditions, and the like, recommend use of previously tried solutions, while conflict, the requirement to justify and optimize, and the like, recommend use of more analytic, perhaps normative, approaches to making the decision.

For example, in the line of duty, firefighters and military officers are often under pressure to make rapid decisions based on their previous training. Examination of these decisions shows that they tend to be unanalytical and heavily based on recognizing the situation as one for which this or that aspect of training provides a solution. In this sense, Klein's findings are very similar to the standard operating procedures described by Simon (1979).

Klein's (1993) RPD model begins with a decision about the familiarity with the situation. If it is not familiar, more information must be obtained. If it is familiar, thinking turns to goals and expectations about what ought to be happening if the situation is correctly recognized. If these expectations are satisfied—that is, the situation is correctly recognized—the question becomes one of what to do. Potential actions are not simply reflexive (although this can happen under extreme time pressure). Rather, the decision maker performs a mental simulation that permits him or her to imagine what might happen if the actions are performed. If the simulation suggests that the actions will successfully deal with the situation, they are implemented. If the simulation reveals potential problems, the actions are modified and the simulation is run again. This is repeated until a set of actions is derived that produces a successful mental simulation. Of course, if the situation is changing over time, this process must be constantly repeated to keep the actions attuned to the changing conditions. Thus, the RPD model has four main components: (1) recognition of the situation, (2) understanding of the situation (as revealed by whether it meets expectations as it unfolds and by recollection of typical actions from past experience), (3) serial evaluation of the potential of various sets of actions for solving the problem, and (4) mental simulation of the possible results of using an action to evaluate its potential.

Recognition-primed decisions research is unlike any research we have described thus far. It is called the critical decision method, in which nonroutine events requiring decisions are obtained from interviews of real-life decision makers, such as firefighters, military commanders, police officers, design engineers. The purpose is to identify the available options, the options actively considered, important information, the goal of the decision as well as how the goal shifted during the course of the decision, and the strategy used to make the decision. Interviews are recorded and raters identify the critical decision points and how the individual went about making the required decision. Results reported by Klein (1989) show that, depending on the expertise of the decision maker and on the degree of latitude he or she has in approaching the decision, from 40% to 80% of the decisions involve recognition in at least the initial stages. The more experience the decision maker has in the area in which the decision arises, the greater the role of recognition.

Recognition-based models of decision making have the advantage that most of us can see ourselves doing what they describe. Moreover, they can draw on a considerable amount of research on memory and learning to provide both examples and mechanisms for their theoretical enrichment. Their disadvantage, however, is that they really never have progressed beyond the level of general description. Even though they inherently are psychological theories, there has been no effort to clearly delineate the psychological mechanisms by which they operate. Recognition is a very complicated process and a great deal of research has been done on it, yet it is taken as a given by these models. Granted, for some applications the lack of specificity of the models is acceptable, but as behavioral theories, they leave much to be desired.

Whatever remains to be done to more fully develop the recognition-based decision models, the fact remains that they highlight an important aspect of decision behavior. It is clearly the case that once they have been made, many decisions are used over and over in similar situations. It is clearly the case that standard operating procedures and policies are similar but not identical, the latter involving more decision latitude. It is clearly the case that once a situation is recognized, the decision maker usually rechecks to make sure the recognition was accurate and that he or she understands what is going on. It is clearly the case that decision makers conceive of solutions (sets of actions) to decision problems and think about them (mental simulations) before implementing them. In short, recognition-based decision models provide a great deal for a comprehensive theory of decision making to deal with.

Narrative-Based Decision Models

When we acknowledge the importance of "thinking about" solutions to decision problems, we must consider the nature of such thinking. It is here that the narrative-based decision models make their contribution. The three most noteworthy models are the scenario model (Jungermann & Thüring, 1987), the story model (Pennington & Hastie, 1986, 1988), and the argument model (Lipshitz, 1993).

Scenario Model

On the presumption that decision making requires forecasting of future events, the scenario model describes how a plausible narrative can be constructed to generate forecasts. The model has four steps. In the first step, the frame within which the decision maker is working and the goal of interest within that frame are used as probes for retrieving relevant knowledge from memory. Relevant means knowledge that permits inferences of cause-and-effect, if-then propositions.

In the second step, the if-then propositions are used to construct a (cognitive) causal model that consists of a network of causal propositions. Construction uses both the known causal relationships that have been retrieved from memory and inferred causal relationships. The latter derive from the four "cues to causality" identified by Einhorn and Hogarth (1986): (1) covariation of events, (2) their temporal order, (3) their spatial and temporal contiguity, and (4) their similarity— to which can be added a fifth, the decision maker's intention to cause events to occur.

In the third step, plausible values are assigned to the "if" part of each of the if-then propositions in the model (i.e., if X were the case, then Y would occur). Each unique set of values assigned to the various propositions constitutes a scenario. Not all possible sets are admissible because the causal relations impose severe constraints.

In the fourth step, the model is run by working through the logical implications of a particular scenario—that is, the logical implications of a set of values assigned to each of the propositions. This produces a forecast for the scenario, which is an answer to the question, "Assuming that my causal model is reasonable, what would happen if X_1, $X_2, \ldots X_n$ were the case?" The "what would happen . . ." is the forecast. A different scenario (a different set of value assignments) would yield a different forecast. Different scenarios can be compared and the sensitivity of the forecasts to differences among them can be assessed. If many different scenarios lead to roughly the same forecast, the decision maker need not be too discriminating about value assignments. If markedly different forecasts are obtained, the decision maker can attempt to discover the crucial if-then propositions in the causal model and focus attention on their careful specification. In short, the causal model permits the decision maker to create multiple scenarios and forecasts. He or she then can select the scenario that most closely represents reality, as it already is or as the decision maker plans to make it, and use that scenario's forecast as a basis for making decisions.

Lest causal models seem so abstract as to be implausible for day-to-day decision making, consider the following rather Machiavellian example: Suppose that I think that the manager of the office where I

work has such a poisonous relationship with the district sales manager
that either of them will do pretty much the opposite of anything the
other suggests. Moreover, suppose I think that the district sales manager has a great deal of influence with the agency head in Phoenix and
that the agency head is in the position to recommend a friend of mine
for a job in our Denver office. Therefore, I can imagine a scenario in
which my office manager tells the sales manager that my friend should
not be hired and, out of spite, the sales manager tells the Phoenix
agency head to recommend my friend to the Denver office. If this chain
of events seems plausible, my decision turns on selecting a way of
getting my office manager to say bad things about my friend to the
sales manager. I now can turn to imagining different ways of inducing
the office manager to say bad things about my friend and how different
actions on my part might influence this chain of events. I can also
imagine what might happen if other events changed the if-then relationships in my causal model—perhaps the Phoenix agency manager
actually knows my friend and does not think much of him and,
therefore, is resistant to pressure from the district sales manager. By
mentally playing with different starting events (ways of getting my
office manager to say bad things) and different states of if-then relationships in my model, I can generate an array of different scenarios.
The one that seems the most plausible, or perhaps the least dangerous
to my own job, can be used to guide my decisions and my actions.

Most causal models exist only in the heads of their authors, and as
a result, they tend to be rather simple, perhaps too simple in many
cases. Of course, it is possible to construct such models on a computer
or using pencil and paper and to have multiple contributors who share
their knowledge and inferences. There are formal procedures for
doing the latter, which go beyond the scope of our discussion, but the
reader should be aware that they exist. Formal models have the advantage of permitting more complex models than individuals can re-
hearse in their heads, and they allow for a degree of objectivity and
the use of multiple contributors' knowledge. On the other hand, they
are complicated, expensive, and somehow coldly analytic. As a result,
they often lose the intuitive compellingness that decision makers need,
to make confident decisions. In short, there is a trade-off between
simplistic, inexpensive, but intuitively compelling mental models and
more realistic, expensive, but rather coldly formal models

Story Model

Causal models of the kind we have been discussing focus on the future. Often, however, decisions flow as a logical consequence of one's interpretation of past events. For example, jury decisions about whether a defendant is or is not responsible for an unlawful event is dependent on knowing about the circumstances leading up to the event. Pennington and Hastie (1986, 1988) examined the way in which jurors use evidence that is presented to them in the course of a trial. The research used volunteers from the jury pool for the Massachusetts Superior Court who had served on an average of three juries prior to the study. They were shown a videotape of a trial and were told that their task was to act as jury members. The tape contained the usual information that is forthcoming in a trial. Afterward, each individual participant talked to the experimenter about the case and his or her thoughts while reaching an individual verdict. This was tape-recorded for later analysis. Results showed that the "jurors" economically organized the information from the tape into a story that was inferred from the testimony, in combination with his or her general knowledge about the world. Moreover, the stories were to the point; irrelevant information was not included. When information was lacking, the jurors made inferences based on the parts of the story they had already constructed.

When completed, the story was used to make a decision about the appropriate verdict; the verdict that most closely "fit" the story was the one decided on. But even though all of the stories shared a general structure, different jurors chose different verdicts depending on the particular version of the story they had constructed. Often, this is because the story was based on what the juror imagined he or she would do in the specific circumstances or what other people might be likely to do. That is, the story was heavily dependent on the juror's implicit theory of human behavior—and not everybody had the same implicit theory.

Pennington and Hastie (1986, 1988, 1992) showed that construction of stories as a method of organizing knowledge and the use of stories for decision making are compatible with other linguistic comprehension models in modern cognitive theory, thereby tying decision making to a larger body of theory and research. They also point out that in contrast to the normative view of decision making, which tends to minimize interpretation and evaluation of information and to focus on direct relations among information and computations of the worth of options on a single dimension (utility), their research results show that the focus, in fact, ought to be on interpretation and evaluation.

It is interesting to compare the scenario model and the story model. They are similar in that they both involve construction of a mental model—a scenario or a story. They appear to be different because scenarios are used to forecast the future and stories are used to understand the past. Nevertheless, scenarios also can be used to explain the past (Beach, Jungermann, & De Bruyn, 1996). This is done by assigning values to the causal model that describe how things were at some point in the past. Then the decision maker uses the scenario to make a "forecast" about the present. By changing either the assigned values or the structure of the causal model itself, the decision maker can generate a series of forecasts. If one of these forecasts resembles the present, the decision maker can assume that the scenario that generated it plausibly describes the chain of events that led to the present state of affairs. In short, the scenario can be regarded as an explanation of how things came to be the way they are. In this sense, the scenario that explains the past is comparable to a story that organizes knowledge about past events. In both cases, knowledge about the past constrains decisions and thus influences what the decision maker will do in the future.

Argument-Driven Models

Models that see arguments about the pros and cons of an option as central to decision making also assume that scenarios and stories are part of the decision process. Nevertheless, they go beyond this to consider how a particular option is thought about, both before it is adopted as the chosen option and afterward when it must be defended to other people.

Lipshitz (1993) has suggested that the metaphor for decision making ought not be gambling or even choice. Instead, it ought to be argument, in which a potential course of action is evaluated in terms of arguments for and against it. This permits one to consider potential outcomes and uncertainty about the eventuation of those outcomes (the components of expected value computations) as arguments, but it does not restrict consideration solely to these elements as does normative decision theory.

Lipshitz's (1993) ideas, called the argument-driven action (ADA) model, are in the process of being slowly crystallized, so it is difficult to characterize them clearly. The general idea is that the decision maker assesses the decision situation and, drawing on past experience and existing knowledge, formulates a course of action that *matches* the demands of the situation: "What should be done in this situation?" This is akin to Klein's idea of recognition, but it involves more than mere recall of past actions in similar situations. At any rate, this first-cut at formulating an action is then *reassessed,* tempered and reshaped, in light of arguments for and against it. This certainly is similar to the scenario-running form of mental simulation considered above, except that the emphasis is on using arguments to reshape the action to increase its match to the demands of the situation. Imagination is a primary tool in reassessment, just as it is in scenario construction. Arguments are phrased in the form, "Do *A* because *R*," in which *A* is an action and *R* is a reason. For example, "Do *A* because there are no objections to doing it or because all objections can be rebutted."

Research on the ADA model, of which there is little thus far, resembles Klein's research on the RPD model. Professional decision makers, often military officers, are asked to describe an important decision and what they thought about when they were making it. Analysis consists of looking at the chain of arguments that result in selecting this or that action as the incident unfolds. Thus, for example, Lipshitz (Beach & Lipshitz, 1993) examined the arguments given by Israeli Air Force General "Motti" Hod for the decisions, in 1973, that led Israeli fighter jets to force a Libyan airliner to crash-land in the Sinai, killing all but one person aboard. The study's results were not the usual statistics to which most of us are accustomed. Rather, they were in the form of a coherent story in which successive decisions are related to one another through supportive arguments, information, and assumptions.

The ADA model has a unique view of how uncertainty influences decision making. Normative theory ties uncertainty to whether or not outcomes will occur if the decision maker selects an action and generally views it in terms of probabilities of future events. The ADA model views uncertainty as the source of motivation for decision making. That is, when there is uncertainty in the assessment of the situation or in whether the formulated action will remedy the situation, the decision maker is motivated to modify the action so that uncertainty is reduced. It is this that moves the decision maker from merely using previously successful actions for this kind of situation to thinking about the action and revising it so it better matches the situational demands. In short, decision problems arise when there are objections to using a previously successful action, motivation to find a better action provided by the uncertainty resulting from those objections, and reassessment (and revision) of the previous action is argument driven with the goal of crafting an action that better matches the situation and thereby reduces uncertainty.

This view of decision making has much in common with the models we have discussed earlier in this chapter and almost nothing to do with the view advanced by normative decision theory. It moves us away from the idea of decisions as gambles because it conceives of uncertainty in an entirely new way, and it places the emphasis on a richer characterization of the cognitive processes underlying decision making. Nevertheless, there is still more to be considered.

Montgomery (1993) and Svenson (1992) have examined how decision makers think about a potential action both before and after it is decided on. In many ways, these authors' views are like Lipshitz's (1993) except that they are a bit broader. The general idea is that the situation "nominates" a course of action, much as Lipshitz describes it. An action may be nominated by some salient characteristic, among which may be that it has worked in the past. The decision maker first *edits* the nominated action to clarify it and make it easier to think about. Then he or she subjects it to *differentiation* to make it sufficiently different from any alternative course of action. This involves stressing its emotional, procedural, or structural attributes in a way that enhances the nominated action's apparent superiority to the alternatives. Moreover, differentiation takes into account future needs to defend the nominated action once it is chosen, thus insulating both the choice and the decision maker from future criticism. Differentiation continues after the action has been chosen, except that now it is called *consolidation*. Consolidation saves the decision maker from the agonies of postdecision cognitive dissonance (Festinger, 1964) or regret by affirming the superiority of the chosen action.

Incremental Models

The notion of incrementalism in decision making is not new. In fact, the first model we will examine was proposed by Lindblom in 1959 and developed further by Braybrooke and Lindblom in 1963. Close reading of this work reveals that, like most decision models, the focus largely is on thought rather than action. Analysis of incremental action came later with the work of Connolly (Connolly, 1988; Connolly & Wagner, 1988). We will begin with the Lindblom model and then move on to the Connolly model. Both models are instructive for any comprehensive theory of decision making.

Incremental Evaluation

Lindblom's (1959) work is based on observation of public policy decisions, focusing on the difference between what is observed and the prescriptions of the normative model of decision making, particularly the way in which options are evaluated prior to decision making.

Consider the conditions surrounding public policy decisions. First, the multiplicity of goals and values that are brought to bear on such a decision by the many different stakeholders make it impossible to derive a single utility function on which to base expected utility computations. Second, the outcomes of almost any public policy decision are so extensive (analogous to the widening circle of ripples when one drops a stone into a pool of water) that it is impossible to enumerate them, let alone evaluate them. Third, public policy decisions frequently are made in the face of absent or inadequate information and daunting ignorance even about their immediate consequences, and often, their remote consequences are completely unknown. Even if the immediate and remote consequences of a decision could be identified, the costs of obtaining precise evaluations are enormous, if only because there are so many of them and because their utilities will differ for different stakeholders. Finally, for any but trivial decisions, it is unlikely that all of the possible (or merely plausible) options will be known to the decision maker(s). Even if they were known, the cost of analyzing all of them, in terms of time, effort, and money, would be prohibitive. The upshot is that the rational evaluation prescribed by normative theory is impossible. On the other hand, policy makers cannot simply give up; they must adopt a strategy that is both realistic and that gets the job done.

Here, we come to one of the hidden gems in the Lindblom (1959) analysis, something that is seldom noted but that makes all the difference. It is that despite the rhetoric of politicians, public policy is shaped less by what policy makers want to move toward than by what they want to move away from. That is, change occurs only infrequently as a result of sweeping reform. Most often it occurs by "nibbling away" at problems, observing the results of small changes, making adjustments in the policy, and so on. Formally, the emphasis is on the undesirable parts of the status quo and options are both generated and evaluated in terms of how those undesirable parts can be remedied. Because predecisional evaluation centers on the flaws in the status quo, it is not surprising that most remedies are very similar to the status quo, differing only in the area of the flaws.

The observation that options are only marginally different from the status quo, and therefore from each other, dictates a change in how we view decision making. We must move away from the normatively prescribed overall analysis of options toward a tighter focus on decisions involving possible solutions to specific problems, from major public policy shifts driven by a universally accepted vision of the future to incremental changes aimed at solving problems without arousing the opposition of some or all stakeholders. These small remedies are provisional in that they can be adjusted in light of feedback about their success in addressing one or another flaw in the status quo or in response to concerted pressure by powerful stakeholders. In some sense, incremental evaluation allows for the planning of small experiments in which success and failure will guide further action as decision making "feels its way along."

The salient features of incremental public policy evaluation are as follows:

- Only those options are considered whose known or expected consequent states differ incrementally from the status quo and from each other.
- Examination of options involves comparative analysis of no more than the marginal (incremental) differences in consequent states rather than a more comprehensive comparison of the options and the states they offer.
- Choice among options is dictated only by the attractiveness of the increments they offer.

- The attractiveness of increments is influenced both by the remedies they offer and by what would be required to effect them.
- The act of exploring increments often leads to greater understanding of the problems being addressed, leading to redefinition of those problems and to previously unsuspected options for solving them.
- Because solutions to problems will be adjusted in light of feedback, decision making must be characterized as a series of small decisions rather than as a single definitive decision.

To summarize,

Since [public] policy analysis is incremental, exploratory, serial, and marked by adjustment of ends to means, it is to be expected that stable long-run aspirations will not appear as dominant critical values in the eyes of the analyst. The characteristics of the strategy support and encourage the analyst to identify situations or ills from which to move *away* rather than goals *toward* which to move. Even short-term goals are defined largely in terms of reducing some observed ill rather than in terms of a known objective of another sort. . . . Policy aims at suppressing vice even though virtue cannot be defined, let alone concretized as a goal; at attending to mental illness even though we are not sure what attitudes and behavior are most healthy; . . . at eliminating inequities in the tax structure even though we do not agree on equity; at destroying slums even though we are uncertain about the kinds of homes and neighborhoods in which their occupants should live. (Braybrooke & Lindblom, 1963, pp. 102-103)

Incremental evaluation pretty much leaves the policy maker buried in thought. It presumes that the decision maker(s) implement(s) the option with the most attractive marginal increments, obtains feedback, and either proceeds or alters the policy in light of the feedback. But it does not provide much detail about how this happens. In this model, options are merely policies not specific courses of action, although Lindblom does not clearly differentiate between the two.

It is one thing to decide to do something and another thing to actually do it. Implementation has to deal with details and circumstances that are not specifically addressed by the policy, because policy cannot anticipate everything that might be encountered in the course of trying to accomplish it. The analogy is that a policy is like a road map, and implementation is like actually driving your car down the bumpy road, detouring around repair crews, and keeping an eye out for landmarks that might signal progress toward the destination. Just as mapmaking and driving are different, formulating an attractive plausible policy is different from executing the series of actions required to produce an acceptable approximation to that policy. What is needed is an incremental implementation model to complement the incremental evaluation model. Just such an implementation model has been provided by Connolly (Connolly, 1988; Connolly & Wagner, 1988), called the "decision cycles model."

Incremental Implementation

Connolly begins his analysis much as Lindblom began his, with an argument against the universal applicability of normative decision theory. "The central image [of normative theory] is that of a single decisive act by which the decision maker hopes to move from a well-specified initial state (the unsolved problem) to a well-specified final state (the solved problem). The problem of felling a single tree highlights these characteristics, and we shall refer to analyses of this sort as 'tree-felling' models" (Connolly, 1988, p. 37). In contrast, he proposes that many decision problems are less like "tree-felling" than like "hedge-clipping." "An unruly hedge and an undesired tree present the householder with rather different types of problems, and different strategies are called for in solving them" (Connolly, 1988, p. 37). The characteristics of problems that call for hedge-clipping—that is, for incremental implementation, are as follows:

1. The elements of the problem are interdependent. Felling a single tree does not affect nearby trees, but clipping a limb of a hedge may have implications for the limbs around it.

2. Iterative solutions are possible. Felling a tree is pretty much all-or-none, but clipping a hedge can be done incrementally, in little bits that nibble away here and there, each bringing the hedge closer to some desired state.

3. Corrections are possible and there is a range of acceptable solutions. Felling the wrong tree or felling it improperly usually cannot be corrected—the tree cannot be restored and mistakes may result in a tree in your living room. Mistakes on hedges, on the other hand,

seldom are serious because incremental clipping means that they are small. Moreover, recovery from errors generally is easy because the end state of hedge-clipping is loosely defined; one can compensate for what might otherwise be an error by making the whole hedge lower or thinner than originally planned and still end with an acceptable result.

4. The sequence of solution steps is flexible and robust to interruptions. There is little latitude in how one goes about felling a tree and once begun it is dangerous to leave the job until it is done. In contrast, one can approach hedge-clipping in a variety of ways, working first here and then there, leaving from time to time to do other things, all without impeding progress or compromising the final result.

To address decisions that have these four characteristics, Connolly extends a perceptual model first proposed by Neisser (1976). The latter posits a "perceptual cycle" that constantly updates a perceiver's knowledge (schema) of his or her environment through new information generated by active exploration guided by the existing schema. The new information results in modification of the guiding schema, which in turn guides new exploration, which generates even newer information, and so on. The strength of the model is the role of active exploration, rather than passive reception of information, in the construction and modification of subjective knowledge about the environment.

Connolly's adaptation of Neisser's (1976) model posits a decision cycle that functions in conjunction with Neisser's perceptual cycle. The decision maker's values, purposes, and goals constitute a cognitive emotive schema that works in tandem with his or her perceptual schema to dictate goal-directed action. When this action is played out in the physical or social environment, it generates new information in the form of consequences. This new information modifies the decision maker's perceptual schema, his or her current knowledge about the environment. The modified schema, together with the decision maker's cognitive-emotive schema (values, purposes, and goals) prescribes changes in further goal-directed action, which generates new information, and so on. This interrelating of perceptual cycles and decision cycles has the effect of shifting the locus of decision making from the isolation of the decision maker's mind to the interaction of information-producing action in a progressively better understood environment. This shift to "decision-makers-in-context" (Connolly & Wagner, 1988, p. 190) produces the desired bridge between incremental evaluation, as described by Lindblom (Braybrooke & Lindblom, 1963; Lindblom, 1959) and incremental implementation.

Incremental implementation often results in revisions of *both* perceptual and cognitive-emotive schemata. That is, feedback from incremental implementation not only provides information that prompts revision of one's knowledge of the environment, it also may prompt revision of one's values, intents, and goals. Tree-felling decisions can produce similar results but usually in the form of regret or guilt because by the time feedback is received it is too late to do anything—the tree is felled. Incrementalism, on the other hand, allows the opportunity to examine where things seem to be going and what is emerging as important. Sometimes the final state is the one that was sought. Often, it is something else; as the process moves along, new opportunities arise, and conditions change that evoke new values and change both tastes and goals. The result is a progressive modification of both the perceptual and the cognitive-emotive schemata that reflect learning from experience and a maturation and refinement of both knowledge and desire.

Incremental implementation also influences commitment to decisions. Tree-felling requires monumental commitment, or at least the semblance of such; there is no turning back once action has begun. In contrast, incremental implementation almost demands low commitment to each small step because each step is merely an experiment, as it were. The results of the experiment inform subsequent action by prompting revisions of the perceptual and cognitive emotive schemata. Because increment implementation is fluid, no step is itself particularly crucial, and commitment lies in loyalty to pragmatics and following the most reasonable (changing) path into the future—even the goals are changing so it is not clear that commitment to any specific goal is appropriate. Indeed, trial periods, simulations, and actions that do not foreclose on future directions are precisely what are called for. All of these can be perverted into decision avoidance, but properly used, they preserve the flexibility that is the genius of incremental implementation while avoiding the dangers of overcommitment inherent in the normative tree-felling prescriptions.

Moral and Ethical Models

The social sciences tend to underrate the importance of morals and ethics in human affairs. Perhaps because what is deemed moral in one culture or by one person may be deemed immoral or amoral by others, we often regard morals and ethics as mere social conventions. This is a mistake. Behavior is very strongly influenced by individuals' bedrock beliefs about what is moral and ethical and therefore proscribed or prescribed. Obligation and commitment are major themes in virtually everyone's life, taking precedence over our preferences and self-interests. Only sociopaths and psychopaths fail to heed these constraints on behavior, and that is why their behavior is regarded as abnormal and potentially dangerous.

In addition to morals and ethics, we must include ideologies and beliefs and values in general. If one is fervently religious, one is obliged to behave in ways that are discernibly different from the behavior of people who are less religious. So too, if one believes that stealing is immoral, one's behavior will be far different from the behavior of those who do not view theft as a moral issue. Similarly, if one values government as a legitimate force in civic affairs, one pays taxes more willingly (and perhaps more honestly) than if one believes the opposite. In general, morals, ethics, ideologies, beliefs, and values all influence the decision process, both by prescription and proscription of particular courses of action and by making some decision outcomes more or less attractive than others.

Deontology

In ethics, *deontology* refers to the influence of moral obligation and commitment on human behavior. Normative decision theory fails to account for such influences, primarily by ignoring their existence. Nevertheless, as we have seen, even casual observation and a little introspection indicates that decisions are greatly shaped by these influences, and that often, it is the major decisions that are most affected.

As discussed in previous chapters, normative decision theory relies on the assumption that all values, whatever their source, can be measured on one scale, called utility. Furthermore, it is assumed that the utility of an anticipated outcome of a decision is some combination (usually the sum) of the utilities of each of the outcome's component parts. These are very convenient assumptions because both theory and applications would become quite complicated if different classes and components of outcomes were to have different kinds of utility, especially if those different kinds of utility did not combine in a simple manner. Of course different kinds of utility are precisely what is implied by Thaler's (1985) work on "mental accounting," discussed in Chapter 7. But the differences that Thaler has identified are perhaps less disruptive to normative theory than those implied by a deontological analysis.

The primary proponent of a deontological imperative in decision making is Amitai Etzioni (1988, 1993). His analyses suggest that decisions are not influenced solely by the pleasure or gain offered by the various options. He begins with the observation that most humans are solidly anchored in a social context. Thus, the normative theory view of a rational decision maker operating alone is seldom appropriate. Even when it is, the decision maker must take others' views into account, if only to avoid their approbation when the decision becomes known. For this reason, Etzioni (1967) proposes three sources of influence on decision making that, for convenience, we will call utilitarian, social, and deontological. The utilitarian influence corresponds to utility in normative theory. The social influence corresponds to both the codes of behavior for the individual's reference group and the cultural values of the larger community. The deonotological influence reflects the moral and ethical considerations that guide the decision maker's behavior. In general, economics and normative decision theory study utilitarian influences, sociology and anthropology study social influences, and ethics studies deontological influences.

The difference between social and deontological influences on decisions is subtle but important. At the risk of oversimplifying, social norms exercise their influence by threatening approbation and ostracism if they are violated. In contrast, morals and ethics, although they derive from the community, are internal to the decision maker, exercising their influence by a sense of obligation, commitment, and duty, with conscience (and perhaps avoidance of guilt) rather than fear, providing the motivation.

Etzioni (1988) begins his exploration of deontological influences on decision making with three questions. The first is about what the decision maker is trying to do. The utilitarian answer is that he or she is trying to maximize pleasure or self-interest. The social answer is that he or she is conforming with social norms and cultural demands to avoid punishment. The deontological view is that, indeed, decision makers evaluate their options in light of utilitarian and social considerations but that both of these are subsidiary to moral and ethical considerations. That is, utility, social norms, *and* morals must be taken into account if we are to understand human decision making.

The second question is about how decision makers choose the means for doing what they are trying to do. The utilitarian view is that they weigh the costs and benefits and select the course of action that promises the greatest net utility. The social view is that they select the course of action that conforms to the expectations of their reference group or the larger community. The deontological view is that they use their emotions and value judgments to reject courses of action that violate their moral or ethical codes or select courses of action that are compatible with, or prescribed by, those codes.

The third question is about who makes decisions. The utilitarian answer is that individual decision makers do so on their own. The social answer is that, in effect, the decision is made by the reference group or community because it sets down the rules about how to behave and the decision maker merely conforms to those rules. The deontological answer is that individuals make decisions in the context of groups and communities, guided by their moral and ethical principles, which derive in large part from those groups and communities. Etzioni concludes, "At issue is human nature: How wise are we and what is the role of morality, emotions, and social bonds in our personal and collective behavior? Also at issue is the extent to which free-standing individuals are the foundation of our society; or does the foundation consist of persons integrated into small groups and communities?" (1988, p. xii).

Summary

We have examined four classes of ideas and models that challenge the normative view of decision making and that require attention from any comprehensive descriptive theory. First are the roles of situation recognition and policy in guiding behavior. Second are the roles of scenarios, stories, and arguments for understanding the past and present, forecasting the future, and justifying decision making. Third are the roles of incremental evaluation, with its emphasis on remedying what is wrong with the present situation and incremental implementation, with its emphasis on decision cycles driven by feedback about progress. Fourth are the roles of morals and ethics in both proscribing unacceptable courses of action and in prescribing actions that the decision maker is obliged or committed to undertake.

This is an impressive list of ideas, especially when taken together with the issues raised in Chapters 8 and 9 about interpersonal, organizational, and group decisions. In the following chapter, we will examine a theory that attempts to accommodate these ideas and issues, at least insofar as it is possible to do so in one framework. This theory, called image theory, is relatively new, but it grew out of the ideas described above, which we have elected to call the naturalistic viewpoint. Having looked at the first part of this naturalistic viewpoint, let us move on to its next chapter.

11 Naturalistic Decision Theory

PART 2

Ralph and Betty sat in a quiet corner of the restaurant. The dinner had been good; perhaps too expensive, but they deserved it. They sipped their coffee and settled down to talk. Dr. Howell had told them a great deal about the new "naturalistic" viewpoint of decision making, and they saw in it much of what they recently had gone through. But the many ideas she described seemed fragmented, disjointed, and vague. Ralph in particular disliked not having a clear picture to help him think about decisions. He wanted to be better prepared when they went through another big one. He wanted a framework to help him streamline the process and avoid the blind alleys and frustrations they had endured last time.

As they talked, Betty took notes until she had covered a page with scribbles and boxes and arrows. She glanced over what she had written and was surprised to find that it was beginning to hang together. In fact, it resembled something Dr. Howell had given her to read, something about images that she had not understood at the time but that somehow seemed to fit in with what she and Ralph had been talking about and the notes she had taken. Suddenly it came to her and she turned to remind Ralph.

* * *

In this chapter we will examine a relatively new theory that addresses some of the issues raised in previous chapters, especially Chapter 10. The goal of the theory, called image theory, is to describe decision making as it occurs rather than to prescribe how it ought to be done. In this, it is a marked departure from the normative, expected value, approach. It builds on the naturalistic decision viewpoint that has itself evolved from behavioral research on how decision making actually takes place.

There are two versions of image theory, one for individual decision making (Beach, 1990) and one for decision making in organizations (Beach & Mitchell, 1990; Weatherly & Beach, 1996). In fact, they are the same theory, in terms of the underlying logic, but the emphasis and some of the vocabulary are different in the two versions. We will begin with the version for individuals and then describe the version for organizations.

Heeding the lessons learned in previous chapters, image theory views decision making as a social act. That is, decisions seldom are made in isolation—the decision maker always must be mindful of the preferences and opinions of other people. However, in all cases, he or she must make up his or her own mind and then differences with others must be resolved in some manner. Thus, whereas groups and organizations are not themselves decision makers, they impose constraints on individuals' decisions. Moreover, often they are the context within which individuals' decisions become consolidated to form a group decision.

Image Theory for Individuals

In a nutshell, decision makers use their store of knowledge (images) to set standards that guide decisions about what to do (goals) and about how to do it (plans). Potential goals and plans that are incompatible with the standards are quickly screened out and the best of the survivors then is chosen. Subsequent implementation of the choice is monitored for progress toward goal achievement; lack of acceptable progress results in replacement or revision of the plan or adoption of a new goal.

The Images

Each decision maker possesses a store of knowledge that is far greater than what is needed for the decision at hand. That store can be conveniently partitioned into three categories, which are called images because they are the decision maker's vision of what constitutes a valuable and properly ordered course of events. The categories are labeled the value image, trajectory image, and strategic image, and they will be explained in a moment.

The constituents of the images can be further partitioned into those that are relevant to the decision at hand and those that are not. The relevant constituents define the decision's frame, which gives meaning to the context in which the decision is imbedded and which provides standards that constrain how the decision will be characterized and interpreted.

Value Image

The first image consists of the decision maker's values, morals, and ethics (Etzioni, 1988) which set standards for how things *should* be and how they and others *ought* to behave. Collectively these are called *principles*. These are "self-evident truths" (a) about what he or she, or the group or organization, stand for and, therefore, about the goals that are worthy of pursuit ("success in my occupation will help my children get a good start in life") and (b) about what are and are not acceptable ways of pursuing those goals ("but success must not come at the price of being away from my family too much"). Even if these principles are difficult for the decision maker to articulate, they are powerful influences on his or her decisions. Whatever they may be, they are the foundation of one's decisions: Potential goals and actions must not contradict them or those goals and actions will be judged unacceptable. Moreover, the utility of the outcomes of decisions derives from the degree to which they conform to and enhance the

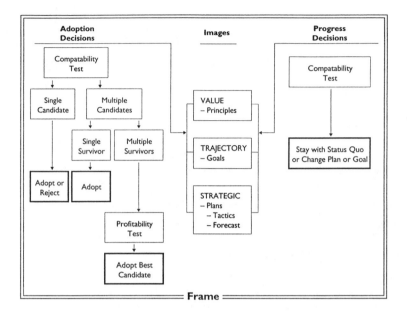

Figure 11.1. Image Theory

decision maker's principles. The decision maker's store of principles is called the value image, because it represents his or her vision about the state of events that would conform most closely to his or her beliefs, values, and ethics (Figure 11.1).

Trajectory Image

In addition to principles, the decision maker has an agenda of goals to achieve. Some goals are dictated by his or her principles ("I must get promoted to unit manager this year in order to progress in my career") and some are dictated by problems encountered in the environment, although principles still influence how these problems are addressed ("because my boss refuses to recommend me for promotion, I must find a new job, but I wouldn't feel right about leaving without giving proper notice"). The decision maker's goal agenda is called the trajectory image, because it is his or her vision about how the future should unfold and, therefore, sets standards for what is and is not appropriate behavior.

Strategic Image

Each goal on the trajectory image has an accompanying plan for its accomplishment. Plans have two aspects. One is tactics, which are their concrete behavioral aspect. Because plans are inherently an anticipation of the future, their second aspect is forecasts. That is, plans require tactics to deal with local environmental conditions and constraints, and they provide a scenario for forecasting what might result if the tactics are successful (Jungermann & Thüring, 1987; Lipshitz, 1993; Pennington & Hastie, 1986, 1988). The various plans for the various goals must be coordinated so that they do not interfere with one another and so that the decision maker can maintain a reasonable orderly pursuit of his or her goals. The collection of plans is called the strategic image, because it represents the decision maker's vision about what he or she is trying to do to achieve the goals on the trajectory image and sets standards for what is or is not appropriate behavior.

The principles, goals, and plans that constitute the three images are called the *constituents* of those images.

Framing

As we saw in Chapter 2, a frame is that portion of his or her store of knowledge that the decision maker brings to bear on a particular situation to endow it with meaning. In image theory, the frame consists of the constituents of the three images that are deemed relevant to the decision at hand and that set the standards that influence that decision.

Framing occurs when the decision maker uses contextual information (cues) to probe his or her memory. If the probe locates a contextual memory that has features that are virtually the same as those of the current context, the current context is said to be *recognized* (Klein, 1989, 1996). Recognition serves two ends: First, it defines which image constituents are relevant to the context and second, it provides information about goals that previously had been pursued in this kind of context and about the plans, both successes and failures, that had been used to pursue them. If the same or a similar goal is being pursued this time, the plan that was used before may either be used again, called a *policy* (Simon, 1979), or used as the foundation for a new plan.

Decisions

There are two kinds of decisions, adoption decisions and progress decisions.

Adoption Decisions

Adoption decisions are about whether to add new goals to the trajectory image or new plans to the strategic image; sometimes new principles are added to the value image, but this is infrequent for adults and need not concern us here. The criterion for adding a new goal or plan is whether it meets the decision maker's standards, as defined by the image constituents that make up the decision frame. That is, is it incompatible with the decision maker's relevant principles or does it interfere with existing goals or ongoing plans? If the answer is "yes," how incompatible is it? If it is not too incompatible, it might work out all right, but there is some point at which it is simply too incompatible and must be rejected rather than adopted.

Adoption decisions are accomplished first by *screening* options (possible goals and plans) in light of relevant principles, existing goals, and ongoing plans and second by *choice* of the best option from among the survivors of screening. If there is only one option and it passes screening, it is adopted without recourse to choice. Similarly, if there are two or more options and only one passes screening, it is adopted without a choice having to be made. But if there are two or more options and more than one passes screening, the best of the survivors must be chosen. The key point here is that choice, the subject of most of the literature on decision making, is rather less common than supposed. Screening is by far the more important decision mechanism, if only because most decisions involve only one option and the question is whether to pursue it, if it is a goal, or to implement it, if it is a plan (Lipshitz, 1993). Choice is, in fact, only a tiebreaker when screening fails to narrow down the field to a single acceptable option.

Progress Decisions

The second kind of decision is about whether a plan is making progress toward achievement of its goal (Connolly, 1988; Connolly & Wagner, 1988). These progress decisions rely on the forecast aspect of plans—the plan is used as a scenario to forecast the future and if that future plausibly includes the goal, the plan is deemed to have met the standard and it is retained (Jungermann, 1985; Jungermann & Thüring, 1987). If the forecast does not include the goal, the standard has not been met and the plan must be rejected and a new or amended plan adopted in its place.

Decision Mechanisms

There are two decision mechanisms in image theory, the compatibility test and the profitability test.

Compatibility Test

The compatibility test screens options for adoption on the basis of their *quality*. This is assayed in terms of the compatibility between the option and the standards defined by the three images. Actually, the focus is on lack of quality, in that the option's incompatibility (I) decreases as a function of the weighted sum of the number of its violations of the standards, in which the weights reflect the importance of the violation. (Note the similarity, but not the identity, between screening and Simon's (1955) concept of "satisficing.")

Violations are defined as negations, contradictions, contraventions, preventions, retardations, or any similar form of interference with the realization of one of the standards defined by the images' constituents. Each violation is all-or-none. The decision rule is, If the weighted sum of the violations exceeds some absolute *rejection threshold,* the option is rejected, otherwise it is adopted. The rejection threshold is that weighted sum beyond which the decision maker regards the option as incompatible with his or her relevant principles, existing goals, and ongoing plans.

The (in)compatibility test can be formally stated as follows:

$$(11.1) \qquad I = \sum_{t=1}^{n} \sum_{c=1}^{m} W_c \, V_{tc} \, ; \, V_{tc} = -1 \text{ or } 0$$

where incompatibility, I, is zero when an option has no violations and decreases (i.e., is more and more negative) as the number of violations increases; t is a relevant attribute of the option; c is a relevant standard; V is a violation of standard c by attribute t of the option; and W is the importance weight for each of the standards.

Thus, whereas the violations are all-or-none (−1 or 0), violations of some standards may count more than others (W_c) and compatibility is a continuous scale between 0 and $-mn$, where m is the number of standards and n is the number of the option's relevant attributes (an attribute may violate more than one standard).

Profitability Test

When more than one adoption option survives screening, the decision maker must choose the best from among them. This is accomplished with the profitability test, which usually focuses on the *quantity* of the outcomes associated with the options rather than the quality of the options' fit with the decision maker's images. The profitability test, in fact, is not a single decision mechanism but a collective term for the individual's repertory of strategies for making choices and the mechanism for selecting one of those strategies for use on a particular choice. Expected value maximization may be one of the strategies, as may any of a number of other strategies (Svenson, 1979); as we shall see, expected value maximization turns out to be the metastrategy for the profitability test.

The underlying assumptions are that each decision maker possesses a repertory of choice strategies and that the strategy that he or she selects for the task at hand depends on three categories of variables: characteristics of the choice, the environment in which that choice is embedded, and the decision maker (Beach & Mitchell, 1978; Christensen-Szalanski, 1978, 1980).

Characteristics of the choice include its unfamiliarity, ambiguity, complexity, and instability—the latter means that the goal of the choice changes over time. Characteristics of the environment consist

of irreversibility of the choice, whether the choice can be made itera-
tively (recall Braybrooke & Lindblom, 1963; Connolly, 1988; Connolly
& Wagner, 1988; Lindblom, 1959), the significance of the choice,
accountability for a choice that fails to yield acceptable outcomes, and
the time and money constraints on the choice process. Characteristics
of the decision maker consist of knowledge of different choice strategies (the breadth of his or her repertory), ability to actually use the
strategies, and motivation to expend the least possible time, effort, and
money on the choice while still doing a good enough job.

The decision maker's repertory is seen as containing strategies that
range from the aided analytic (e.g., decision analysis) to unaided
analytic (e.g., balancing pros and cons in one's head) to nonanalytic
strategies (e.g., coin tossing, asking others for advice).

As formulated by Christensen-Szalanski (1978, 1980), the metalogic
of the selection process is cost-benefit, with benefit in terms of subjective expected utility. The utility of choosing a strategy that will
produce what ultimately will prove to be a correct choice is designated
U_c, the utility of an incorrect choice is U_i, the cost of using a given
strategy is U_e, the subjective probability of a given strategy yielding a
correct choice is P_c, and the subjective probability of that strategy
yielding an incorrect choice is $1 - P_c$.

Assume that the decision maker believes that, in general, the more
analytic a strategy the higher the probability that it will yield a correct
choice (an assumption for which there is evidence). Also assume that
the decision maker believes that more analytic strategies are more
costly in terms of time, effort, and money to use. It follows, then, that
the subjective expected utility for any strategy in the decision maker's
repertory is

[11.2] $$SEU = P_c U_c + (1 - P_c) U_i = P_c(U_c - U_i) + U_i$$

which is the equation for the straight line in Figure 11.2. The abscissa
is a probability scale and the ordinate is a utility scale. The straight line
demarcates the range from the utility of an incorrect adoption choice,
U_i, which is seen by the decision maker to be virtually assured at $P_c = 0$,
to the utility of a correct choice, U_c, which is seen as virtually assured
at $P_c = 1.00$. (U_i is a positive number in the figure, but it could be
negative if an incorrect choice would result in a loss.) The slope of the

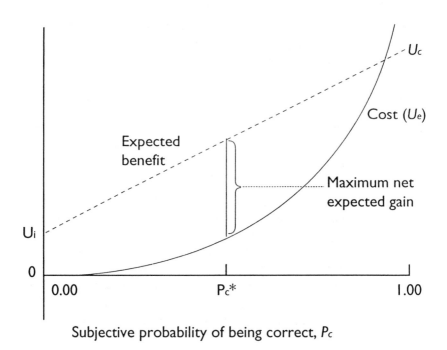

Figure 11.2. The Logic of Strategy Selection
SOURCE: Reproduced from Christensen-Szalanski (1978) by permission of the author and Academic Press, Inc.

line is $U_c - U_i$, the difference between the utility of a correct choice and the utility of an incorrect choice.

The decision maker's repertory of choice strategies can be arrayed along the abscissa of the figure according to the decision maker's subjective probabilities, P_c, that they will yield a correct adoption choice in the present situation. On the left will be the simple, nonana-lytic strategies, perceived to have low P_c, and on the right will be the aided analytic strategies, perceived to have high P_c. The unaided-analytic strategies will be somewhere in the middle. Of course, which strategies are in the array and where they lie on the P_c scale depends on the individual decision maker's repertory and his or her beliefs about the efficacy of each strategy.

Assume that the strategies (which are arrayed from nonanalytic to aided-analytic), and the perceived cost of using them (which varies from quite low, for the nonanalytic strategies to quite high for aided-analytic strategies) result in the increasing cost curve, U_e, in the figure. (The cost curve could be illustrated as a negative utility, but doing so complicates the rather simple picture that this method permits.)

The straight line in the figure represents the expected utility (benefit) of each strategy on the probability scale. The cost curve represents the cost of using each of those strategies. The difference between the expected benefit line and the cost curve represents the net expected gain of using each strategy. The optimal strategy for use on the adoption choice at hand is the one for which the net expected gain is maximal—which is the strategy that lies closest to the point at which the difference between the line and the curve is largest. This point, called P_c^*, is the optimal probability level for the choice strategy that is to be used. That is, using a strategy with a higher P_c would increase the expected benefit, but it would increase the cost more, thereby reducing the net gain. Using a strategy with a lower P_c would decrease the cost, but it would decrease the expected benefit more, thereby reducing the net expected benefit. Of course, the decision maker may not have a strategy in his or her repertory with a P_c that corresponds to P_c^*, in which case he or she should select the strategy whose P_c most nearly corresponds to P_c^*.

At the moment the strategy is selected, the decision maker need not take into account anything about the individual adoption options that have survived screening by the compatibility test. The utilities of making a correct (U_c) or incorrect (U_i) choice derive from the various characteristics of the decision environment vis-à-vis the decision maker's principles (value image constituents), rather than from the features of the options themselves. Thus, irreversibility, significance, accountability, and constraints on time and money induce a high utility for making a correct choice and a low (or negative) utility for making an incorrect choice. The decision maker's job is to balance these perceived utilities against the probabilities and costs associated with each of the choice strategies in his or her repertory to select the strategy that offers the best hope of success at the lowest cost in resource expenditure.

Research

There is a growing research literature on image theory. Rather than reviewing it all (see Beach 1990, 1993a, 1996), let us examine a primary experiment, which is on screening, and then summarize the findings of the rest.

Beach and Strom (1989) asked undergraduate students to assume the role of a newly graduated student who was looking for a job. The job seeker's preferences about 16 job characteristics were provided so that all participants were using the same standards. Then each student was presented with an array of jobs. The 16 characteristics of each job were presented on 16 successive pages of a small booklet, one booklet for each job. Each characteristic violated or did not violate one of the job seeker's 16 standards. The characteristics violated different standards for different jobs and each job had a different number of violations. The student read the information on the successive pages in a booklet until he or she decided to reject the job or to save it for his or her short list. By noting where the student stopped looking through a particular booklet, the experimenters were able to calculate the numbers of violations and nonviolations that had been observed before the student made the decision to reject the option or to place it in the choice set.

The results showed that rejection of options regularly occurred after observation of roughly four violations; this is the rejection threshold. There was no comparably constant number of nonviolations for deciding to place options on the short list. In fact, nonviolations played virtually no role in screening except to stop the information search when no violations were observed (or else a perfect option never would be accepted because the search for violations would never stop).

The Beach and Strom (1989) study supports the image theory position that screening relies almost exclusively on violations of standards. It also demonstrates the existence of a rejection threshold, and suggests that for a specific decision task the rejection threshold may remain fairly constant. Subsequent research showed that screening not only turns solely on violations of decision standards, it is regarded as so different from choice by the decision makers that they often do not carry forward the information used in screening when they evaluate surviving options before choosing the best (van Zee, Paluchowski, & Beach, 1992). They also may use the same information differently in screening and choice (Potter & Beach, 1994). In short, screening is a different process from choice and requires a different way of thinking about it than is commonly used in thinking about choice.

Beach, Smith, Lundell, and Mitchell (1988) investigated compatibility in three business firms. The first firm, which manufactured athletic shoes, was in financial difficulty and experiencing a large turnover among its executives. The second firm, a winery, was relatively new and growing and changing in a rapid but planned manner. The third firm, which manufactured ski wear, was old and stable, with most of its workers employed there for a long time.

To begin, the executives of each firm were interviewed about the principles that were important to their firm, which turned out to be surprisingly different. Then, for each firm, various plans were drawn up for the introduction of a hypothetical new product. The plans were designed to violate more or fewer of the firm's principles. Then the plans were given to the executives, who rated each plan in terms of its compatibility with their firm's values. Results showed that the greater the number of violations the lower the compatibility rating, but of equal interest was the finding that the agreement among the executives differed from firm to firm. Agreement was less among the executives of the athletic shoe manufacturer than among the executives of the winery, which in turn was less than among the executives of the ski wear manufacturer. In fact, as you might expect, the less the agreement among the executives about their firm's principles, the less the agreement among them about whether a plan was compatible with those principles.

This experiment makes two contributions. First, it is a nonlaboratory study of compatibility, showing that compatibility is linked to violations of principles. Second, it shows that the more the members of an organization share a common view of what is important to that organization (culture), the more they agree about the appropriateness of a plan of action for that organization—which relates to the organizational version of image theory that we will review shortly.

Research on strategy selection for the profitability test demonstrates that decision makers possess repertoires of choice strategies, and that their selection of which strategy to use in a particular decision context is contingent on the characteristics of the decision itself, the decision environment, and the decision maker. In a series of experiments, Christensen-Szalanski (1978, 1980) manipulated the payoffs for correct choices and the costs for executing various strategies and found that as the payoffs for correct choices increased subjects used more analytic strategies. In addition, he examined the effects of individual differences on decision makers' ability to execute strategies of differing degrees of analytic complexity and found profound effects on strategy selection and choice accuracy. That is, subjects who admitted avoiding mathematics and similar forms of disciplined, analytic thought were less inclined to select analytic strategies than were business school students (who had high mathematical scores on entry exams). Moreover, when participants became tired as a result of prolonged participation in experiments, they selected less analytic strategies, which Christensen-Szalanski interpreted as resulting from an increased cost to execute the more demanding strategies.

McAllister, Mitchell, and Beach (1979), using both practicing managers and business students as participants, found that increases in irreversibility, significance, and accountability resulted in increases in the use of more costly, analytic strategies. Huffman (1978) showed that these same three variables and familiarity and complexity of the task influenced strategy selection. As environment and task demands increased, participants' willingness to expend resources on more analytic strategies increased.

Images also have been investigated, but not to the degree that is demanded by their central position in the theory. It is not clear exactly how images are best studied—by having individuals describe the relevant constituents or by looking at the impact of images on decisions. Of course, both are plausible, but the first is difficult because, often, participants cannot put images into words very well. In one study (Bissell & Beach, 1996), workers in three firms were presented with a questionnaire that elicited their descriptions of "ideal" supervisory behavior and the behavior of their real supervisor. Presuming that the description of the ideal embodies their standards for supervision, the difference between it and the description of their own supervisor's behavior should indicate the compatibility of the two descriptions. It was found that the rejection threshold was at about 10 to 12 violations of the ideal by the supervisor's actual behavior. Above this point workers were satisfied with supervision, with their jobs, and with the firm as a whole; below this point satisfaction with all three aspects of the workplace was low.

In contrast, Dunegan (1993, 1995, in press; Dunegan, Duchon, & Ashmos, 1995) asks subjects to "conjure up two images," one of the desired state of affairs and the other of the existing or expected state of affairs. Then they answer a series of questions about the compatibility of the two images. Dunegan (1993, 1995, in press) finds that image compatibility has a major impact on how information is used in decision making about such things as funding allocations and amounts of penalties to impose for deceptive business practices. This research also suggests that the positive and negative formulation effects so often observed in the research on prospect theory (Kahneman & Tversky, 1979) are mediated by images and image compatibility. For example, when subjects are told that a group has failed in 20 of its last 50 projects, the image of how things can be expected to turn out is more negative than if they are told that the group has succeeded in 30 of its last 50 projects. Because of this the image is less compatible with the ideal and subjects tend to be less generous in allocating additional funds to continue work.

Clearly, there is a great deal more to be done to explore the limits of image theory and to make the appropriate changes. It does, however, offer a vehicle for consolidating the ideas that are described in Chapter 10 and earlier, and it provides the beginning of a research agenda that promises to be interesting. Now, having said that, it is time to review, however briefly, the organizational version of image theory.

Image Theory for Organizations

The reasoning underlying the organizational version of image theory is the same as for the individual version. That is, there are three images, adoption and progress decisions, and the compatibility and profitability tests for screening and choice. The difference lies in how the images are characterized and the implications of this characterization.

The image theory view is that organizations do not themselves make decisions (Davis, 1992). Rather, the individual members make decisions, either as agents of the organization or as participants whose individual decisions are in some way combined with the individual decisions of the other participants to arrive at a collective decision. The degree to which the decisions made by an agent of the organization make sense to other members, and the ease with which a collective decision can be reached depends on the degree to which the organization's members have similar underlying beliefs, values, goals, and plans. It is here that the images become crucial.

Images

The organizational counterparts of the value, trajectory, and strategic images are called the organization's culture, its vision, and its strategy.

Culture

Like the value image, an organization's culture consists of beliefs and values. Here, however, they are the organizationally related beliefs and values that are shared, to one degree or another, by the members of the organization. The culture prescribes what is true, necessary, and desirable and, therefore, the goals that the organization and its members ought to pursue and how they should be pursued. By the same token, it proscribes what is false, unnecessary, and undesirable and, therefore, the goals and actions that the organization and its members ought not pursue and that they ought to resist when proposed by others. The culture provides answers to the question, "Who are we and what do we stand for?" (Weatherly & Beach, 1996).

Harrison (1972) described the functions of organizational culture: It specifies what is important to the organization, the criteria for success and failure. It dictates how resources are to be used and to what ends. It defines where power lies and how it is to be used. It establishes what the organization and its members can expect from each other and how the members are to be rewarded and punished. And it instructs members about how they are to deal with each other and with the external environment. In short, the culture provides the guidelines for member's expectations and for their behavior.

Vision

Like the trajectory image, an organization's vision consists of its agenda of goals and their time lines for accomplishment. It may or not be formally articulated by the organization's leaders—often, it is simply understood throughout the organization. When it is formally stated, it provides guidelines for planning activities. Vision provides answers to the question, "Where are we going and what are we trying to become?"

Strategy

Like the strategic image for individuals, an organization's strategy provides the general blueprint for accomplishing the goals encompassed in its vision (trajectory image). The strategy consists of numerous specific plans for accomplishment of specific goals—with different emphases for different parts of the organization but all contributing to the overall strategy and dedicated to realization of the vision. Strategy provides answers to the question, "How are we striving to achieve the goals that constitute our vision?"

Research

Thus far, there has been little research on the organizational version of image theory. What there is has been motivated by the hypothesis that the greater the agreement among the members about the culture, the more agreement there will be among them about what constitutes appropriate goals and plans for the organization.

Using employees of an electric power company and of a commercial finance company as participants, Weatherly (1995; Weatherly & Beach, 1996) presented options that were and were not compatible with the individuals' company culture and asked them which options should be chosen by their organization. The more compatible an option was with the individuals' perceptions of their organization's culture, the more likely they were to endorse it as the appropriate choice, from a high of about 98% endorsement of compatible options to a low of about 20%, with a rejection threshold of about 5.5 violations.

In a second study, when options were presented to subjects as having been chosen by management, the more compatible the option with the culture the greater the willingness of subjects to endorse it, from a high of 98% for the most compatible options to a low of 59% for the less compatible options (suggesting a general tendency to go along with management decisions even when they are not truly acceptable). Both this result and the one described in the previous paragraph are congruent with the Beach et al. (1988) results for the executives of the athletic shoe manufacturer, the winery, and the ski wear manufacturer discussed earlier.

In the third study, it was found that the less the compatibility between employees' descriptions of their organization's culture *as it is* and their descriptions of the culture *as it ought to be,* the less satisfied they reported themselves to be with their jobs, the less committed they reported themselves to be with the organization, and the more strongly they reported themselves to feel about leaving their jobs.

The results of the third study complement the findings of Shockley-Zalabak and Morley (1989), who examined the relationship between individuals' images of an ideal organization and these same persons' images of the organization for which they worked. It was found that larger discrepancies between these two images led to lower satisfaction with the organization, lower evaluations of the organization's quality, and lower estimates of the chances that the organization would survive.

These studies are merely a beginning. Clearly, a great deal more needs to be done to investigate both the organizational and the individual version of image theory. In addition, studies that integrate the two versions more tightly are called for. The goal, of course, is to produce a descriptive theory that covers both individual and organizational decisions with one small set of concepts and mechanisms, thus giving some degree of unity to what are now fairly different views of decision making.

Summary

Image theory is a naturalistic decision theory; it attempts to describe how decision makers actually make decisions rather than prescribe how they should make decisions, which is what normative theory attempts to do. Image theory draws on the empirical research from traditional behavioral decision theory, but its more immediate antecedents are outlined in the previous chapter—the small, descriptive, naturalistic decision ideas and models. It certainly is not the end of the line; it is but a first step in the development of a comprehensive naturalistic theory.

Image theory assumes that decision makers come to the decision with a store of knowledge that conveniently can be divided into three categories, the three images. These are knowledge about what truly matters (beliefs and values), what constitutes a desirable future (goals), and how to go about securing that future (plans). The process by which relevant knowledge is brought to bear on a decision is called framing.

Decisions consist of either augmenting one's knowledge (adoption decisions) or assessing the effectiveness of one's actions (progress decisions). The most frequently used decision mechanism is the compatibility test (screening and progress decisions). When the compatibility test fails to provide an unequivocal decision, the decision maker turns to the profitability test, which in fact is a repertory of strategies for making choices. The selection of a strategy from the repertory is contingent on the characteristics of the decision, the environment in which the decision is embedded, and of the decision maker. Unfortunately, the present formulation of strategy selection relies on the expected utility model to evaluate benefits, which are then compared to costs. Given the evidence against the descriptive adequacy of the expected utility model, this part of image theory needs revision.

The organizational version of image theory presumes that decisions are made by individuals in the organization and amalgamated to create an "organizational decision." The theory is the same as for individuals except that the relevant parts of the individual's knowledge base are specific to the organization. Thus, knowledge about the organization's culture is part of the individual's value image, knowledge about the organization's vision is part of the individual's trajectory image, and knowledge about the organization's strategic plan is part of the individual's strategic image. When making decisions for and about the organization, the framing assures that these organizationally relevant parts of the individual's knowledge contribute to the decision process.

12 Looking to the Future

The light turned green and Ralph headed his car toward home. It had been a long couple of months but he felt good about the outcome. The new salespeople were working out well. So that problem was solved, and he thought he somehow was better prepared for whatever came up next.

He had learned a lot in this short time, especially about decision making. On the other hand, impressed as he was by all the theory and research that Dr. Howell had taught him, he was disappointed by how little help it was to folks like him. True, the multiple regression (cloning) stuff had worked well, but it left them with a large pool of qualified candidates, and the process of choosing from that pool had been brutal. Decision trees with all their fancy computations were too cold and cumbersome for him to even consider; he doubted he would feel comfortable with their prescriptions even if he used them. Behavioral decision work was not much better; it simply wasn't advanced enough to give guidance where it was needed. And the heuristic and biases stuff just made him feel stupid and depressed.

On the positive side, however, now he could think more objectively about how he approached decisions and he could understand where some of his frustrations had come from. If nothing else, he had learned to make his goals and decision criteria explicit, so he could tell how and where he disagreed with other people and could detect contradictions in his own thinking. Next time, perhaps, he could make things go a little smoother.

* * *

The purpose of this final chapter is to outline some research questions arising from previous chapters and, in the process, address some of Ralph's complaints. Before doing this, let us recall where we have been: After the introduction in Chapter 1, we examined the nature of decision framing, reframing, and shared frames in Chapter 2. In Chapter 3, we discussed the use of polices in situations that have been encountered previously, followed by, in Chapter 4, a discussion of the lens model and multiple regression as a way of examining policies. In Chapter 5, we examined the most frequently cited normative model for choice, the expected value model, followed by, in Chapters 6 and 7, a discussion of the research on the two major components of that model, subjective probability and utility. After so much on individual decision making, in Chapter 8 the focus turned to interpersonal decisions within the frameworks of game theory and research on negotiations. In Chapter 9, this social theme continued with examination of work in organizational and group decision making. In Chapter 10, we reviewed naturalistic ideas about decision making. And, in Chapter 11 we looked at image theory, an attempt to use some of the naturalistic ideas for describing both private and organizational decisions as they actually occur, rather than prescribing how they ought to occur. This brings us to the present chapter, an agenda for future research.

Frames

If you read the latest journal articles, you might think that framing pertains solely to prospect theory (Kahneman & Tversky, 1979) and to putting a positive or negative spin on identical payoffs for gambles (e.g., 60% successes vs. 40% failures). If on the other hand, we view framing as it has been viewed historically (Minsky, 1968), as the process of bringing relevant knowledge to bear on a situation, several research questions suggest themselves.

First, what are the general principles that govern how information influences framing? This includes current information about the situation as well as knowledge the decision maker has about what led to the situation. Perhaps advertising provides a source of ideas about this; a great deal of effort has been put into ways of grasping consumers' attention and influencing how they perceive (frame) decisions about products. Are there principles from advertising and, say, the management of political campaigns, which generalize to the framing of everyday decisions? In short, perhaps there are natural situations that could provide useful suggestions for a theory of framing that can be tested in scientific laboratories. As part of this, studies of how experts frame decisions must be broadened to include areas other than just occupation-related decision making; we are all experts in our own lives, and clearly, experience has an effect on how each of us frames situations.

Research also is needed on how frames influence the construction and use of scenarios and mental models, how they affect the stories we tell ourselves and thereby affect subsequent decisions. Part of this involves how people communicate frames, to influence another person's frame and to promote understanding of their own frames by other people. This in turn raises questions about how shared frames influence confidence in decisions; perhaps we are more confident if we know that other people see things in the same way we do. It also raises questions about what happens when people who must work together have different frames for the same situation but do not realize it and how resolution of the differences is handled.

Reframing also requires attention. If a problem is framed in a certain way and subsequent events prove that frame to have been inaccurate, how does reframing take place? Under what conditions do decision makers resist reframing—how wrong must the first frame be to prompt reframing?

Finally, framing need not always be intuitive and private. Sometimes frames are carefully and thoughtfully constructed, and often, this is done in concert with other people. For example, when a committee or team is charged with examining a particular problem, much of their early effort may be invested in reaching a common understanding of what the problem is and what its possible ramifications may be. In some cases, this exploration is done systematically (or at least in an orderly manner), and the question is whether there are ways of doing this that are efficient and that make subsequent decision making easier and ensure more satisfying results.

Policy

If we conceive of policies as preformulated action strategies for classes of similar situations, research must focus on how we recognize that a situation is a member of one or another class. This might draw on what has been learned about stimulus and response generalization in learning theory, but the stimulus-response framework is perhaps too restrictive. Alternatively, cognitive research on memory certainly is relevant, and tying policy to this research would strengthen the rather tenuous links between cognitive science and decision research.

It is also important to learn more about the nature of behavioral policies, particularly their detail and breadth. One can imagine that for very repetitive, well-structured situations the policy might be highly detailed and prescriptive, whereas for more variable situations the policy might consist of guidelines that allow for changing conditions or for the uniqueness of a particular instance of the situation. Of course, organizational policies, as distinct from an individual's behavioral policies, also range from highly prescriptive to general guidelines and, therefore, may provide ideas about how to think about individuals' policies that could result in useful theory and interesting research.

The lens model and multiple regression have been valuable in studying individuals' policies, and they will probably continue to be so, particularly in applied research aimed at a rough sketch of what is going on. Nevertheless, for more detailed research they both may have outlived their usefulness. The lens model must be conceived of in greater complexity if we are to better appreciate the nuances of decision makers' policies, and this will demand equally complex analytic techniques. Multiple regression provides a very simple picture of the structure of a decision maker's policy, but advances in structural modeling can provide richer pictures.

An interesting area of research about the nature of cues has been opened by Connolly (1977; Connolly & Srivastava, 1995). Sometimes cues are "clues," and sometimes they are "components" of the thing being evaluated, and the two interpretations have different implications. Clues are information about some unobserved state and, as such, they help in diagnosing what that state might be. In our example of Ralph and Betty trying to clone their good salespeople, the information on job applications was treated as clues about an unobserved sales ability.

Component information is quite different. Connolly's (1977) example involves two men who have purchased new cars, each of whom finds a defect in the ashtray of his car. One regards the defect as a clue about the quality of his car's construction; the defective ashtray suggests lower than hoped-for quality. The other man regards the ashtray as a component of the car and the defect as a negligible decrease in his car's value.

Connolly (1977) showed that these different interpretations of cues require quite different policies: averaging of clue information and adding of component information. Connolly and Srivastava (1995) demonstrated that decision makers, in fact, are sensitive to the distinction between clues and components, as evidenced by the predicted difference in their policies for the two kinds of information, and by subsequent behavior that reflects these policy differences. Moreover, whether a decision maker interprets cues as clues or components depends on how he or she frames the situation. The researchers could manipulate the decision maker's frame by the way in which they described the situation. The attractiveness of Connolly's differentiation and the empirical results of Connolly and Srivastava's research, both on policy and on framing, suggest this as an important area of research.

Choice

The normative, subjective expected utility model does not show any signs of going away. It is seductive. It is reasonable to think that people behave in their own best interests. It is convenient to characterize these interests as the product sum of subjective probability and utility and to describe choice as simply the selection of the option with the largest product sum. Even when research shows that this is an inaccurate description, the model's predictions often are not too far off the mark anyway (remember, accurate prediction is not necessarily accurate description). To tip the scales even further, the decision-aiding technology (decision trees, computer programs and all the rest) derived from the expected utility model is highly developed and salable, and it is unlikely that its users willingly will abandon it anytime soon.

On the other hand, the failures of normative theory are so well documented that virtually no one who is familiar with the research believes it to be an adequate descriptive model, and only a few still believe it to be an adequate normative model. One way of addressing this is represented by prospect theory; keep the general idea of subjective expected utility and make massive changes in the logic of the components, in order to make it descriptive. Prospect theory has generated a quantity of interesting research. Nevertheless, as valuable as it has been, many researchers find it as constricting as the normative theory it seeks to replace, if only because it, too, relies on the gamble metaphor, and that metaphor is only narrowly applicable.

Another way of addressing the failure of normative theory is to regard it as merely one out of many possible strategies for making choices, albeit the most thoroughly researched and logically well-developed strategy. Then the question becomes one of who actually uses the strategy, under what conditions it is used, and how closely does its use follow the prescriptions of the normative model. Because the strategy is highly analytic, a good place to begin is with an examination of the conditions that generally promote analytic thought. Such work was begun in the 1980s (e.g., Barnes, 1984; Nisbett, Krantz, Jepson, & Kunda, 1983) but little has been done since.

Subjective Probability

Even if we demote expected utility to merely being one of many strategies, subjective probability retains its importance. Be it a representation of uncertainty, risk, unpredictability, or whatever, it is clear that subjective probability influences decisions. Early research attempted to use probability theory as a normative model, and the conclusion was that subjective probability does not behave as the theory demands. One result was that probabilities were replaced by decision weights in prospect theory. Nevertheless, the weights are merely a transform on probability (a transform that comes from a gambling study in which participants treated the high and low probabilities presented to them by the experimenter as though they were less extreme than they were actually [Preston & Baratta, 1948]). If we presume that decision makers use these weights, we must assume that they know the probabilities in the first place in order to know which decision weights to use. How, then, do we deal with situations in which there are no objective probabilities to be subjected to the transform. Are decision weights in this case the same as when individuals know the objective probabilities? This concept of decision weights is not at all as straightforward as it at first seems, and because it is so central to a major theory, it deserves to be more thoroughly examined.

There has been a great deal of research on risk, risk perception, and risk communication (e.g., Rück, 1993; Slovic, 1987), but naturalistic theories have virtually ignored it, which is unacceptable. If we think of decisions as involving both screening and choice, the role of risk in each must be considered (see Potter & Beach, 1994). If we acknowledge that decision makers have numerous strategies for making choices, the role of risk in each of them must be examined. If we recognize that a belief in luck influences many (most?) peoples' decisions, its links to perceived risk and to subjective probability deserve attention. Nevertheless, before all of this is undertaken, researchers must become more sophisticated about what probability is (and is not) and how it relates to risk, lest they simply repeat the errors of the past. Hacking's (1975) book on the development of the concept of probability is a good place to start, and Gigerenzer's research (1991) is a good follow-up. Not every proportion is a probability, and not every event has a clearly defined probability, and not all uncertainty is perceived as riskiness. These concepts are substantially more elusive than generally imagined.

Utility

From a behavioral viewpoint, utility is not so much a useful concept as it is a conversation stopper. There is not much to be said when the complex factors that drive decision making are presumed to result in a single point on a single scale. This impoverished description may be useful for economics, although Etzioni (1988) has argued persuasively to the contrary, but it is a liability for behavioral decision theory.

The roles in decision making of the decision maker's various principles (beliefs, values, morals, ethics, obligations, and duties) are so important that it is counterproductive to oversimplify them. Add to this the distinct need to account for the contributions of emotions and feelings to decisions, and the idea of reducing everything to a point on a single scale becomes somewhat absurd. If for no other reason, advances in the neurosciences (Damasio, 1994) demand that decision theorists and researchers (and economists) look beyond mere convenience to acknowledge that things are far richer, if less tractable, than has been admitted.

The upshot, perhaps, is that research on utility, per se, is not needed because the concept no longer is required. In contrast, research is sorely needed on all of the principles that utility has obscured and on how they contribute to decision makers' evaluations of subjective worth. In contrast to utility, subjective worth is bound to be multidimensional, and framing is likely to influence how it is evaluated and why it shifts as conditions change. Certainly, these issues merit research.

Finally, Thaler's (1985) work on "mental accounting" opens a potentially rich new research area. His theoretical work is linked to prospect theory, but it has implications for any theory of decision making. The observation that different categories of money are treated differently probably applies to the worth of things other than money; familiar possessions are often worth more than their market price, for example. Indeed, it is likely that the worth of different categories is tied to how those categories relate to various of the decision maker's bedrock principles, which means that mental accounting relates to naturalistic theory and research as much as to prospect theory.

Interpersonal and Organizational Decisions

Insofar as principles derive from culture, studying their influences on decision making leads us beyond the decision maker as an isolated being to broader social and organizational influences. It also raises interesting questions about the assumptions people make about other people's principles and, as a result, about the reliability of their behavior. This in turn leads to issues about the origins of trust and the role of trust in interpersonal and organizational decision making. Trust is discussed a good deal in management research, but it is seldom mentioned in decision research.

Trust also is linked to fairness and cooperation, which feature so prominently in the results of game theory and negotiation research and, in turn, to research on equity and attribution. Of particular interest, because it has such broad implications for the rest of decision making, is the game theory finding that players can "earn" the right to disproportionate shares of resources. This, of course, is a common idea in everyday life, but rights have never played a role in decision theory or research. This has implications for the study of subjective worth, discussed a moment ago, because it sets reference points for all of the participants about the "natural" distribution of resources. If, as is probably true, the prospect theory notion that gains and losses are relative to a reference point, then "earned" rights are important. At any rate, trust, fairness, cooperation, and rights are such ubiquitous concepts in day-to-day interactions with other people that they deserve to be examined closely.

Game theory holds considerable potential, but it has few ties to other areas that could make it richer. Social psychologists study many of the same problems as game researchers (e.g., the dilemma of the commons), but the two seem to have little communication. In part, this is because social research is not as rigorous as game research, and game researchers appear to be put off by this. On the other hand, that rigor often makes game research very formal and abstract, and social psychologists appear to be put off by this. The two groups ought really to talk to each other; little harm could result and there is a potential for something good evolving (Selten, 1990).

Negotiation research also frequently is viewed as separate from mainline decision research. A potential point of intersection, however, is afforded by the role of negotiation in the consolidation of group members' individual decisions into a single decision. Whether it be by voting, consensus, the leader recognizing the sense of the meeting, or powerful members dominating the others, group members engage in complicated negotiations to combine their views and present the result to outsiders. There has been research on voting and conditions that promote consensus, but they have not been brought together theoretically and neither of them integrates well with negotiation research or decision research. In part, this is because negotiation and voting research use different formal models, and consensus research focuses on situation variables and process. Because there is neither common focus nor common language, the research does not fit together very well. Someone should put them together to create a theory of group decision negotiation.

Discussions of organizational decision making often suffer from a failure to clearly specify their level of analysis and then to stay on that level rather than moving back and forth. Work at the highest molar level consistently should treat the organization as a single decision-making unit, the decisions of which are implemented in an environment populated by other organizations. Work at the middle level consistently should treat the organization as a structured collection of members or employees, each of whom makes decisions that contribute to a collective one that is then implemented according to the dynamics of the organization's structure and the situation. Work at the molecular level consistently should treat members of the organization as individuals working within the constraints and imperatives of the organization, with an emphasis on the cognitive and emotive processes that contribute to their decision making. The garbage can model (Cohen, March, & Olsen, 1972) is an example of what happens when the discussion switches among levels; it is neither molar, middle or molecular, but a mix of all three. As a result, in my opinion, it does not enlighten us about either the organization or the members, and therefore it is difficult to imagine how it could guide behavioral research.

If molar-level discussions have a common fault, it is that they tend to reify what is really only a useful fiction, that the organization itself makes decisions. If the middle-level discussions have a common fault, it is that they seem to revel in the disorder in organizational decision making, overlooking the role of theory in identifying order in apparent chaos. If molecular-level discussions have a common fault, it is that they ignore the fact that individuals are enmeshed in a social environment and that the forces in that environment contribute hugely to decision making.

Some might argue that the foundations for organizational decision theory exist, citing the garbage can model, participation research, groupthink, or the risky shift research. I have already commented on the garbage can model and, contrary to how it is discussed in textbooks, the Vroom (1973; Vroom & Yetton, 1973) participation model is not really about group or organizational decision making. It is about the decision on the part of a manager about whether to invite the participation of members in an organizationally relevant decision. As such, it is an interesting and perhaps valuable model, but it does not contribute much to our understanding of what happens when decisions are made in groups or organizations.

Similarly, groupthink (Janis, 1972) might seem promising for studying individuals in a group decision setting, but it has not delivered on the promise. Thousands of students and business people have been warned about the dangers of groupthink, but the relative paucity of research makes the warnings rather difficult to justify.

Things are better for risky shift. Even though the risky shift seems a bit elusive and its causes are not altogether clear, research on it continues, as does other research on small groups. It is to be hoped that the results eventually will be of value to a broad theory of organizational decision behavior.

Paradoxically, the greatest promise for molar- and middle-level theories of group and organizational decision making may lie in advances in theory and research at the molecular level. That is, it may be impossible to understand what happens in groups and organizations until we better understand the individuals who belong to them. Until we have a better grasp of the role of principles, emotions, and feelings on individuals' decision making, until we see how people infer these same things in those around them, and until we see how the trust (or lack of it) engendered by these inferences influence individuals' decisions, we cannot understand the raw material that goes into group deliberations and the forces that influence its negotiated choices.

Naturalistic Theory

Policy

In addition to questions of situation recognition, discussed above, policy research must address the fact that blind application of a previously successful response to a decision problem is unlikely to turn out well. Indeed, any policy must be modified to fit the unique demands of the situation at hand and, be it characterized as a scenario, a story, or a script, the mechanisms for appropriate modification are central to a useful theory of policy use. One approach to doing research on this might be to give subjects descriptions of a policy for a familiar, real situation and observe how they revise it in light of changes in circumstances.

Narratives

In addition to the role of narratives in policy, there is the larger question of their role in providing continuity; in explaining the past and forecasting the future. Add to this the degree to which they are argument-driven, which implies purposefulness in their construction, and the degree to which they are shaped by emotion, and the research agenda becomes very rich. In my view, narratives hold the key to progress in studying decision making. They encompass the past, the present, and the future. They provide a platform for expression of the decision maker's principles. They are colored by assumptions about social norms and interpersonal expectations. They may well be the primary vehicle for both understanding and decision making, in which decisions grow "naturally" from the progressive development of the narrative. In short, the stories decision makers tell themselves may be central to how they pursue their futures, which, after all, is what decision making is all about.

Incrementalism

The gamble analogy has led to the mischaracterization of decisions. Seldom is the decision maker required to subscribe to a course of action and then wait passively for the results; most of us take pains to avoid such decisions. Most often, we can experiment with what we do, advancing or retreating in light of how things are working. Indeed, the whole purpose of implementation is to influence events, to take command of the future, to work toward ends that fit with our vision of the future, no matter how ill-defined and fluid that vision may be. Passivity has no place in this. Commitment seldom is to the course of action itself; it is to the ends toward which one is striving. Consequently, only an extremely stupid or extremely desperate decision maker would irrevocably lock into a course of action, willingly foregoing the opportunity to revise both the ends and the means in light of information about progress and about the dynamic state of the environment. Most decisions "feel their way along," and in the course of so doing change the narrative that drives them. As things change, both as a result of what the decision maker does and external reasons, strategies and goals change. Often, the decision maker ends up having done things and achieving ends that were totally unanticipated when the process began. Clearly, this process requires our attention. Research can be done if we do not try to force this dynamic process into a static model—if we begin to think of decision making as an ongoing story rather than as a single episode.

Principles

It is high time that theory and research acknowledge the powerful impact of decision makers' beliefs, values, morals, ethics, obligations, and duties. This is not the same as research on moral behavior, which tends to focus on lapses, or studies of courage, which tend to focus on heroism, although lapses and heroism are not unimportant. More to the point is how principles are invested with emotion and feeling and how this, in turn, influences such things as preemptive rejection (screening) of unacceptable options. Beyond this, however, is the contribution of principles to the perceived worth of potential consequences of decisions. Utility theory has nothing to say about what makes things valuable. Similarly, principles influence the means selected to achieve worthwhile consequences. Some acts are less worthy than others and some are simply unthinkable.

Related research questions involve how framing defines some principles and not others as relevant to the decision at hand and what happens when the frame changes. Moreover, how are principles integrated into narratives to influence meaning and the direction of the narrative's development? And, how do principles influence the interpretation of feedback about implementation as well as changes in the goal of implementation? These sorts of questions lead to research on individual differences, which, aside from risk aversion and mixed results on self-efficacy, has never been a particularly strong feature of decision work.

Image Theory

Most of the research questions discussed above are relevant to image theory, but there are also questions specific to the theory.

Images

Basic to the theory is the idea that knowledge is contained in mental representations called images. These are captured in part by concepts such as stories, scenarios, or scripts, but they are more than narratives. For many people, visual imagination is part of their mental images, as is emotion. Cognitive science and neuroscience are beginning to explore issues relevant to images and decision making, and behavioral decision research can contribute to this effort.

Attempts have been made to measure images, but they tend to boil down to lists of important factors, which rather misses the essence of things and probably obscures the emotional content of images. Techniques similar to those used for projective tests might be a better approach, although the results are less amenable to quantification than one might wish. Still, the goal is to understand images rather than find convenient ways of doing research, so a little creativity is to be encouraged.

Adoption Decisions

Most image theory research has focused on screening of options and the compatibility test, and most of it has been done in the laboratory. The results indicate that screening is perhaps the most important part of the decision process, if only because it dictates which options end up in the set from which a choice is made. The next step in this research should be to move from the laboratory to decision making in organizations. Because organizations require decision making to be semipublic, in that someone other than the decision maker must understand the decisions, often the process is more open to examination than is that of private decisions.

Choice has been studied in the context of the strategy selection model, which constitutes the profitability test portion of image theory. Unfortunately, the strategy selection model, while acceptable in principle, is flawed in detail—its driving mechanism is maximization of subjective expected utility, which is increasingly untenable. Whereas it is clearly true that decision makers have numerous strategies for making choices, there must be an alternative to expected utility for describing the way in which they match a strategy to a choice situation.

Progress Decisions

Image theory describes implementation monitoring in terms of ongoing decisions about whether acceptable progress is being made toward goals. The theory must be able to account for changes in goals and plans as implementation proceeds. This means that the role of information about progress is richer than mere feedback. It informs the images that define the goal and the plan and changes them in ways that are governed by the decision maker's principles. This takes place in an ongoing flow of interacting behavior and information, and image theory must be developed to deal with it.

Organizations

Viewing the organization's culture, vision, and strategy as the counterpart of the individual's value image, trajectory image, and strategic image permits use of the same decision mechanisms for both versions of image theory. Research is needed to examine both the value and the descriptive adequacy of this parallel. The first step is to see whether the compatibility and profitability tests—that is, screening and choice—work the same way for private and organizational decisions. For example, does the organization's culture exert the same kind of influence on its members' decisions, as agents of the organization, as their private value images exert on their decisions for themselves? This requires studies of cultural influences both on screening decisions and on choice, perhaps having subjects make the same decision for themselves and for the organization when their private principles differ in some significant way from the organization's culture. The decisions should reflect the difference.

Research also should explore the parallels between an organization's vision and individuals' trajectory images. How do they guide both decision making and information seeking in support of both adoption and progress decisions? Similarly, what are the parallels between organizational strategy formulation and what individuals do when they set out to achieve goals. Individuals' strategies are unlikely to look like the formal strategic plans that some organizations generate each year, but they may resemble the plans that smaller businesses use—often encapsulated in the heads of a few top executives. In the latter case, both vision and plans are flexible and opportunistic, and in this sense they are very like their counterparts for individuals. Research should explore these parallels.

The Future

A reader of a draft of this book asked me what I thought its table of contents would look like if it was to be revised 20 years from now. Of course, I can only guess, but I think that decision research, like psychology in general, will continue to have two dominant paradigms, analytic and descriptive. The analytic paradigm is driven by a taste for mathematical models and for using logical puzzles as vehicles for studying cognition in general and problem solving and decision making in particular. Investigators who prefer this paradigm want their science to appear rigorous and orderly. The descriptive paradigm is driven by a taste for verbal models (with abundance of boxes and arrows) and for using real-world situations as vehicles for studying cognition, problem solving, and decision making. Investigators who prefer this paradigm want their science to avoid illusory precision and premature formalization. It would be a mistake to regard one paradigm as more scientific than the other, the difference is more in how they tell their stories than in actual substance.

Some Speculation

I think that framing will become more important and that its link with policy will be a feature of future books on decision making. Work on policy will increase, but the lens model and multiple regression will be superseded by more flexible methods. Moreover, the definition of policy will broaden to permit ties to research on public policy and business policy. When this happens, the psychology of policy may become a special field of its own.

The expected value model will continue to play a role in the analytic paradigm, but its days are numbered for the descriptive paradigm.

Whether it will rate more than passing mention in future texts depends on whether the author favors analysis or description. Similarly, subjective probability as a surrogate for subjectively experienced uncertainty or risk will disappear from descriptive accounts but be retained by analytic accounts—the mathematics of probability theory is simply too seductive for analytic theorists to give it up easily. Much the same will happen for utility, which is mathematically convenient but sterile; it will remain part of analytic accounts but disappear from descriptive accounts.

Game theory and negotiation theory are presently at the crossroads. They both are spawn of the analytic paradigm, but empirical evidence is forcing them toward softer, less analytic descriptions of the behaviors of interest. Few game theorists accept maximization as descriptive, but it is not clear what they will put in its place. Indeed, most of the research consists of demonstrating that people do not behave as game theory and negotiation theory prescribe (although, as Selten, 1990, points out, "Too many experimentalists are in search for a confirmation of orthodox theory and go to great lengths in explaining away deviations which cannot be overlooked," p. 650). Like the heuristic and biases studies, this research is in danger of producing nothing but examples of the theory's shortcomings, which soon loses its intellectual appeal. More to the point, if people do not behave as game theory or negotiation theory prescribe, what do they do? Is it orderly and coherent? Can it be theoretically described, with or without mathematics? In short, what happens in these research areas?

Organizational and group decision making is a treasure-trove of unrealized research opportunities. My impression is that current research merely describes the conditions under which various kinds of group decision outcomes are more or less likely to occur, but it seldom looks at decision making per se. This makes the existing research of little interest to decision researchers because it is seen as social psychology rather than decision psychology. One could argue, quite correctly, that you cannot have the latter without some appreciation of the former, but as things stand now it is not at all clear that the two literatures have much to say to each other. However, this is going to change as descriptive decision theory develops, if only because it tends to be interested in real-life decision making, and real-life decisions mostly occur in groups and organizations. I predict that the textbook of the future will be largely devoted to just this topic and that new researchers would be wise to get in on the ground floor; this is going to be big.

Finally, naturalistic decision theories will dominate the descriptive paradigm for the immediate future. I can only hope that the awful name, "naturalistic," gets dropped along the way (for some reason it reminds me of someone looking into a coffin and remarking that the corpse looks so "natural"). Aside from that, however, the naturalistic viewpoint has allowed researchers who favor the descriptive paradigm to escape from the oppression of the normative model view of decision making. This has been very liberating, but it has been slow to produce developed theories to fill the void. Image theory is the most advanced, but clearly it is only a stopgap; much more sophisticated theorizing is on the way and it will be a major feature of that future textbook. Eventually, the naturalistic view and the descriptive paradigm will become the same thing, and the protest movement that has called itself naturalistic theory will become the new establishment, only to be protested against by someone else. I have no idea what these new protesters will be championing, but it is bound to be interesting.

Summary

These research directions are only the high points, but they are what seems to me to be the most important directions. The history of the field shows a steady retreat from normative models imported from economics and statistics and the beginnings of descriptive theories that may help us get a handle on what people are trying to do when they make decisions, thereby suggesting ways in which they can do it better (or at least less painfully). Many naturalistic ideas derive from observations of real-life decision making and from observed failures of the normative theories when confronted with day-to-day decision problems. It is my firm belief that decision research is on the brink of substantial advances as it departs from its normative roots and sets out on its own. Links with cognitive science must be maintained, and organizational research results must be taken into account, but it is time for a little risk taking and some creativity. It is a good time to be working in this area, to be building theory and doing research. The enterprise is exciting and fun, it is worthwhile, and the future looks bright.

References

Anderson, J. R. (1981). *Cognitive skills and their acquisition.* Hillsdale, NJ: Lawrence Erlbaum.

Anderson, N. H. (1970). Functional measurement and psychophysical judgment. *Psychological Review, 77,* 153-170.

Asch, S. E. (1956). Studies of independence and conformity: A minority of one against a unanimous majority. *Psychological Monographs, 70* (Whole No. 416).

Barclay, S., & Beach, L. R. (1972). Combinatorial properties of personal probabilities. *Organizational Behavior and Human Performance, 8,* 176-183.

Barnes, V. E. (1984). *The quality of human judgment: An alternative prospective.* Unpublished doctoral dissertation, University of Washington, Seattle.

Bayes, T. (1958). Essay towards solving a problem in the doctrine of chances. *Biometrika, 45,* 293-315. (Reprinted from *Philosophical Transactions of the Royal Society,* 1763, *53,* 370-418)

Beach, L. R. (1967). Multiple regression as a model for human information utilization. *Organizational Behavior and Human Performance, 2,* 276-289.

Beach, L. R. (1974). A note on the intrasubject similarity of subjective probabilities obtained by estimates and by bets. *Organizational Behavior and Human Performance, 11,* 250-252.

Beach, L. R. (1990). *Image theory: Decision making in personal and organizational contexts.* Chichester, UK: Wiley.

Beach, L. R. (1993a). Broadening the definition of decision making: The role of prechoice screening of options. *Psychological Science, 4,* 215-220.

Beach, L. R. (1993b). *Making the right decision: Organizational culture, vision and planning.* Englewood Cliffs, NJ: Prentice Hall.

Beach, L. R. (Ed.). (1996). *Decision making in the workplace: A unified perspective.* Mahwah, NJ: Lawrence Erlbaum.

Beach, L. R., Barnes, V. E., & Christensen-Szalanski, J. J. J. (1986). Beyond heuristics and biases: A contingency model of judgmental forecasting. *Journal of Forecasting, 5,* 143-157.

Beach, L. R., Christensen-Szalanski, J. J. J., & Barnes, V. E. (1987). Assessing human judgment: Has it been done, can it be done, should it be done? In G. Wright & P. Ayton (Eds.), *Judgmental forecasting* (pp. 49-62). Chichester, UK: Wiley.

Beach, L. R., Jungermann, H., & De Bruyn, E. E. J. (1996). Imagination and planning. In L. R. Beach (Ed.), *Decision making in the workplace: A unified perspective* (pp. 143-154). Mahwah, NJ: Lawrence Erlbaum.

Beach, L. R., & Lipshitz, R. (1993). Why classical decision theory is an inappropriate standard for evaluating and aiding most human decision making. In G. A. Klein, J. Orasanu, R. Calderwood, & C. E. Zsambok (Eds.), *Decision making in action: Models and methods* (pp. 21-35). Norwood, NJ: Ablex.

Beach, L. R., & Mitchell, T. R. (1978). A contingency model for the selection of decision strategies. *Academy of Management Review, 3,* 439-449.

Beach, L. R., & Mitchell, T. R. (1990). Image theory: A behavioral theory of decisions in organizations. In B. M. Staw & L. L. Cummings (Eds.), *Research in organizational behavior (Vol. 12)* (pp. 1-41). Greenwich, CT: JAI.

Beach, L. R., & Phillips, L. D. (1967). Subjective probabilities inferred from estimates and bets. *Journal of Experimental Psychology, 75,* 354-359.

Beach, L. R., Smith, B., Lundell, J., & Mitchell, T. R. (1988). Image theory: Descriptive sufficiency of a simple rule for the compatibility test. *Journal of Behavioral Decision Making, 1,* 17-28.

Beach, L. R., & Strom, E. (1989). A toadstool among the mushrooms: Screening decisions and image theory's compatibility test. *Acta Psychologica, 72,* 1-12.

Beach, L. R., & Wise, J. A. (1969). Subjective probability estimates and confidence ratings. *Journal of Experimental Psychology, 79,* 438-444.

Behn, R. D., & Vaupel, J. W. (1982). *Quick analysis for busy decision makers.* New York: Basic Books.

Ben-Yoav, O., & Pruitt, D. G. (1984a). Accountability to constituents: A two-edged sword. *Organizational Behavior and Human Performance, 34,* 282-295.

Ben-Yoav, O., & Pruitt, D. G. (1984b). Resistance to yielding and the expectation of cooperative future interaction in negotiation. *Journal of Experimental Social Psychology, 20,* 323-353

Bernoulli, D. (1738). Specimen theoriae novae de mensura sortis. *Comentarii Academiae Scieniarum Imperiales Petropolitanae, 5,* 175-192.

Bissell, B. L., & Beach, L. R. (1996). Supervision and job satisfaction. In L. R. Beach (Ed.), *Decision making in the workplace: A unified perspective* (pp. 63-72). Mahwah, NJ: Larence Erlbaum.

Boje, D. M., & Murnighan, J. K. (1982, October). Group confidence pressures in iterative decisions. *Management Science,* pp. 1187-1196.

Braybrooke, D., & Lindblom, C. E. (1963). *A strategy of decision: Policy evaluation as a social process.* New York: Free Press.

Brehmer, B., & Joyce, C. R. B. (Eds.). (1988). *Human decision: The SJT view.* Amsterdam: North-Holland.

Brown, F. W., & Finstuen, K. (1993). The use of participation in decision making: A consideration of the Vroom-Yetton and Vroom-Jago normative models. *Journal of Behavioral Decision Making, 6,* 207-219.

Brunswik, E. (1947). *Systematic and representative design of psychological experiments, with results in physical and social perception.* Berkeley: University of California Press.

Camerer, C. F. (1990). Behavioral game theory. In R. M. Hogarth (Ed.), *Insights in decision making: A tribute to Hillel J. Einhorn* (pp. 311-336). Chicago: University of Chicago Press.

Chase, W. G., & Simon, H. A. (1973). Perception in chess. *Cognitive Psychology, 4,* 55-81.

Christensen-Szalanski, J. J. J. (1978). Problem-solving strategies: A selection mechanism, some implications, and some data. *Organizational Behavior and Human Performance, 22,* 307-323.

Christensen-Szalanski, J. J. J. (1980). A further examination of the selection of problem-solving strategies: The effects of deadlines and analytic aptitudes. *Organizational Behavior and Human Performance, 25,* 107-122.

Christensen-Szalanski, J. J. J., & Beach, L. R. (1982). Experience and the base-rate fallacy. *Organizational Behavior and Human Performance, 29,* 270-278.

Cohen, M. D., March, J. G., & Olsen, J. P. (1972). A garbage can model of organizational choice. *Administrative Science Quarterly, 17,* 1-25.

Cohen, M. S. (1993). The naturalistic basis of decision biases. In G. A. Klein, J. Orasanu, R. Calderwood, & C. E. Zsambok (Eds.), *Decision making in action: Models and methods* (pp. 36-50). Norwood, NJ: Ablex.

Connolly, T. (1977). Cues, components, and causal structure in laboratory judgment studies. *Educational and Psychological Measurement, 37,* 877-888.

Connolly, T. (1988). Hedge-clipping, tree-felling and the management of ambiguity: The need for new images of decision-making. In L. R. Pondy, R. J. Boland, Jr., & H. Thomas (Eds.), *Managing ambiguity and change* (pp. 37-50). New York: John Wiley.

Connolly, T., Jessup, L. M., & Valacich, J. S. (1990). Effects of anonymity and evaluative tone on idea generation in computer-mediated groups. *Management Science, 36,* 698-703.

Connolly, T., & Srivastava, J. (1995). Cues and components in multiattribute evaluation. *Organizational Behavior and Human Decision Processes, 64,* 219-228.

Connolly, T., & Wagner, W. G. (1988). Decision cycles. *Advances in Information Processing in Organizations, 3,* 183-205.

Davis, J. H. (1992). Some compelling intuitions about group consensus decisions, theoretical and empirical research, and interpersonal aggregation phenomena: Selected examples, 1950-1990. *Organizational Behavior and Human Decision Processes, 52,* 3-38.

Davis, J. H., Stasson, M., Ono, K., & Zimmerman, S. (1988). Effects of straw polls on group decision making: Sequential voting pattern, timing, and local majorities. *Journal of Personality and Social Psychology, 55,* 918-926.

Davis, J. H., Tindale, R. S., Nagao, D. H., Hinsz, V. B., & Robertson, B. (1984). Order effects in multiple decisions by groups: A demonstration with mock juries and trial procedures. *Journal of Personality and Social Psychology, 47,* 1003-1012.

Dawes, R. M. (1971). A case study of graduate admissions: Application of three principles of human decision making. *American Psychologist, 26,* 180-188.

Dawes, R. M. (1979). The robust beauty of improper linear models in decision making. *American Psychologist, 34,* 571-582.

Dawes, R. M., & Corrigan, B. (1974). Linear models in decision making. *Psychological Bulletin, 81,* 95-106.

de Grott, A. D. (1965). *Thought and choice in chess.* The Hague: Mouton.

Diehl, M., & Stroebe, W. (1987). Productivity loss in brainstorming groups: Toward the solution of a riddle. *Journal of Personality and Social Psychology, 53,* 497-509.

Dinsmore, J. (1987). Mental spaces from a functional perspective. *Cognitive Science, 11,* 1-21.

Dougherty, T. W., Ebert, R. J., & Callender, J. C. (1986). Policy capturing in the employment interview. *Journal of Applied Psychology, 71,* 9-15.

Dunegan, K. J. (1993). Framing, cognitive modes and image theory: Toward an understanding of a glass half-full. *Journal of Applied Psychology, 78,* 491-503.

Dunegan, K. J. (1995). Image theory: Testing the role of image compatibility in progress decisions. *Organizational Behavior and Human Decision Processes, 62,* 79-86.

Dunegan, K. J. (in press). Fines, frames, and images: Examining formulation effects on punishment decisions. *Organizational Behavior and Human Decision Processes.*

Dunegan, K. J., Duchon, D., & Ashmos, D. (1995). Image compatibility and the use of problem space information in resource allocation decisions: Testing a moderating effects model. *Organizational Behavior and Human Decision Processes, 64,* 31-37.

Edwards, W (1954). The theory of decision making. *Psychological Bulletin, 51,* 380-417.

Edwards, W. (1955). An attempt to predict gambling decisions. In J. W. Dunlap (Ed.), *Mathematical models of human behavior* (pp. 12-32). Stamford, CT: Dunlap and Associates.

Einhorn, H. J., & Hogarth, R. M. (1986). Judging probable cause. *Psychological Bulletin, 99,* 3-19.

Etzioni, A. (1967). Mixed-scanning: A "third" approach to decision-making. *Public Administration Review, 27,* 385-392.

Etzioni, A. (1988). *The moral dimension: Toward a new economics.* New York: Free Press.

Etzioni, A. (1993). *The spirit of community.* New York: Crown.

Festinger, L. (1964). *Conflicts, decision and dissonance.* Stanford, CA: Stanford University Press.

Fischhoff, B., Slovic, P., & Lichtenstein, S. (1980). Knowing what you want: Measuring labile values. In T. Wallsten (Ed.), *Cognitive processes in choice and decision behavior* (pp. 64-85). Hillsdale, NJ: Lawrence Erlbaum.

Fisher, R., & Ury, W. (1981). *Getting to yes: Negotiating agreement without giving in.* Boston: Houghton Mifflin.

Follett, M. P. (1940). Constructive conflict. In H. C. Metcalf & L. Urwick (Eds.), *Dynamic administration: The collected papers of Mary Parker Follett* (pp. 36-47). New York: Harper.

Fryback, D. G., Goodman, B. C., & Edwards, W. (1973). Choices among bets by Las Vegas gamblers: Absolute and contextual effects. *Journal of Experimental Psychology, 98,* 271-278.

Galanter, E. (1962). The direct measurement of utility and subjective probability. *American Journal of Psychology, 75,* 208-220.

Gigerenzer, G. (1991). How to make cognitive illusions disappear: Beyond "heuristics and biases." In W. Stroebe & M. Hewstone (Eds.), *European review of social psychology, Vol. 2* (pp. 83-115). Chichester, UK: Wiley.

Gigerenzer, G., Hoffrage, U., & Kleinbolting, H. (1991). Probabilistic mental models: A Brunswikian theory of confidence. *Psychological Review, 98,* 506-528.

Gray, C. A. (1975). Factors in students' decisions to attempt academic tasks. *Organizational Behavior and Human Performance, 13,* 147-164.

Gruder, C. (1971). Relationships with opponent and partner in mixed-motive bargaining. *Journal of Conflict Resolution, 15,* 403-416.

Hacking, I. (1975). *The emergence of probability.* New York: Cambridge University Press.

Hammond, K. R. (1955). Probabilistic functioning and the clinical method. *Psychological Review, 62,* 255-262.

Hammond, K. R. (1971). Computer graphics as an aid to learning. *Science, 172,* 903-908.

Hammond, K. R., & Adelman, L. (1976). Science, values, and human decision. *Science, 194,* 389-396.

Hammond, K. R., Harvey, L. O., Jr., & Hastie, R. (1992). Making better use of scientific knowledge: Separating truth from justice. *Psychological Science, 3,* 80-87.

Hammond, K. R., Rohrbaugh, J., Mumpower, J., & Adelman, L. (1977). Social decision theory: Applications in policy formation. In M. Kaplan & S. Schwartz (Eds.), *Human decision and decision making in applied settings* (pp. 1-30). San Diego: Academic Press.

Hammond, K. R., Stewart, T. R., Brehmer, B., & Steinmann, D. O. (1975). Social decision theory. In M. Kaplan & S. Schwartz (Eds.), *Human judgment and decision processes* (pp. 54-63). New York: Academic Press.

Hardin, G. R. (1968). The tragedy of the commons. *Science, 162,* 1243-1248.

Harrison, R. (1972, May-June). Understanding your organization's character. *Harvard Business Review,* 119-128.

Heath, C., & Gonzalez, R. (1995). Interaction with others increases decision confidence but not decision quality: Evidence against information collection views of interactive decision making. *Organizational Behavior and Human Decision Processes, 61,* 305-326

Heller, F. A., Drenth, P. J. D., Koopman, P. L., & Rus, V. (1988). *Decisions in organizations: A three-country comparative study.* Newbury Park, CA: Sage.

Hickson, D. J., Hinnings, C. R., Lee, A. C., Schneck, R. E., & Pennings, J. M. (1971). A strategic contingency theory of intra-organizational power. *Administrative Science Quarterly, 16,* 216-229.

Hoffman, E., & Spitzer, M. (1985). Entitlements, rights, and fairness: An experimental examination of subjects' concepts of distributive justice. *Journal of Legal Studies, 14,* 259-297.

Hoffman, P. J. (1960). The paramorphic representation of clinical judgment. *Psychological Bulletin, 57,* 116-131.

Huffman, M. D. (1978). *The effect of decision task characteristics on decision behavior* (Technical Report No. 78-16). Seattle, WA: University of Washington, Department of Psychology.

James, W. (1983). *The principles of psychology.* London: Macmillan. (Original work published 1890)

Janis, I. L. (1972). *Victims of groupthink.* Boston: Houghton Mifflin.

Janis, I. L. (1982). *Groupthink: Psychological studies of policy decisions and fiascoes.* Boston: Houghton Mifflin.

Johnson-Laird, P. N. (1983). *Mental models.* Cambridge, MA: Harvard University Press.

Jungermann, H. (1983). The two camps on rationality. In R. W. Scholz (Ed.), *Decision making under uncertainty* (pp. 63-86). Amsterdam: North-Holland.

Jungermann, H. (1985). Inferential processes in the construction of scenarios. *Journal of Forecasting, 4,* 321-327.

Jungermann, H., & Thüring, J. (1987). The use of causal knowledge for inferential reasoning. In J. L. Mumpower, L. D. Phillips, O. Renn, & V. R. R. Uppuluria (Eds.), *Expert judgment and expert systems* (pp. 131-146). New York: Springer.

Kahneman, D., Slovic, P., & Tversky, A. (1982). *Judgment under uncertainty: Heuristics and biases.* Cambridge, UK: Cambridge University Press.

Kahneman, D., & Tversky, A. (1979). Prospect theory: An analysis of decision under risk. *Econometrica, 47,* 263-291.

Katzenbach, J. R., & Smith, D. K. (1993). *The wisdom of teams.* New York: McKinsey.

Keren, G. B., & Wagenaar, W. A. (1985). On the psychology of playing blackjack: Normative and descriptive considerations with implications for decision theory. *Journal of Experimental Psychology: General, 114,* 133-158.

Keren, G. B., & Wagenaar, W. A. (1987). Violation of utility theory in unique and repeated gambles. *Journal of Experimental Psychology: Learning, Memory and Cognition, 12,* 387-396.

Keysar, B., Ginzel, L. E., & Bazerman, M. H. (1995). States of affairs and states of mind: The effect of knowledge of beliefs. *Organizational Behavior and Human Decision Processes, 64,* 283-293.

Klayman, J. (1988). On the how and why (not) of learning from outcomes. In B. Brehmer & C. R. B. Joyce (Eds.), *Human decision: The SJT view* (pp. 115-162). Amsterdam: North-Holland.

Klein, G. (1996). *Sources of power: The study of naturalistic decision making.* Mahwah, NJ: Lawrence Erlbaum.

Klein, G. A. (1989). Recognition-primed decisions. *Advances in Man-Machine Systems Research, 5,* 47-92.

Klein, G. A. (1993). A recognition-primed decision (RPD) model of rapid decision making. In G. A. Klein, J. Orasanu, R. Calderwood, & C. E. Zsambok (Eds.), *Decision making in action: Models and methods* (pp. 138-147). Norwood, NJ: Ablex.

Kolmogorov, A. N. (1950). *Foundations of the theory of probability* (N. Morrison, Trans.). New York: Chelsean. (Original work published in 1933)

Koopman, P. L. (1980). *Besluitvorming in organisates.* Assen: Van Gorcum.

Koopman, P., & Pool, J. (1991). Organizational decision making: Models, contingencies and strategies. In J. Rasmussen, B. Brehmer, & J. Leplat (Eds.), *Distributed decision making: Cognitive models for cooperative work* (pp. 19-46). Chichester, UK: Wiley.

Kort, F. (1968). A nonlinear model for the analysis of judicial decisions. *American Political Science Review, 62,* 546-555.

Kuhn, T. S. (1962). *The structure of scientific revolutions.* Chicago: University of Chicago Press.

Lichtenstein, S., & Newman, J. R. (1967). Empirical scaling of common verbal phrases associated with numerical probabilities. *Psychonomic Science, 9,* 563-564.

Lindblom, C. E. (1959). The science of "muddling through." *Public Administration Review, 19,* 79-88.

Lipshitz, R. (1993). Decision making as argument-driven action. In G. A. Klein, J. Orasanu, R. Calderwood, & C. E. Zsambok (Eds.), *Decision making in action: Models and methods* (pp. 172-181). Norwood, NJ: Ablex.

Locke, E. A., & Schweiger, D. M. (1979). Participation in decision-making. One more look. In B. M. Shaw (Ed.), *Research in organizational behavior.* (pp. 265-339). Greenwich, CT: JAI.

Lopes, L. L. (1981). Decision making in the shortrun. *Journal of Experimental Psychology: Human Learning and Memory, 1,* 377-385.

Luce, R. D., & Raiffa, H. (1957). *Games and decisions: Introduction and critical survey.* New York: John Wiley.

March, J. G. (1978). Bounded rationality, ambiguity, and the engineering of choice. *Bell Journal of Economics, 9,* 587-608.

March, J. G., & Shapira, Z. (1982). Behavioral decision theory and organizational decision theory. In G. R. Urgson & D. N. Braunstein (Eds.), *Decision making: An interdisciplinary inquiry* (pp. 52-68). Boston: Kant.

March, J. G., & Simon, H. A. (1958). *Organizations.* New York: John Wiley.

Marcus, H., & Nurius, P. (1986). Possible selves. *American Psychologist, 41,* 954-969.

Marcus, H., & Wurf, E. (1987). The dynamic self-concept: A social psychological perspective. *Annual Review of Psychology, 38,* 299-337.

McAllister, D., Mitchell, T. R., & Beach, L. R. (1979). The contingency model for selection of decision strategies: An empirical test of the effects of significance, accountability, and reversibility. *Organizational Behavior and Human Performance, 24,* 228-244.

McCauley, C., Stitt, C. L., & Segal, M. (1980). Stereotyping: From prejudice to prediction. *Psychological Bulletin, 87,* 195-208.

McGrath, J. E. (1984). *Groups: Interaction and performance.* Englewood Cliffs, NJ: Prentice Hall.

McKelvey, R. D., & Palfrey, T. R. (1992). An experimental study of the centipede game. *Econometrica, 60,* 803-836.

Messick, D., & Sentis, K. P. (1979). Fairness and preference. *Journal of Experimental Social Psychology, 15,* 418-434.

Minsky, M. (1968). *Semantic information processing.* Cambridge: MIT Press.

Mintzberg, H., Raisinghani, D., & Theoret, A. (1976). The structure of "unstructured" decision processes. *Administrative Science Quarterly, 21,* 246-275.

Montgomery, H. (1993). The search for a dominance structure in decision making: Examining the evidence. In G. A. Klein, J. Orasanu, R. Calderwood, & C. E., Zsambok (Eds.), *Decision making in action: Models and methods* (pp. 172-181). Norwood, NJ: Ablex

Mullen, B., Anthony, T., Salas, E., & Driskell, J. E. (1994). Group cohesiveness and quality of decision making: An integration of tests of the groupthink hypothesis. *Small Group Research, 25,* 189-204.

Nash, J. (1950). The bargaining problem. *Econometrica, 28,* 155-162.

Nash, J. (1951). Non-cooperative games. *Annals of Mathematics, 54,* 286-295.

Neale, M. A. (1984). The effect of negotiation and arbitration cost salience on bargainer behavior: The role of arbitrator and constituency in negotiator judgment. *Organizational Behavior and Human Performance, 34,* 97-111.

Neale, M. A., & Northcraft, G. B. (1986). Experts, amateurs, and refrigerators: Comparing expert and amateur negotiators in a novel task. *Organizational Behavior and Human Decision Processes 38,* 305-317.

Neisser, U. (1976). *Cognition and reality.* New York: Freeman.

Neisser, U. (1982). *Memory observed: Remembering in natural contexts.* New York: Freeman.

Nisbett, R. E., Krantz, D., Jepson, C., & Kunda, Z. (1983). The use of statistical heuristics in everyday inductive reasoning. *Psychological Review, 90,* 339-363.

Nisbett, R. E., & Wilson, T. D. (1977). Telling more than we can know: Verbal reports on mental processes. *Psychological Review, 84,* 231-259.

Nordhoy, F. (1962). *Group interaction in decision making under risk.* Unpublished master's thesis, Massachusetts Institute of Technology, Cambridge.

Osborn, A. F. (1957). *Applied imagination.* New York: Scribner.

Park, W. W. (1990). A review of research on groupthink. *Journal of Behavioral Decision Making, 3,* 229-245.

Pennington, N., & Hastie, R. (1986). Evidence evaluation in complex decision making. *Journal of Personality and Social Psychology, 51,* 242-258.

Pennington, N., & Hastie, R. (1988). Explanation-based decision making: Effects of memory structure on judgment. *Journal of Experimental Psychology: Learning, Memory and Cognition, 14,* 521-533.

Pennington, N., & Hastie, R. (1992). Explaining the evidence: Tests of the story model for juror decision making. *Journal of Personality and Social Psychology, 2,* 189-206.

Peterson, C. R., & Beach, L. R. (1967). Man as an intuitive statistician. *Psychological Bulletin, 68,* 29-46.

Peterson, C. R., DuCharme, W. M., & Edwards, W. (1968). Sampling distributions and probability revisions. *Journal of Experimental Psychology, 76,* 236-243.

Peterson, C. R., Schneider, R. J., & Miller, A. J. (1965). Sample size and the revision of subjective probabilities. *Journal of Experimental Psychology, 69,* 522-527.

Peterson, C. R., Ulehla, Z. J., Miller, A. J., Bourne, L. E., & Stilson, D. W. (1965). Internal consistency of subjective probabilities. *Journal of Experimental Psychology, 70,* 526-533.

Phelps, R. H., & Shanteau, J. (1978). Livestock judges: How much information can an expert use? *Organizational Behavior and Human Performance, 21,* 209-219.

Phillips, L. D., & Edwards, W. (1966). Conservatism in a simple probability inference task. *Journal of Experimental Psychology, 72,* 346-354.

Plott, C. R., & Levine, M. E. (1976). A model of agenda influence on committee decisions. *American Economic Review, 68,* 146-160.

Potter, R. E., & Beach, L. R. (1994). Imperfect information in pre-choice screening of options. *Organizational Behavior and Human Decision Processes, 59,* 313-329.

Preston, M. G., & Baratta, P. (1948). An experimental study of the auction-value of an uncertain outcome. *American Journal of Psychology, 61,* 183-193.

Prinzmetal, W. (1995). Visual feature integration in a world of objects. *Current Directions in Psychological Science, 3,* 90-98.

Quinn, J. B. (1980). *Strategies for change: Logical incrementalism.* Homewood, IL: Irwin.

Raiffa, H. (1968). *Decision analysis.* Reading, MA: Addison-Wesley.

Raiffa, H. (1982). *The art and science of negotiation.* Cambridge, MA: Harvard University Press.

Rapoport, A. (1966). *Two-person game theory: The essential ideas.* Ann Arbor: University of Michigan Press.

Rapoport, A. (1988). Provision of step-level public goods: Effects of inequality in resources. *Journal of Personality and Social Psychology, 54,* 432-440.

Rohrbaugh, J. (1988). Cognitive conflict tasks and small group processes. In B. Brehmer & C. R. B. Joyce (Eds.), *Human decision: The SJT view* (pp. 199-226). Amsterdam: North-Holland.

Roose, J. E., & Doherty, M. E. (1976). Decision theory applied to the selection of life insurance salesmen. *Organizational Behavior and Human Performance, 16,* 231-249.

Rorer, L. G., Hoffman, P. J., Dickman, H. D., & Slovic, P. (1967). Configurational judgments revealed. *Proceedings of the 75th Annual Convention of the American Psychological Association, 2,* 195-196.

Rosch, E. (1976). Classification of real-world objects: Origins and representations in cognition. In S. Ehrlich & E. Tolving (Eds.), *La memorie semantique* (pp. 24-32). Paris: *Bulletin de Psychologie.*

Rubin, J. Z., & Brown, B. R. (1975). *The social psychology of bargaining and negotiation.* San Diego: Academic Press.

Rück, B. (Ed.). (1993). *Risk is a concept: Perceptions of risk perception.* Munich: Knesebeck.

Rummelhart, D. E. (1977). Understanding and summarizing brief stories. In D. LaBerge & S. J. Samuels (Eds.), *Basic processes in reading: Perception and comprehension* (pp. 62-93). Hillsdale, NJ: Lawrence Erlbaum.

Samuelson, P. A. (1963). Risk and uncertainty: A fallacy of large numbers. *Scientia, 9,* 108-113.

Schank, R. C., & Abelson, R. P. (1977). *Scripts, plans, goals and understanding.* Hillsdale, NJ: Lawrence Erlbaum.

Schoemaker, P. J. H. (1980). *Experiments on decision under risk: The expected utility hypothesis.* Boston: Nijhoff.

Selten, R. (1990). Bounded rationality. *Journal of Institutional and Theoretical Economics, 146,* 649-658.

Shanteau, J. (1992). The psychology of experts: An alternative view. In G. Wright & F. Bolger (Eds.), *Expertise and decision support* (pp. 11-24). New York: Plenum.

Shanteau, J., & Anderson, N. H. (1969). Test of a conflict model for preference judgment. *Journal of Experimental Psychology, 103,* 680-691.

Sheridan, J. E. (1992). Organizational culture and employee retention. *Academy of Management Journal, 35,* 1036-1056.

Shockley-Zalabak, P., & Morley, D. D. (1989). Adhering to organizational culture: What does it mean? Why does it matter? *Group and Organizational Studies, 14,* 483-500.

Simon, H. A. (1945). *Administrative behavior.* New York: Macmillan.

Simon, H. A. (1947). *Administrative behavior.* New York: Free Press.

Simon, H. A. (1955). A behavioral model of rational choice. *Quarterly Journal of Economics, 69,* 99-118.

Simon, H. A. (1957). *Models of man.* New York: John Wiley.

Simon, H. A. (1979). Rational decision making in business organizations. *American Economic Review, 69,* 493-513.

Slovic, P. (1987). Perception of risk. *Science, 236,* 280-285.

Slovic, P., & Lichtenstein, S. (1983). Preference reversals: A broader perspective. *American Economic Review, 73.* 596-605.

Slovic, P., Rorer, L. G., & Hoffman, P. J. (1971). Analyzing use of diagnostic signs. *Investigative Radiology, 6,* 18-26.

Sniezek, J. A. (1992). Groups under uncertainty: An examination of confidence in group decision making. *Organizational Behavior and Human Decision Processes, 52,* 124-155.

Sniezek, J. A., & Henry, R. A. (1989). Accuracy and confidence in group judgment. *Organizational Behavior and Human Decision Processes, 43,* 1-28.

Sniezek, J. A., & Henry, R. A. (1990). Revision, weighting, and commitment in consensus group judgment. *Organizational Behavior and Human Decision Processes, 45,* 66-84.

Sniezek, J. A., Paese, P. W., & Furiya, S. (1990). *Dynamics of group discussion to consensus judgment: Disagreement and overconfidence.* Unpublished Manuscript, University of Illinois at Urbana-Champaign.

Srivastava, J., Connolly, T., & Beach, L. R. (1995). Do ranks suffice? A comparison of alternative weighting approaches in value elicitation. *Organizational Behavior and Human Decision Processes, 63,* 112-116.

Stasser, G., & Titus, W. (1985). Pooling of unshared information in group decision making: Biased information sampling during discussion. *Journal of Personality and Social Psychology, 48,* 1467-1478.

Stoner, J. A. F. (1961). *A comparison of individuals and group decisions involving risk.* Unpublished master's thesis, Massachusetts Institute of Technology, Cambridge.

Svenson, O. (1979). Process descriptions in decision making. *Organizational Behavior and Human Performance, 23,* 86-112.

Svenson, O. (1992). Differentiation and consolidation theory of human decision making: A frame of reference for the study of pre- and post-decision processes. *Acta Psychologica, 80,* 143-168.

Thaler, R. (1985). Mental accounting and consumer choice. *Marketing Science, 4,* 199-214.

Thaler, R. (1992). *The winner's curse: Paradoxes and anomalies of economic life.* New York: Free Press.

Thomas, J. C. (1990). Public involvement in public management: Adapting and testing a borrowed theory. *Administration Review, 50,* 435-445.

Thompson, L. (1990). Negotiation behavior and outcomes: Empirical evidence and theoretical issues. *Psychological Bulletin, 108,* 515-532.

Thüring, M., & Jungermann, H. (1986). Constructing and running mental models or inferences about the future. In B. Brehmer, H. Jungermann, P. Lourens, & G. S. Sevòn (Eds.), *New directions in research in decision making* (pp. 163-174). Amsterdam: North-Holland.

Tjosvold, D. (1977). Commitment to justice in conflict between unequal status persons. *Journal of Applied Social Psychology, 7,* 149-162.

Tjosvold, D. (1978). Control strategies and own group evaluation in intergroup conflict. *Journal of Psychology, 100,* 305-314.

Trice, H. M., & Beyer, J. M. (1993). *The cultures of work organizations.* Englewood Cliffs, NJ: Prentice Hall.

Tversky, A. (1967). Additivity, utility, and subjective probability. *Journal of Mathematical Psychology, 4,* 175-202.

Tversky, A. (1969). The intransitivity of preferences. *Psychological Review, 76,* 31-48.

Tversky, A., & Kahneman, D. (1974). Judgment under uncertainty: Heuristics and biases. *Science, 185,* 1124-1131.

Tversky, A., & Kahneman, D. (1981). The framing of decisions and the psychology of choice. *Science, 221,* 1124-1131.

Tversky, A., & Kahneman, D. (1982). Causal schemas in judgments under uncertainty. In D. Kahneman, P. Slovic, & A. Tversky (Eds.), *Judgment under uncertainty: Heuristics and biases* (pp. 117-128). Cambridge, UK: Cambridge University Press.

Tversky, A., & Kahneman, D. (1992). Advances in prospect theory: Cumulative representation of uncertainty. *Journal of Risk and Uncertainty, 5,* 297-323.

Valacich, J. S., Dennis, A. R., & Connolly, T. (1994). Idea generation in computer-based groups: A new ending to an old story. *Organizational Behavior and Human Decision Processes, 57,* 448-467.

Valacich, J. S., Dennis, A. R., & Nunamaker, J. F. (1991). Electronic meeting support: The GroupSystems concept. *International Journal on Man-Machine Studies, 34,* 261-282.

Van, J. (1983, April 17). That "sweet tooth" may be a " fat tooth." *Chicago Tribune,* Section 4, p. 3.

van Zee, E. H., Paluchowski, T. F., & Beach, L. R. (1992). The effects of screening and task partitioning upon evaluations of decision options. *Journal of Behavioral Decision Making, 5,* 1-23.

von Mises, R. (1957). *Probability, statistics, and truth.* Sydney, Australia: Allen and Unwin. (Original work published 1928)

von Neumann, J., & Morgenstern, O. (1947). *Theory of games and economic behavior.* Princeton, NJ: Princeton University Press.

von Winterfeldt, D., & Edwards, W. (1986). *Decision analysis and behavioral research.* Cambridge, UK: Cambridge University Press.

Vroom, V. H. (1973, Spring). A new look at managerial decision making. *Organizational Dynamics,* 66-80.

Vroom, V. H., & Jago, A. G. (1978). On the validity of the Vroom-Yetton model. *Journal of Applied Psychology, 63,* 151-162.

Vroom, V. H. & Jag, A. G. (1988). *The new leadership: Managing participation in organizations.* Englewood Cliff, NJ: Prentice Hall.

Vroom, V. H., & Yetton, P. W. (1973). *Leadership and decision-making.* Pittsburgh: University of Pittsburgh Press.

Wagenaar, W. A. (1988). *Paradoxes of gambling behavior.* Hillsdale, NJ: Lawrence Erlbaum.

Wagenaar, W. A., & Keren, G. B. (1986). The seat belt paradox: Effect of adopted roles on information seeking. *Organizational Behavior and Human Decision Processes, 38,* 1-6.

Wagenaar, W. A., & Keren, G. B. (1988). Chance and luck are not the same. *Journal of Behavioral Decision Making, 1,* 65-75.

Wagenaar, W. A., Keren, G. B., & Pleit-Kuiper, A. (1984). The multiple objectives of gamblers. *Acta Psychologica, 56,* 167-178.

Wagner, J. A., & Gooding, R. Z. (1987). Shared influence and organizational behavior: A meta-analysis of situational variables expected to moderate participation-outcome relationships. *Academy of Management Journal, 30,* 524-541.

Wallach, M. A., Kogan, N., & Bem, D. J. (1962). Group influence on individual risk taking. *Journal of Abnormal and Social Psychology, 65,* 77-86.

Weatherly, K. A. (1995). *The rapid assessment of organizational culture using the Organizational Culture Survey: Theory, research and application.* Unpublished doctoral dissertation, University of Arizona, Tucson.

Weatherly, K. A., & Beach, L. R. (1996). Organizational culture and decision making. In L. R. Beach (Ed.). *Decision making in the workplace: A unified perspective* (pp. 117-132). Mahwah, NJ: Lawrence Erlbaum.

Wheeler, G., & Beach, L. R. (1968). Subjective sampling distributions and conservatism. *Organizational Behavior and Human Performance, 3,* 36-46.

Wise, J. A. (1970). Estimates and scaled judgments of subjective probabilities. *Organizational Behavior and Human Performance, 5,* 85-92.

Wright, G., & Bolger, F. (1992). *Expertise and decision support.* New York: Plenum.

Yantis, S. (1995). Perceived continuity of occluded visual objects. *Psychological Science, 6,* 182-186.

Yates, J. F. (1990). *Judgment and decision making.* Englewood Cliffs, NJ: Prentice Hall.

Zimmer, R. J. (1978). Validating the Vroom-Yetton normative model of leader behavior in field sales force management and measuring the training effects of TELOS on the leader behavior of district managers. Unpublished doctoral dissertation, Virginia Polytechnic Institute, Blackburg.

Index

About The Author

Lee Roy Beach is McClelland Professor of Management and Policy, and Professor of Psychology in the College of Business and Public Administration at the University of Arizona, Tucson. He received his PhD in experimental psychology from the University of Colorado and began his professional career as a human factors researcher for the U.S. Navy, followed by service at the Office of Naval Research. After leaving the Navy, he completed two years of postdoctoral work at the University of Michigan before taking a position in the Department of Psychology at the University of Washington, where he moved from assistant to full professor and served as Chair. He has been a Visiting Scholar at Cambridge and Leiden Universities and a Visiting Professor at the University of Chicago. He is the author of over 125 scholarly articles and three books on organizational behavior and human decision making. He has been the recipient of numerous awards for research and teaching.